T0385741

Citizens in Motion

Citizens in Motion

Emigration, Immigration, and Re-migration

Across China's Borders

Elaine Lynn-Ee Ho

Stanford University Press
Stanford, California

Stanford University Press
Stanford, California

Printed in the United States of America on acid-free, archival-quality paper

Library of Congress Cataloging-in-Publication Data

Names: Ho, Elaine Lynn-Ee, author.
Title: Citizens in motion : emigration, immigration, and re-migration across China's borders / Elaine Lynn-Ee Ho.
Description: Stanford, California : Stanford University Press, 2019. | Includes bibliographical references and index.
Identifiers: LCCN 2018009227 | ISBN 9781503606661 (cloth : alk. paper) | ISBN 9781503607460 (epub)
Subjects: LCSH: China—Emigration and immigration. | Chinese—Foreign countries. | Chinese diaspora. | Citizenship—China.
Classification: LCC JV8701 .H6 2018 | DDC 304.8/20951—dc23
LC record available at https://lccn.loc.gov/2018009227

Typeset by Westchester Publishing Services in 10/14 Minion Pro

Cover design: Rob Ehle

Cover photo: City workers, tolgart | iStock

In memory of Connie Lim

Contents

Preface

THIS BOOK ARGUES THAT the multidirectional aspects of migration routes—emigration, immigration, and re-migration—can and should be analyzed alongside one another. Its focus on contemporaneous migration departs from conventional approaches that study migration sites in isolation or as snapshots in time. This approach directs us toward examining how temporal periodization structures migration and the citizenship constellations that are forged across migration sites, shaping the lives of citizens in motion. The book develops new arguments that contribute to our theorization of citizenship and territory, fraternity and alterity, ethnicity, and the co-constitution of time and space.

The chapters in the book examine how state accounts of migration and citizenship in China, Canada, and Singapore compare with the experiences of fraternity and alterity articulated by migrants and nonmigrants. This combination of cases may seem unusual, but what links China, Canada, and Singapore analytically is their status as societies characterized by existing cultural diversity, even as they simultaneously experience a range of new migration trends that add newfound challenges to maintaining social cohesiveness. Central to the analyses of migration in these countries are past and present accounts of emigration, immigration, and re-migration.

This book is based on more than a decade of field research, including participant observation, semistructured interviews, and analysis of news reports and other textual or visual sources. From 2008 to 2010 I conducted a two-stage research project, first considering skilled Mainland Chinese immigration to Vancouver, Canada, followed by research on skilled immigrants who had re-migrated to China from Canada and were based in the cities of Beijing, Shanghai, and Guangzhou. The latter group was labeled "return migrants" (*huiliu zhongguo huaren*) by the Chinese state, even if they had naturalized elsewhere. While searching the library archives of the All-China Federation of Returned Overseas Chinese (*Qiaolian*) in Beijing for reports of Chinese return migration, I chanced upon a news article describing an earlier cohort of forced migrants from Southeast Asia, which the Chinese state had resettled as returnees (*guiguo nanqiao*, or refugee-returnees). My curiosity piqued, I began to find out more about them.

From 2010 to 2013 my research focused on the refugee-returnees who had been resettled in the state-owned farms established by the Chinese state (*huaqiao nongchang*). I conducted research at two farms in rural Guangdong province and Hainan Island, and subsequently in the cities of Shenzhen, Guangzhou, and Xiamen. I extended my research from the farms to the cities for two reasons: First, I learned that during the 1980s post-reform period, groups of young people from the state-owned farms had been dispatched to work in state-owned enterprises in the cities and they resettled there. Second, of those who remained on the farms, their children (1.5 and second generations) later re-migrated to look for work in the cities independently after the rules restricting internal mobility through the household registration system (*hukou*) were relaxed.

In 2011 an academic colleague who was visiting Singapore introduced me to his Burmese companion. He remarked, "You do research on the Chinese, you will find many Chinese in Myanmar!" The possibility of carrying out research in Myanmar proved appealing because Myanmar had been closed to most of the international community for decades and little was known about the Chinese living there. The transition to partial civilian rule through the general elections in 2010 proved timely for starting new research there. From 2012 to 2014 I carried out research on Chinese migration to Myanmar. I began by sourcing for contacts in Yangon, but it was in Mandalay, known colloquially as Myanmar's "Chinatown," where research access proved most productive. From Mandalay, I went to Lashio in Shan state, a key trading route between Myanmar and China, and as such a key node for Chinese migrant communities as well. In Lashio, the Chinese I met urged me to do further research at the border town of Ruili in Yunnan province of China, thus enhancing my knowledge of the social interactions between Chinese diasporic descendants from Myanmar and the domestic Mainland Chinese.

From 2013 to 2016 I conducted new research on Africans in China, as I had started to notice new immigration trends in Chinese cities. I focused on educational migration routes and the social lives of African students who had enrolled in Chinese university degree programs. My fieldwork was in Guangzhou and Wuhan, cities with an agglomeration of universities that appealed to African students. As a hub of China-Africa trade, Guangzhou was further attractive to African students who wanted to do business or work alongside studying. As a second-tier city, Wuhan attracted students who desired a lower cost of living than in metropolitan cities like Guangzhou, Beijing, or Shanghai, or those who were dispatched there by Chinese scholarship agencies that funded their studies.

Throughout 2008 to 2016 I maintained an interest in deepening my understanding of Singaporean migration. Prior to 2008 I had conducted research on overseas Singaporeans in London and Singapore's diaspora strategies (2003 to 2007). During my trips to China I would meet overseas Singaporeans who were working and living there. In Singapore I got to know Singaporeans who had returned from an earlier working stint in China or were commuting regularly between China and Singapore to balance their work commitments and family life. In 2012 I conducted interviews in Singapore with government agencies and organizations reaching out to Singaporeans abroad. Dividing my time between Singapore and China meant that I was in a trans-territorial environment that allowed me to be an ethnographer even as I went about my daily life.

At the same time, in Singaporean society a sense of urgency had developed over social tensions between Singaporeans and the new immigrants living in Singapore. Much of the coverage in the Singaporean media, reflected in everyday life, focused on the perspectives of Singaporeans who expected the new immigrants to integrate. In 2015 I started research on the attitudes of new Chinese immigrants toward integration in Singapore. This research is ongoing, complementing my overall research engagement on the migration connections between China and Singapore, and more generally between China and the world.

This book brings together these different research projects conceptually. The multisited ethnographic approach informing the work pieces together a picture of migration flows that connect China to the world, and the world to China.

Acknowledgments

THIS BOOK HAS BENEFITED GREATLY from the advice and inputs of colleagues and friends. The research projects informing the book's arguments extend across more than a decade of academic learning, for which I am especially grateful to Claire Dwyer, Shirlena Huang, David Ley, Katie Willis, and Brenda Yeoh, who guided me through different stages of the journey. Rhacel Parreñas, Dhooleka Raj, and Henry Yeung gave timely encouragement during various stages of writing, thus steering the book to fruition.

I am thankful to Lynette Chua, Mark Boyle, Mary Gilmartin, and Rob Kitchin for providing insightful comments on early drafts of the book proposal. Glen Peterson and Lee Kah Wee also generously gave time to read individual chapters, which helped sharpen the writing subsequently. I extend my thanks to the reviewers and Marcela Maxfield, my editor at Stanford University Press, for the constructive feedback they shared as the manuscript developed.

Adrian Bailey, Tim Bunnell, Neil Coe, Romit Dasgupta, Jamie Gillen, Hoon Chang Yau, Eleonore Kofman, Lily Kong, Wei Li, Kelvin Low, Fiona McConnell, Anne McNevin, Kamalini Ramdas, Jonathan Rigg, James Sidaway, Rachel Silvey, Robert Vanderbeck, and Woon Chih Yuan have enriched my academic life with thought-provoking conversations and their good wishes. I am grateful to Gao Weinong, Khin Maung Soe, Li Zhigang, Min Min Oo, Wang Lei, and Zhang Jijiao, who kindly introduced me to research contexts that were unfamiliar and challenging to access in China and Myanmar. Kezia Barker, Chng Nai Rui, Russell Hitchings, Priya Kissoon, Ben Lampert, Daniel Large, Leo Minuchin, Eileen Sullivan, Tan Shzr Ee, and Valerie Viehoff have been crucial pillars of a supportive community while I lived abroad and up till today. Their friendships will always be deeply cherished.

Cai Xiaocun, Foo Fang Yu, Jin Xin, Loo Wenbin, Shona Loong, Veronica Tang, Zhang Jie, and Claire Zhao helped as research assistants for the projects mentioned in this book. My thanks and good wishes to them all. Special thanks to Madeleine Lim, who assisted in preparing the manuscript for production. I am also deeply grateful to the research participants who shared their lifeworlds with me, without which this book would not have been possible.

Last but not least, I am grateful to my family for their unfailing support and understanding. To Connie, we will always miss your loving and affirming presence in our lives.

Citizens in Motion

1 Migration and Citizenship

Introduction

A taxi driver in Beijing, noting that my intonation of Mandarin did not identify me as someone from northern China, asked curiously if I was from southern China. Not feeling particularly chatty that day, I replied, "I'm from Singapore." He probed next, "Which part of China is that?" To which I explained, "It's not in China—Singapore is in Southeast Asia." Without missing a beat, he retorted, "You should come back to serve the country (*huiguo weiguo fuwu*)."[1]

A seemingly casual encounter such as this one, which happened during my first visit to China in 2008, captures the complex relations that tie emigrants and their descendants to China as an ancestral land. Whether through one's personal decision to emigrate or through one's being several generations removed from China (through ancestral emigration), the Chinese abroad continue to be regarded as co-ethnics who should serve the ancestral land. At the same time, the countries in which they reside see them as immigrants or citizens—that is, subjects in which national identity and loyalty should be cultivated and mobilized to serve their country of immigration or natal belonging.

Transnationalism theorists have long argued for the need to study the links between emigration and immigration societies.[2] This book takes Chinese emigration as the starting point to consider how multidirectional migration flows have shaped and continue to shape nation building both in China and the countries to which cohorts of Chinese have migrated. My approach brings seemingly distinct emigration, immigration, and re-migration trends under the same analytical framework to conceptualize the *contemporaneous aspects of migration*, illuminating how citizenship formations in different national contexts are drawn into a constellation of relations (henceforth citizenship constellations[3]).

A handful of scholars, such as Susan Coutin and Filomeno Aguilar, have proposed that immigration debates should be reconsidered through the lens of emigration.[4] For Coutin, this analytical shift shows that "it is no longer clear which migrant movements consist of going and which coming."[5] Studies of re-migration also trouble the dichotomy that is often drawn of emigration and immigration contexts. For example, the re-migration of diasporic descendants (i.e., descendants of emigrants) to an ancestral land is normally labeled "return migration," but this label becomes a misnomer when it is projected on migrants who have never lived in the ancestral land before. For Anastasia Christou and Russell King, the re-migration of diasporic descendants to the ancestral land is more suitably referred to as "counter-diasporic migration."[6] Re-migration reverses the directionality of movement between two countries, switching the sites of origin and destination. It also challenges accounts that presume migrants and their descendants will assimilate into their countries of residence in the long term.[7]

With these arguments in mind, I develop the concept of "contemporaneous migration" as an analytical framework to draw together multidirectional migration routes as they converge in a national territory or forge interconnections across global space. This analysis situates the migration and citizenship politics of national societies in a trans-territorial context to signal how concurrent global events (i.e., temporal simultaneity) taking place in different parts of the world can forge citizenship constellations that interconnect migration sites.

Theoretically, this book advances migration and citizenship scholarship in four ways. First, it draws out how states, migrants, and nonmigrants exercise claims of membership (henceforth fraternity) or social difference (henceforth alterity) flexibly to advance their claims to belonging, identity, and rights. I deploy the vocabulary of fraternity and alterity throughout the book to creatively juxtapose discourses and practices of membership with social difference. Such dynamics are illuminated in new ways when emigration and immigration contexts are analyzed in tandem, rather than in isolation. Second, I consider the co-ethnic tensions that ensue when different cohorts of migrants from the same ancestral land advance their own versions of fraternity or alterity alongside interethnic hierarchies that exist in multicultural societies. Such an approach marks a distinctive departure from studies that consider fraternity and alterity through the lens of interethnic relations only. This provides a significant and timely intervention for scholarship on migration and citizenship, because the assumed cultural compatibility of migrant co-ethnics has been challenged in different immigration contexts, such as Korea, Japan, Taiwan, Macau, and Hong Kong.[8] Yet the academic vocabulary we have for analyzing such trends remains deficient compared to interethnic relations. In response to these deficiencies, this book underlines how temporal periodization (i.e., temporality) is deployed to differentiate the membership and rights of newer immigrants,[9] particularly toward co-ethnics.[10]

Third, the book examines how migrants engage in re-migration journeys and their aspirations for recognition and rights in different countries during distinct life stages. Re-migration journeys render such migrants susceptible to dissonances in membership and identity. They also become conscious that their social reproduction concerns regarding family closeness and retirement planning will extend across different nation-states in their lifetime.[11] Few researchers have considered the long-term implications of re-migration patterns for the rights and duties associated with citizenship. As compared to normative framings of national citizenship that assume sedentariness, accounts of re-migration prompt us to analyze how citizenship inclusion or exclusion is experienced across the life course in a trans-territorial context. Fourth, the book contrasts the partial acceptance of immigrants in a country with the recognition extended to emigrants from the same country (i.e., the diaspora). Immigrants may be physically present but accorded only partial recognition by the nation-state, whereas emigrants can be physically absent yet sustain an emotional and political presence in a society that values them.[12] Examining emigration, immigration, and re-migration trends in conjunction directs attention to how the territorial premises of citizenship are undergoing spatial change.

To develop the above arguments, the chapters in this book examine how state accounts of migration and citizenship in China, Canada, and Singapore compare with the actual experiences of fraternity and alterity expressed by migrants and nonmigrants. The culturally diverse societies of those three countries are experiencing migration patterns that add newfound challenges to maintaining social cohesiveness. Studying those countries together will allow us to draw out the spatial connections and temporal considerations that would be otherwise elided in compartmentalized approaches to migration trends. In addition to multisited ethnography and interviews, the writing also draws on wider historical and ethnographic studies to develop the breadth and depth critical to elucidating the diverse forms of migration and global events addressed here.

Emigration and Diaspora: Contextualizing Chinese Migration

Emigration creates diasporas when people move from one part of the world to settle elsewhere but they retain a sense of belonging to the countries they left, often referred to as the homeland. Diaspora can counteract narrow-minded framings of "race," ethnicity, and nation, but diasporic imaginaries may also be appropriated by chauvinist agendas.[13] The lineages and social relations undergirding diaspora create cognitive and material taxonomies of inclusion or exclusion in conceptions of the nation and diaspora. Hence critical race scholars, such as Avtar Brah, argue that diasporas should be examined conceptually from a historically informed perspective, rather than being taken as a primordial condition.[14]

Such debates on diaspora, membership, and belonging inform my analyses of migration trends pertaining to China. Scholars of Chinese migration have questioned using "diaspora" as a referent for the Chinese abroad given the assumptions of origin, membership, and belonging that it connotes.[15] The "Chinese diaspora" is conventionally associated with the Han Chinese ethnic group, which represents only one of the fifty-six officially classified ethnic groups in China.[16] The Han Chinese comprise the majority population in China, but their culture is also characterized by regional, linguistic, and cultural distinctions. I use the label "overseas Chinese" (huaqiao) to refer to the Chinese who consider China their natal land while reserving "Chinese diaspora" (sanju huaren) or "Chinese abroad" (i.e., persons of Chinese ethnicity) as more encompassing terms that also include Chinese diasporic descendants (huayi) who were born abroad, bear foreign nationality status, and consider a country other than China their native land. The heterogeneity of the social groups contained within these labels and the changing nature of the label "Chinese diaspora" will be discussed. I employ the emic labels that were mentioned during research so as to capture the specific aspects of identity brought up by the research participants.

Chinese emigrants of the nineteenth and early twentieth centuries were mainly young and poorly educated male peasants from five major dialect groups (Cantonese, Hokkien, Hakka, Hainanese, and Teochew) in coastal China (Guangdong, Fujian, and Hainan Island). They ventured to Southeast Asia and the Americas as laborers and are referred to as the "overseas Chinese" by both the Chinese state and in academic literature. They brought their families to join them or intermarried with the resident population in their destination countries. This group is now referred to as the "old diaspora," differentiating it from the "new Chinese diaspora," made up of migrants who left China after 1979. Whereas first-generation emigrants have a personal identification with the country they left, diasporic descendants harbor only distant identification with the ancestral land. Their knowledge of the ancestral land is accrued through stories and memories of the older generation or through short visits rather than longer-term residency.

Engaging Chinese emigrants and diasporic descendants has been central to successive political regimes in China, whether it is the late Qing dynasty, Sun Yat-sen's short-lived republican administration, or the communist government that succeeded it.[17] Political rhetoric oscillated between seeing the Chinese abroad as resources for nation building, co-ethnics deserving protection by the ancestral land, or foreign spies and threats to the prevailing political ideology. Mobilizing the Chinese abroad to promote nation building and China's role in the world led consecutive Chinese political regimes to assert an extraterritorial reach toward the Chinese diaspora, re-territorializing the geo-body from afar.[18] The extraterritorial reach of the Chinese state is enabled through diaspora engagement policies that capitalize on the transnational identifications of the Chinese abroad.[19]

Diaspora engagement by China must be analyzed on three levels: first, the "old Chinese diaspora" and Chinese diasporic descendants with foreign nationality; second, overseas Chinese from the "new Chinese diaspora" who have naturalized abroad; and third, overseas Chinese from the "new Chinese diaspora" who retain Chinese nationality. Each of these emigrant populations can be analyzed in relation to immigration trends perceptible in China today. Diasporic descendants with foreign nationality status (*huayi*) are moving to China to work, study, or live. Unlike earlier policy that recognized the right of "return" for the Chinese abroad even if they no longer have Chinese nationality status, Chinese diasporic descendants today are required to apply for temporary work or study visas. Nonetheless, they are tacitly acknowledged as co-ethnics who bear a cultural affinity to China. The ties that the Chinese state maintains with diasporic descendants are loose but resilient, as it recognizes that their affiliations to their natal lands are likely to be more prominent than their attachment to the ancestral land.

The other two groups of Chinese left China after 1979 and are referred to as *xinyimin* (new Chinese immigrants). However, the collective label of *xinyimin* belies the distinct identities that different cohorts of emigrants embody, depending on whether they left the country when China was a low-income or middle-income developing country. Another marker of differentiation pertains to their nationality status. Of the *xinyimin*, those that have naturalized abroad are required to apply for immigrant visas to re-migrate to China. The third group of emigrants retained Chinese nationality (*huaqiao*) and went abroad intending to study or work temporarily. They represent the accrual of global competencies and international networks for China's domestic agendas, and the means through which the Chinese state extends its reach to places as diverse as Africa, North America, Europe, Latin America, and Southeast Asia. Through this third group the Chinese state exports national ideologies, development models, and modernization.[20] Long-distance nationalism extends the extraterritorial influence of one country into another.[21]

Production of national identity and community in China has to be viewed alongside global events that interconnect the ancestral land to the countries where the Chinese abroad have migrated across the generations.[22] As Adam McKeown argues, the "mutual entanglement" of flows and border is "key to most understandings of contemporary globalization."[23] Historically, the Chinese in Southeast Asia represented the conduits by which political revolution and notions of modernity circulated from China to destinations abroad, and from those destinations back to China. Circulatory histories, genealogies, and concurrent events prompt us to examine the interlinked aspects of migration within and across national contexts.[24] For example, Chinese emigration and Chinese development abroad today are precipitating new immigration trends in China.

Chinese globalization and its extraterritorial reach into other countries expand capital circuits that connect not only goods and services but also people globally. As China transitions from an emigration nation to an immigration nation, the racial categorizations that shape its external engagement with the world influence its treatment of immigrant populations too. More importantly, China's experience exemplifies how the territorial underpinnings and norms of citizenship are being reconfigured through the domestic and global events experienced by emigrants, immigrants, and re-migrants.

Territory and Extraterritorial Reach: China's Worldview of Ethnic Stratification

While territory is associated with physically delimited space, territoriality refers to a strategy to "affect, influence, or control [the] actions and interactions (of people, things, and relationships) by asserting and attempting to enforce control over a geographic area."[25] When a state exercises an extraterritorial reach, it is practicing territoriality that extends beyond its political jurisdiction. Arguments examining the extraterritorial conduct of state or non-state power have been deployed to analyze political, economic, urban, or social activities that transcend the national territory or contravene state sovereignty,[26] but juridical and political economy approaches occlude analyses of how membership and belonging are extended contingently to sojourning populations. This book considers the way that territory as a legal concept intersects with identity and subjectivity. By manipulating identity and subjectivity, the extraterritorial conduct of state power can be used to "claim" diaspora populations.[27] Such extraterritorial reach is conducted through flexible rules and norms that result in the "elasticity of territory."[28] In the case of China, ethnic privilege and ethnic stratification feature prominently in how territoriality is exercised within and outside of the national territory.

The idea and practice of citizenship in China combine multiple international antecedents of citizenship with Chinese political thought about the nature of the state and nation.[29] Reunification with Hong Kong and Macau also complicated the political-legal, sociocultural, and territorial assumptions of Chinese citizenship,[30] leading to novel ways of constructing political and cultural membership in China. Peter Harris identifies three streams of thought influential in Chinese conceptions of the state, nation, and citizenship: the Chinese philosophy of *tianxia* (all under heaven), which seeks to forge a culturalist world united in moral harmony; an affirmation of nationhood shared among different ethnic groups; and balanced against that a form of racial nationalism that privileges Han Chinese identity.[31] *Tianxia* connotes a distinctive geographical worldview of how international relations between political units should be organized. It attributes centrality to China as the "Middle Kingdom," with a system of tributary states throughout the rest of the world.

The contemporary iteration of *tianxia*, as popularized by Chinese scholar Zhao Tingyang, prescribes an internal hierarchy of social relations that extends to foreign policy orientations.[32] This Chinese political philosophy, which has been compared to Western notions of cosmopolitanism,[33] is regaining intellectual and foreign policy traction in China today. *Tianxia* resembles the Kantian vision that seeks to manage difference and international relations through a unitary government.[34] The center-periphery relations that *tianxia* invokes and its underlying Confucian principles of loyalty and belonging are also similar to Martha Nussbaum's concentric circles of affiliation (extending from self to family, community, and nation).[35] Yet, a Kantian interpretation of cosmopolitanism has been critiqued for reifying difference and suppressing the political dimensions of inequality, while Nussbaum's concentric-circles model masks the global exploitation of "darker races."[36] Logics of alterity and subjugation of difference are as pervasive in Chinese philosophy and social practice as they are in European enlightenment and colonialism.[37] International relations scholar William Callahan argues that current debates about *tianxia*, as reflected in China's domestic and foreign policies, serve to reinforce a Chinese version of world hegemony.[38]

Tracing the emergence of racial discourse in China, Frank Dikötter highlights that the Chinese philosophy of *tianxia* advocates using (Han) Chinese ways to civilize other races. In this spherical concept of the world with China at the center, "the degree of remoteness from the imperial center corresponded to levels of cultural savagery and physical coarseness."[39] Racial stratification established the privilege of Han Chinese lineage. During the end of the nineteenth century, racialized discourses reached emotional heights as Chinese nationalism premised on the lineage of the Yellow Emperor (the "Han Race") sought to counteract the external threats posed to China by Western imperialism. A hierarchical ordering of the world was popularized in China in the 1890s by reformers such as Kang Youwei and Liang Qichao. Under Kang's philosophical treatise of *datongshu* (One World), darker races were considered unequal.[40] Subsequently, Liang's political thought helped normalize racial classifications in Chinese society and disseminate Han Chinese nationalism by enrolling the Chinese abroad in the service of the ancestral land.

Crucially, Liang excluded ethnic minorities in China from the "genuine yellows" or the majority Han race.[41] Nonetheless, ethnic minorities living within the territorial jurisdiction of China were and continue to be considered key to maintaining the territorial integrity of the nation. For example, the Ethnic Classification Project of 1954 sought to unify ethnic diversity under the leadership of the communist regime.[42] This nation-building project promoted class solidarity as the social glue of China's territorial integrity and national unity. Scholars of China Studies such as Elena Barabantseva and Dru Gladney argue that the promise of ethnic equality under the communist state was subordinated by Han Chinese privilege in both the economic and cultural spheres.[43] Ethnic minorities such as the Uighurs and Tibetans continue to be portrayed as potential threats to national security.[44] But what has changed today is the way the Chinese state now considers emigration among certain ethnic minority groups as a resource for extending China's soft power into new frontiers, just as with the Han Chinese emigrants of the nineteenth and twentieth centuries.

Accompanying the racial nationalism that underpins China's domestic approach toward ethnic diversity is its view of the external world. Barry Sautman argues that racial stereotyping popularized by reformers Liang Qichao and Kang Youwei gave "scientific basis" to beliefs that "blacks were seen as lazy, stupid and incapable of progress."[45] White Westerners were referred to as "foreign devils" (*yangguizi*) but remained socially distinguished from the Africans, who were considered "black ghosts" (*heigui*). Black symbolized the most remote part of the geographically known world and Africans were placed at the lowest rank of the racial hierarchy.[46] After 1949, Chairman Mao Zedong reframed racial discourse as class struggle that builds solidarity with "colored" people in Asia and Africa against white imperialism.[47] Under Mao, China contributed foreign aid and scholarship opportunities to African and Asian nations. Nonetheless, Africans studying in China at that time complained of racial prejudice.[48] From the 1960s to the 1980s, episodic outbursts of racial hostility between African and Chinese students attest to difficult relations arising from the former's dissatisfaction with the low living standards in China and mutual racial antagonism.[49]

How might these debates on racial classification and self-orientalism inform analyses of China's treatment of the new immigrants and long-standing Chinese emigration? A growing variety of immigrants with different visa situations and motivations for migrating to China present unprecedented challenges for the state and society. Distinctive racial hierarchies are observable in Chinese attitudes toward the different ethnic and nationality groups. Anti-black prejudice is resurging in China with the arrival of African traders and immigrants,[50] brought on paradoxically by the external reach of Chinese politics and economics into African countries.[51] Meanwhile, extending an extraterritorial reach toward the Chinese diaspora continues to be legitimized by the ethnic privilege associated with Han Chinese racial discourses. But the Chinese state's developmental goals today give greater weight to the potential economic contributions of the Chinese diaspora.

From Extraterritorial Reach to Citizenship Constellations: China in the World

Emigration received far less scholarly attention than immigration concerns over citizenship[52] until the turn of the millennium, when new optimism about diaspora-centered development[53] became a mantra for national governments and international institutions alike. Migrant-sending countries now strengthen ties with emigrants and/or diasporic descendants to encourage their investments, economic and social remittances, and knowledge transfer to the homeland.[54] Such states redesign citizenship to confer selective rights to diasporas and solicit their duties.[55] Emigrants also actively shape their relationships with migrant-sending states by engaging in practices like voting abroad and long-distance lobbying.[56] These changes to citizenship have been described as extraterritorial, emigrant, or external citizenship.[57] The substance of extraterritorial citizenship varies across countries, but the flexible decoupling of membership, rights, or responsibilities from national territory features prominently throughout.

When states exercise an extraterritorial reach to regulate membership and political life, they engage in transnational practices.[58] Transnationalism scholarship addresses aspects of community life that extend across national borders, but it does not adequately theorize the "membership manifest in the relationship between states and migrants or does so, only implicitly."[59] Inasmuch as extraterritorial citizenship is a function of transnational citizenship, it also deserves theory building in its own right. The focus of political sociologists and political geographers has been on the institutional restructuring of the nation and state, or on political transnationalism and international relations.[60] I adopt a different approach of foregrounding how identity and subjectivity contribute to the extraterritorial restructuring of political and legal state power. Analyzing extraterritorial citizenship brings greater precision to how we understand citizenship engagement and the way that state power cuts across multiple levels of analyses and domains.

Also distinctive about how citizenship is asserted extraterritorially today is the way it is increasingly drawn into immigration and citizenship debates. Coutin observes that examining immigration through the lens of emigration can undermine the constructs and apparatus through which immigration is conceptualized.[61] Rainer Bauböck further points out that migrant rights are constituted by citizenship norms and policies in both the countries of origin and settlement.[62] In separate writing, Bauböck deploys the term "citizenship constellations" to describe how citizenship norms and practices in two or more countries can become entangled when migrants claim legal status, biographical ties, or belonging to multiple national societies.[63] How should we analyze citizenship formations that extend across distance and are constituted by both migrant-sending and migrant-receiving countries? This book addresses three analytical routes through which citizenship constellations can be traced in the study of Chinese migration.

First, through successive periods of emigration and subsequent re-migration, multiple sites of origin and destination now characterize the journeys of the Chinese abroad. As Laurence Ma and Carolyn Cartier observe, "Re-migration has expanded the areal extent of the Chinese diaspora, created new paths of transnational circulation of people and capital, and contributed to the diaspora's social heterogeneity."[64] Second, the re-migration routes of migrants reverse the origin and destination sites. When migrants naturalize abroad, then return to the country of origin (now the site of immigration), they form diaspora populations that claim a second affiliation to the country in which they have naturalized (now the site of emigration). Their re-migration creates new questions for how ancestral or natal lands should treat returnees with foreign citizenships. It also generates new dilemmas for the countries where they had immigrated, naturalized, and then subsequently left. Third, countries experiencing migration rarely function as only origin or destination sites. They experience immigration and emigration simultaneously and seek to enroll both types of migration in their nation-building projects. Thus transnationalism and integration debates in migrant-receiving countries must be analyzed alongside such patterns of spatial interaction.

Fraternity and Alterity in Citizenship Projects: Ordering Chinese Co-ethnicity

This complex canvas of migration patterns creates new citizenship struggles, especially in nation-states whose societies are characterized by both immigration histories and contemporary immigration flows. Catherine Dauvergne describes nations built through extensive migration as "settler societies" that subscribe to a mythology of immigration.[65] In such societies earlier immigrants are considered the progenitors of the national community. But each cohort of immigrants is also a diaspora from another country. Settler nations contain multiple diasporas with affiliations to different origin sites or who identify with a different period of migration even if they are from the same ancestral land. What appears to be "new migrations" to postcolonial nation-states are already linked through "old migrations" (from the same source countries) that transpired during colonial times.[66] But the identity and affiliations of both types of migrants are refracted through decolonization and postcolonial nation building, and emigrants and diasporic descendants maintain lingering cultural ties with the migrant-sending country.

Cognitive taxonomies stratify people into categories of ethnicity, nationality, class, and more. They create internal borders that define social inclusion or exclusion and hierarchies of difference.[67] Differential treatment is given to categories of migrants and co-ethnics based on their presumed potential to contribute to the economic well-being of the nation-state and/or based on an "'imagined community' bound by blood or kinship."[68] In a study of Mainland Chinese immigrant wives in Hong Kong, Nicole Newendorp observes that immigrants are expected to adopt purported qualities of Hong Kong citizens.[69] Civilizing processes like this exemplify enactments of cultural citizenship, referring to the "qualitative distinctions in senses of belonging, entitlement, and influence that vary in distinct situations and in different local communities."[70] Such distinctions emerge through cultural encounters that are "contingent, improvisational, and transformative,"[71] thus reformulating identities relationally.

The biopolitical power of the state operationalizes a variety of cognitive taxonomies and internal borders as it asserts migration management toward *not only immigrants but also emigrants*. The state institutionalizes immigration as a necessary pillar of nation building yet undermines it in at least two ways: first, by creating greater differentiation between citizenship, permanent residency, and temporary residence rights; and second, by privileging natal ties, thereby rendering the belonging of later cohorts of immigrants as always secondary to those of earlier cohorts. Hence, as Dauvergne observes, despite official statements and policies that promote multiculturalism, an "immigration hierarchy" prioritizing earlier immigrant arrivals still exists, even in paradigmatic settler societies like Canada and Australia.[72] Comparatively, the state extends membership to emigrants selectively by privileging ancestral or natal belonging despite the physical absence of such migrants from the national territory.

This book critically examines the manner in which states, migrants, and nonmigrants flexibly mobilize fraternity and alterity claims. Exemplifying this are the tensions between "old" and "new" migration found in Canada and Singapore, two postcolonial nations that are experiencing contemporary immigration from China even as their own citizens emigrate to live, study, or work abroad. On the one hand, these states couch nation building in arguments of national vulnerability and survival, and they mobilize these arguments to urge new immigrants to integrate and court their own emigrants. On the other hand, these same states extend membership to their emigrants outside of the national territory but deny such fraternity to immigrants by invoking their alterity instead.

Analyzing alterity through entrenched racial hierarchies only accounts for one manifestation of how fraternity is withheld from newcomers. Interracial divisions do not account for how alterity operates in the context of co-ethnicity or how alterity mutates spatially and temporally. The concept of *suzhi* ("quality" or human capital) in China, normally invoked in discussions of rural migration,[73] proves key to understanding how alterity is operationalized spatially during international migration too. For Chris Vasantkumar, the "contingent amalgamations of class, 'quality,' place of origin, degree of developedness [sic] and a host of other linked factors" function as markers of difference that are assembled through localized and non-localized ways.[74] Even though internal migration is not the focus of this book, it informs analyses of the international migration trends discussed here. Internal migration is interlinked with international migration trends, but it presents citizenship tensions of its own that merit fuller discussion elsewhere.[75]

This book undertakes a different task of tracing the spatial dispersion and interconnection of Chinese migration historically through to the present day so as illuminate how migration triggers alterity dynamics among co-ethnics. Identities such as class, *suzhi*, place of origin, nationality, and degree of development take on importance in contingent ways as national societies and migrants alike struggle to define fraternity and alterity. In one respect, alterity can operate on the basis of territorial belonging (i.e., the country one comes from) and its perceived correlation to developmental and moral superiority or inferiority. In another respect, the contingent nature of fraternity and alterity also means that both can be potentially spatially recalibrated during migration (e.g., the new importance of emigrants as developmental resources).

Contemporaneous Migration: Spatial and Temporal Interconnections

To conclude, the temporal simultaneity of global events and the spatial connections that interlink migration sites propel personal migration decisions that have a collective impact on those sites. Attentiveness to the contemporaneous aspects of migration prompts us to link the domestic management of migration and citizenship to external events and engagement. The rise of China and its overtures to disseminate Chinese language and culture has triggered new interest in the global spread of Chinese philosophy, modern thought, and business conduct. Chinese developmental models and norms circulate globally when individuals and social groups interact with one another through migration.

Contemporaneity is signaled in two prominent ways in this book: First, studying emigration, immigration, and re-migration trends concurrently underlines not only the co-presence of migrant populations or multiple diasporas within a migration site, but also the significance of emigrants in national citizenship debates despite their absence from the national territory (i.e., an absent presence). Second, analyzing the temporal meanings that different stakeholders of citizenship construct illuminates the way in which fraternity and alterity work through operationalizing racial hierarchies or alleged cultural differences between co-ethnics. Foregrounding notions of co-presence alongside manifestations of social difference directs attention to the possibility of an emergent cosmopolitan sociability that values shared experiences and aspirations without seeking to essentialize or erase difference.[76]

The chapters that follow unpack how the logics of fraternity and alterity manifest in China, Canada, and Singapore when Chinese migration patterns interface with other ways of understanding diversity and citizenship in those societies. Chapter 2 sets out the context of China's diaspora engagement during the period from 1949 to 1979. In the same period, suppression of communism in British-ruled Malaya and ethno-nationalism in newly decolonized Indonesia and Vietnam prompted the expulsion of Chinese populations in those countries. Circumstances forced them to seek readmission to China as "returnees" even though many had not lived in the ancestral land before. The Chinese state framed their move as the "return" of co-ethnics, resettled them in state-owned farms, and provided economic and social entitlements. The chapter highlights the tensions and challenges they faced, troubling claims to co-ethnic affinity. The recognition extended to them was conditional on their political and cultural re-integration into socialist China. Their pasts and familial relationships in Southeast Asia positioned them as subjects belonging to but placed at the periphery of both social worlds. Subsequent domestic political events reinforced their cultural alterity. The co-ethnic privilege perceptible from 1949 to 1979 receded as the Chinese state's subsequent diaspora strategies prioritized scientific skills and economic contributions to advance national development. The chapter argues that only by examining the historical context of China's diaspora engagement can we grasp the continuities or discontinuities apparent in contemporary diaspora strategizing.

Chapter 3 directs the discussion toward how contemporary emigration and return trends in China are entwined with the policies of migrant-receiving countries. It focuses on first-generation Mainland Chinese emigrants who had immigrated to Canada, experienced de-skilling and integration challenges, and subsequently returned to China. Such de-skilled returnees are not considered part of the highly skilled diaspora desired by China's contemporary diaspora strategizing. Since China restricts dual citizenship, those who naturalized in Canada are compelled to seek readmission to the natal land using immigrant visas. Despite claiming biographical ties and stakeholdership, legally they are considered foreigners in China. While in China, they develop a secondary identification as part of the Canadian diaspora. Transnationalism theory provides one way of understanding their dual affiliations, but deliberate policies by both China and Canada to mobilize their respective diasporas provide a new lens to examine such citizenship formations. The chapter highlights the citizenship constellations that interlink emigration and immigration contexts. It also examines the reversal of source and destination countries when migrants engage in repeated re-migration across the life course, troubling premises of citizenship such as territorial presence or duration to deepen fraternity ties.

Building on these arguments, Chapter 4 draws out the migration flows interconnecting Singapore and China. Singapore, a country birthed through the agglomeration of multiple past diasporas, is now facing new immigration pressures alongside concerns over Singaporean emigration. The chapter pays attention to the tensions between the "old" Chinese diaspora, which considers Singapore a natal land, and the post-1979 "new" Chinese diaspora. Co-ethnicity is downplayed by Singaporeans of Chinese ethnicity, who emphasize a version of multiculturalism that is associated with earlier waves of immigration to

Singapore. The chapter argues that color-coded and allegedly color-blind racism can coexist in multicultural Singapore because of such framings of territoriality and temporality. Responding to popular pressure, the Singaporean state has stepped up immigrant integration efforts. Furthermore, it is extending nation building to overseas Singaporeans through diaspora engagement. The alterity of new immigrants in Singapore is heightened when set against the fraternity claims extended to Singaporeans abroad on account of natal ties despite their territorial absence. The chapter draws together the themes of diaspora, identity, fraternity, and alterity by discussing how territoriality and temporality are invoked to legitimize and prioritize natal belonging.

Chapter 5 analyzes how China manages both domestic ethnic diversity and the convergence of a variety of foreigners in the country today. Whereas China was once known primarily as an emigration country, today it is both a site of return or re-migration and new immigration. This chapter considers three distinct manifestations of alterity arising from those intersecting migration trends: phenotypical difference as evinced through African immigration to China; diversification of co-ethnicity as reflected through the re-migration of Chinese diasporic descendants; and the spatial recalibration of alterity brought about by emigrating ethnic minorities. Analyzing the contemporaneous aspects of migration in China signals ways to reconsider the global nature of Chinese society, not in the classic sense of China as represented through the Chinese diaspora, but in the sense of the world as immanent in China yet contingent on events elsewhere. It shows that contemporaneous migration fosters China as an active site of global interconnections with the world, compelling it to reconsider both its domestic policy and its foreign policy toward migration governance and diversity.

Overall, this book provides a conceptual approach for studying and theorizing the multidirectional journeys that impact and deepen articulations of fraternity or alterity between interethnic and co-ethnic groups. Analyzing the contemporaneous aspects of migration draws out citizenship struggles within a country and the citizenship constellations that connect the countries in which migrants claim stakeholdership at different stages of their lives.

2 Chinese Re-migration

Introduction

Counter-diasporic migration,[1] or the return of diasporic descendants to an ancestral land,[2] has become a noticeable global trend, signaling that over time major shifts can occur in the direction of migration.[3] Such migration routes are linked to the development agendas of ancestral lands that seek to capitalize upon the resources represented by the descendants of emigrants (henceforth diasporic descendants). From the perspective of the migrants, counter-diasporic migration symbolizes their enduring ties with the ancestral land. This chapter considers China's extraterritorial reach toward both the overseas Chinese (*huaqiao*) and diasporic descendants (*huayi*), which it labels as the "Chinese diaspora" (*sanju huaren*). In 1978 the Overseas Chinese Affairs Office of the State Council was established; that year is normally taken as the starting point of China's strategic outreach to contemporary diasporic communities.[4] However, the extraterritorial reach of the Chinese state has a genealogy that predates 1978, and it is crucial to study China's contemporary diaspora strategies in the context of past diaspora engagement.

Diaspora engagement by China dates as far back as the late Qing dynasty, which reigned from 1644 to 1912.[5] But the focus of this chapter is on the events that transpired from 1949 to 1979, a period considered significant because it marked the inauguration of communist rule in China. During the same period, the Chinese in Southeast Asia became embroiled in decolonization conflicts as newly minted political elites sought to advance nation building in those countries while negotiating the vestiges of colonial rule and fending off threats of communist encroachment.[6] Consequently, Chinese diasporic descendants in Malaya,[7] Indonesia, and Vietnam were compelled to leave their countries of residence. As a show of co-ethnic fraternity and given wider geopolitical considerations, China resettled the expelled diasporic descendants on state-owned farms in the ancestral land even if they had not lived there before and were not considered nationals of the People's Republic of China.[8]

This chapter begins the task of challenging linear narratives of emigration and immigration by examining the re-migration of diasporic descendants to an ancestral land. Migrant-sending states construct narratives that reach into the past to legitimize their extraterritorial reach toward diaspora populations. But the social realities of exclusion experienced by those who re-migrated expose the cognitive taxonomies that were used to privilege alleged cultural purity over hybridity. Contestations over presumed kinship and co-ethnic identity underline the complex relationship that Chinese diasporic descendants have with the ancestral land. Such contestations are also seen in Japan, South Korea, Hong Kong, Macau, and Taiwan, where the re-migration of co-ethnics has challenged assumptions of kinship.[9]

Subsequent political events and domestic concerns in China further impacted how the Chinese state and society treated the Chinese abroad and the domestic populations that had ties to them. After 1978, China's diaspora strategizing gradually shifted from privileging co-ethnicity to efforts concerned with inviting foreign capital through the connections of the Chinese abroad. From the 1990s onward the Chinese state stepped up efforts to minimize brain drain and tap the Chinese scientific diaspora for development purposes.[10] China's diaspora engagement reveals its perceptions of the Chinese abroad and shows how citizenship formations in China were linked to the circulatory histories, genealogies, and events of its regional neighbors in Southeast Asia.[11] The discussion draws on historical research from overseas Chinese studies and original ethnographic research and oral history interviews conducted with the Chinese diasporic descendants who resettled in China from 1949 to 1979.

Spatiotemporal Connections and China's Extraterritorial Reach

A fertile scholarship on the Chinese in Southeast Asia has debated the framing of Chinese migration and the identity of the Chinese living outside of China.[12] Should they be referred to as the Chinese diaspora, overseas Chinese, or Chinese overseas?[13] Prasenjit Duara argues that officially circulated histories tend to "occlude, repress, appropriate, and sometimes, negotiate with other modes of depicting the past, and thus, the present and future."[14] Grasping the processes through which historically constructed labels are appropriated, hidden, or suppressed is important for uncovering alternative histories and social narratives.

Chinese migrants of the nineteenth and twentieth centuries traveled as far as North America and Europe, but many more ventured to Southeast Asia. Stories about riches to be found in *Nanyang* (the South China Sea) and migration networks connecting coastal provinces in China with Southeast Asia facilitated chain migration.[15] The relationship of China to the Chinese abroad has always been a subject of contention for the different political regimes. Chinese emigration during the eighteenth century was governed by the Qing government, which tried to enforce exit controls, fearing emigrants would collude with foreigners. Following China's defeat during the First Opium War (1839–1842), European governments developed regulations to encourage voluntary emigration and ensure that brokers of indentured labor would be licensed. The Qing government negotiated for the extraterritorial protection of Chinese subjects who departed, arguing that "they should be considered as if China were loaning them to foreign countries to use."[16]

Scholars of overseas Chinese studies regard the 1860 Treaty of Beijing between Britain and China as a milestone that marked both the legitimate recognition of Chinese emigration and regulation of Chinese labor migration.[17] Subsequent treaties were signed with other foreign powers to formalize the legal status of Chinese migrants.[18] The Qing government grew to value the financial resources and Western technological knowledge represented by emigrants. From the 1880s onward policies were introduced to involve emigrants in the reform and modernization of China. The Qing government gave the Chinese abroad special privileges and protection, which it extended to their dependents (*qiaojuan*) in China and returnees (*guiqiao*). Its 1909 nationality law recognized all children born to Chinese parents as nationals regardless of their birthplace.[19] Subsequently, the Chinese abroad played a significant role in supporting the revolutionary overthrow of the Qing dynasty in favor of Sun Yat-sen's republican regime. Sun recruited Chinese emigrants and diasporic descendants, particularly those in Southeast Asia; he gave them representation in political decision making and established administrative functions to handle the affairs of the Chinese abroad.[20]

The new communist government continued this approach of engaging the Chinese diaspora when it took power in 1949. The political leaders established the Committee of Overseas Chinese Affairs—subsequently renamed the Overseas Chinese Affairs Commission (OCAC) of the People's Republic of China—and it continued to function until it was abolished in 1970. The government also supported the formation of a non-governmental organization known as The All-China Federation of Returned Overseas Chinese, similarly tasked with reaching out to the Chinese abroad. In 1955 the Chinese Communist Party (CCP) issued two significant decrees: the first protected the rights of returned overseas Chinese (*guiqiao*) and the dependents of the overseas Chinese (*qiaojuan*) to receive remittances, and the second extended investment privileges to the overseas Chinese and returnees. These decrees sought to protect the *guiqiao* and *qiaojuan* from the social and economic effects of rural socialist transformation, and to encourage the development of tropical agriculture through the wealth and expertise brought by the return of the Southeast Asian Chinese.[21] Even though China introduced a law barring dual nationality in 1958,[22] the Chinese state maintained an extraterritorial reach over co-ethnics abroad by using provisions in domestic law, and it continued to facilitate the re-migration of the Chinese abroad to the ancestral land.

Across the nineteenth and early twentieth centuries, Chinese diasporic descendants in Southeast Asia adopted the customs and languages of the countries in which they lived. Emigrant Chinese and those born in Southeast Asia were part of decolonization histories in the region, but the Chinese state appropriated historical narratives to suit its needs at that time. Its version of linear history portrayed the anti-Chinese climate of decolonization and assimilation pressures in those countries as a threat to the safety of the Chinese abroad[23] and to China's own nation building and extraterritorial reach.[24] Such narratives contained a temporal structure which offered "story statements that connect the action with beliefs about actual past events and desires and expectations about future events."[25] The Chinese state's narrative structures framed Chinese emigrants and diasporic descendants as an extension of the nation abroad both spatially and temporally. Such expressions of solidarity enabled the state to legitimize their return and convince domestic publics of its repatriation and resettlement policies. Concurrent events linked developments in Southeast Asia with those in China and shaped the lived realities of those who moved between the two contexts.

Return, a Sleight of Hand

Sovereignty projects mobilize symbolic resources (linguistic, aural, visual, textual) to emphasize alleged enduring kinship links between emigrants or diasporic descendants and the ancestral land.[26] Even as transnational migration patterns reinforced purported connections between kinship and nation building, they also destabilized idealized narratives of kinship and national belonging.[27] After the CCP took power in 1949, its political leaders tacitly encouraged the Chinese abroad to re-migrate to China. Those who re-migrated between 1949 and 1979 can be categorized into two groups: the intellectuals who returned voluntarily to study or to serve the ancestral land, and the deportees and refugees who were compelled to seek sanctuary in China.[28] For the first group, about fifty thousand overseas Chinese voluntarily re-migrated to China to receive a Chinese-language education during the 1950s.[29] The Chinese political leadership initially considered them intellectuals who would contribute to building the new socialist nation, but it gradually saw and depicted the students (*qiaosheng*) as troublemakers with capitalist leanings that contradicted communist ideology.[30] As part of socialist re-education efforts, a number of those who returned voluntarily were dispatched to state-owned farms, where they lived and worked alongside the deportees and refugees.

Toward this second group of involuntary migrants (henceforth refugee-returnees), China adopted the role of a protector by facilitating their return and resettlement in the ancestral land. The Chinese leadership had faced criticism from the Chinese abroad during the 1950s for not responding promptly to reports of anti-Chinese discrimination in Indonesia and Vietnam. The OCAC and the Chinese Foreign Ministry wavered between encouraging Chinese emigrants and diasporic descendants to integrate in their countries of residence and repatriating those who were unable or unwilling to do so.[31] Official pronouncements by CCP members represented on the OCAC urged the Chinese abroad not to expect "special consideration" from the ancestral land and discouraged them from sending their children back to China for education.[32] Yet from 1959 to 1969, the Chinese state sent ships to repatriate those who chose to leave Indonesia's climate of anti-Chinese hostilities. It also accommodated a mass exodus of Chinese fleeing ethnic persecution in Vietnam after 1978.

From 1949 to 1979, China received more than a half-million co-ethnics, who arrived under forced migration circumstances from countries such as

Malaya, Indonesia, and Vietnam.[33] The circumstances of these episodes of forced migration differed,[34] but some commonalities can be drawn out of China's diaspora engagement and resettlement policies at that time. The first batch of refugee-returnees that China resettled in the years between 1949 and 1953 were from Malaya; about fifteen thousand economic and political refugees from Malaya went to China during the 1950s.[35] The British colonial government had deported them for participating in the communist insurgency in Malaya. Between 1959 and 1969, another batch fleeing anti-Chinese actions in Indonesia arrived in China. The last batch of Vietnamese-Chinese came during 1978 and 1979, following repressive policies enacted by the Vietnamese government (but discrimination against the Chinese in Vietnam had been ongoing since the 1950s).

The refugee-returnees were resettled in state-owned farms (*huaqiao nongchang*) and given farming equipment to support their families through agricultural labor. Considered of *huaqiao* background, the deportees and refugees were granted special status in Chinese society: they were treated as "refugee-returnees" (*guiguo nanqiao*) and offered protection and privileges on the premise of co-ethnicity. As Stephen Fitzgerald puts it, "These people were accorded a special, and sometimes very privileged, status, and the sole justification for this status was their relationship with the Chinese abroad."[36] The term *huaqiao* had been popularized by the Qing regime to encourage Chinese sojourners to identify with China.[37] Together with the intellectuals who re-migrated to China, the refugee-returnees helped consolidate for the new political regime the identity of the Chinese nation through a collective identity known as *guiqiao*, translated as a generic category of "returnees."

Portraying the diasporic descendants as returnees proved to be a sleight of hand, however, since they had never lived in China before. How then could they have "returned?" Their nationality status also posed complications for the Chinese authorities, because many of the deportees and refugees had naturalized abroad or acquired the citizenship of a foreign country at birth. China should have extended protection only to those holding Chinese nationality status, but it did not limit its repatriation efforts to this group. In deciding to "return" to China, the refugee-returnees had to relinquish their foreign nationality status. They then became a stateless population within China for decades until they were eventually given *hukou* status by the Chinese state.[38] Tracing these historical events signals the "hardening (or softening) of porous social and cultural boundaries around a particular configuration of self in relation to an

Other,"[39] the latter referring to social groups that are perceived as distinct from one's own identity.

When the portrayal of national history is set against the histories of the people most affected by such events, it reveals the social differences or alterity that developed across space and time. The refugee-returnees found that the membership or fraternity extended to them by the Chinese state and society was conditional. Political events in China circumscribed their economic participation and social integration. They experienced the logics of fraternity and alterity simultaneously. Etienne Balibar notes that racism can function in equivocal ways and that it proliferates through culture, nationality, and class.[40] As it merges with those social formations, racism constructs and institutionalizes patterns of behavior that combine intellectual bases with affect. Although normally associated with phenotype, racism is at its core about how cognitive taxonomies manifest as systematic modes of exclusion, stigmatization, and repression. Exclusion removes the Other from recognition, status, dignity, rights, and access to normal social relations and activities.

Read this way, our analysis can shift from approaching racism as biological coding (i.e., "race" or "ethnicity") to how racism manifests itself by naturalizing cultural codes. Among co-ethnics, this means projecting hierarchies of difference onto the social construct of "co-ethnicity." The refugee-returnees who re-migrated to China were considered culturally and morally inferior by the domestic Chinese, who grew to despise their foreign connections. Difference, otherness, and exclusion are categories open to their own transformations.[41] The stories that the refugee-returnees shared represent attempts to make sense of their transnational journeys and "engage in the construction of a moral vision."[42]

Spatiotemporal Disconnections and Alterity

I met Auntie Liu by chance when I was exploring the village one afternoon during my first visit to one of the state-owned farms where the refugee-returnees had been resettled. Walking past a two-story house in the village, I noticed a young man puttering around the front porch, so I stopped and asked him about the village. I had already seen a Thai-style roof, Balinese pavilion, and a small plot of land described by a sign as the "Malaysian garden," which I thought was a peculiar combination of Southeast Asian influences. Overhearing my questions, Auntie Liu joined the conversation from the balcony of the house.

I learned that the young man was her son, and that she was originally from Malaya. She had come to China in 1961 at the behest of her husband, who had returned earlier during the 1950s because the Chinese state had encouraged the Chinese abroad to re-migrate to the ancestral land. She was only twenty-seven years old at that time. Her return coincided with the period of the social upheavals of the Cultural Revolution. Auntie Liu declined to speak further about those episodes, except to say that it was a difficult time for all. When I told her that I was from Singapore she became sentimental, and tears welled up in her eyes. She had not seen her siblings in Sabah, Malaysia, for more than forty years, and I represented memories of her life in Malaya, since historically Singapore was part of British-ruled Malaya, together with the states in the Malay peninsula. A lady in a *batik* blouse who passed by the house as we were chatting joined our conversation and told me she was from Indonesia.[43] A fire disaster in her village caused by hostilities against the Chinese led to her resettlement in China. The Chinese state had "recruited" people like her who were affected by the anti-Chinese climate in Indonesia during the 1960s. Over subsequent fieldwork visits, I learned more about the people living in that village—their stories and the political events and economic reforms that underpinned the pockets of Southeast Asian architecture and cultural influences I had seen in the village.

Most of the refugee-returnees arrived in China with few personal belongings because they had left their countries of residence hastily. With nowhere to live and no means of livelihood, they could only rely on the patronage of the Chinese state, which resettled them in what were known colloquially as the "overseas Chinese farms."[44] Earlier cohorts of Chinese from Malaya and Indonesia (1949–1969) were sent to coastal provinces in Guangdong, Fujian, and Hainan Island, where there was undeveloped land to be farmed. Over the years, other refugee-returnees who had experienced anti-Chinese nationalism in Thailand and Myanmar were also resettled on those farms,[45] but their numbers were few compared to the cohorts from Malaya and Indonesia. The next significant influx of refugee-returnees was from Vietnam. New state-owned farms were built for them in Guangxi province, which shares a land border with Vietnam. Others were sent to existing farms in the coastal provinces of China.[46] Over time the state-owned farms in coastal China came to house a diverse population of Chinese diasporic descendants who had re-migrated to the ancestral land.

Although the refugee-returnees were not Chinese nationals, as returnees[47] they were granted better privileges than domestic populations in the neighboring communes.[48] The Malayans and Indonesians I interviewed recalled that the refugee-returnees received more rice and dried food rations, even though agricultural reforms restricted the food packages that were distributed to each family.[49] As agricultural conditions worsened in the period leading up to the Great Leap Forward, the food packages for the refugee-returnees were reduced. But unlike the domestic Chinese, they could still receive food parcels and re-mittances from abroad,[50] linking them with family members they had left behind in Southeast Asia.

Many of the refugee-returnees did not speak Mandarin (*putonghua)*, the official language in China, since they grew up in Southeast Asia. They had been socialized into the language and cultural norms of their natal lands in South-east Asia.[51] Some retained their ancestral dialects, such as Hokkien, Hakka, or Cantonese, but the resettlement plans of the Chinese state did not relocate them to places where those dialects were spoken. The Chinese state projected on them a historical consciousness of co-ethnic belonging from an earlier pe-riod. At the same time, it sought to insert them into a contemporary period characterized by reforms to instill a "laboring outlook" (*laodong guannian*) in the people.[52] Fervent communist cadres and the domestic Chinese expected the refugee-returnees to conform to the social norms associated with the tran-sition to socialism. Consequently, the refugee-returnees experienced both spatial and temporal displacement as they navigated multiple pasts and the present, each associated with different places.

The refugee-returnees sought to recreate a familiar home environment in China. The sub-tropical climate in the Chinese coastal province allowed them to plant crops found in tropical countries, such as jackfruit, pandan leaves, and lemongrass.[53] The expansion of coffee plantations in China became associated with the returnees from Southeast Asia, who introduced coffee-growing and -roasting techniques into local landscapes. The extraterritorial state power that brought the refugee-returnees back to China facilitated the production of transnational spaces. During my visits to the farms, the older refugee-returnees from Malaya or Indonesia would proudly show old photographs of how they recreated a semblance of their lives in Southeast Asia through at-tire, food, dance, and music. My visits gave them reason to gather old friends to reminisce about the past. They were delighted at my interest in the memo-ries they shared from places long gone and times long past; their children and grandchildren had no such orientations. On those social occasions, a few older ladies would bring along home-cooked dishes such as jackfruit curry and pergedil (potato patty) as a treat for their friends. During my visits I stayed with a Vietnamese family who would regularly serve sticky rice or Vietnamese stews to their homestay guests alongside other Chinese dishes. On any ordinary day if one walked past the homes in the village during the late morning before lunch-time, the aroma of food cooked in Southeast Asian spices would fill the air.

Differences in taste, fashion, and cultural training constituted the alterity of the refugee-returnees. For example, one of the refugee-returnees told me that they preferred to sport tidy hairstyles and wear covered shoes habitual to the colonial-ruled countries they had left, unlike the domestic Chinese in rural China, who he said did not comb their hair and wore open-toed slippers every-where. The refugee-returnees disliked austere communist attire and longed for the colorful patterns of the clothes they associated with Southeast Asia, but their cultural habitus and historical consciousness became associated with for-eign influences and capitalist practices. The domestic Chinese and the politi-cal leadership thought the refugee-returnees enjoyed decadent pleasures more than the collective labor they contributed to the socialist society, and so they would need to be culturally assimilated and purged of capitalist influences.

Counter-diasporic migration or diaspora ethnic return documented in other parts of the world are similarly characterized by displacement experi-ences rather than homecoming.[54] What stands out in the Chinese case is the divergent ways the refugee-returnees were treated by the state and society dur-ing different political episodes in China. The poor treatment they endured underscored how definitions of Chineseness and co-ethnicity had "less to do with blood than with politics."[55] A phobia of degeneracy creates cognitive tax-onomies and hierarchies of difference.[56] Tensions over diasporic ethnic return illustrate how a deterministic view of purity can be privileged over hybridity.

Spatiotemporal Upheavals and Adaptation

Few escaped the socialist reforms leading to the Great Leap Forward of 1958, which permeated both the economy and the society in China.[57] The refugee-returnees, unaccustomed to agricultural labor, were nevertheless made to toil in the state-owned farms. As Glen Peterson documents, the "state farms were run with military discipline, with people awakened each morning and marched off to work. . . . [The workers] toiled in the fields in military-style formations [and] lived in military barracks and ate together in large mess halls."[58] Similar accounts of forced labor were shared by the refugee-returnees I met during my repeat visits to the farms. One of them was Uncle Fang, a second-generation

Malayan refugee-returnee who had re-migrated to China as a child. He recounted a sorry tale an Indonesian-Chinese had told him. After the Indonesian-Chinese arrived in China they stayed for a short time in the cities but were subsequently trucked to the state-owned farms. As the trucks approached the farms, the passengers, seeing the desolation around them, came to the realization that they would be subject to agricultural labor. In tears, they begged the drivers and communist cadres accompanying them to take them back to the city. But there was no turning back. Another Indonesian-Chinese told me the farms were uncultivated when they first arrived. With only sparse farming tools and machinery available, they were forced to dig the soil with their bare hands. At the end of the day those hands were smeared with their own blood, and yet the next day they had to carry on working in the fields.

During the Cultural Revolution (1966–1976) the refugee-returnees experienced stigmatization on account of their foreign ties, and they became targets of political campaigns. The land reforms of the early 1950s had produced a collective consciousness that labeled those that belonged to special status groups, such as the *huaqiao* and *guiqiao*, as "bourgeois" or "bad." The stigma intensified during the Cultural Revolution, bringing suffering to the refugee-returnees, who also fell subject to the surveillance of communist cadres known as the Red Guards (*hongweibing*).[59] Under the political climate of the Cultural Revolution, the OCAC fell apart and so did the protection and privileges it extended toward the returned overseas Chinese (*guiguo huaqiao*). The returnees were subjected to the political and social reforms, even as they yearned for the natal lands they had left behind in Southeast Asia.

Decades later, such interconnections to Southeast Asia continued to remind the refugee-returnees of the transnational family histories and spaces they had left behind. Uncle Fang, who came from Malaya with his parents during the 1950s, recalled the tins of Jacob's cream crackers they used to receive in the food parcels sent by relatives. Mimicking the excitement of a young child opening a gift, he told me those biscuits, considered a treat from abroad that was unavailable to the domestic Chinese, helped stave off hunger pangs during times when the family's food rations were low. But the biscuits also symbolized their lingering ties to Western capitalism. On the verge of tears, he continued, "My parents were later imprisoned for alleged ties to 'capitalists.' Even though I was a child, when I brought food to them the prison guards would make me eat a mouthful first to ensure it was not laced with poison." He explained, "Poison meant the prisoners would experience a quick death," a punishment considered inadequate for those with capitalist connections. In recounting this sorrowful episode from the past, Uncle Fang was visibly angry at the treatment his family had endured despite the Chinese government's rhetoric of blood, kinship, and homecoming.

Acts of speech such as those narrated by Uncle Fang reflect what John Frow describes as "heterogeneous clusters of time."[60] For Frow, heterogeneous assemblages of time are made up of diverse temporalities that "run at different speeds and according to different social imaginaries."[61] First, they include what he describes as "the time of enunciation, with its two-fold division between the time of speaking and the time spoken of." They capture the double pasts of the refugee-returnees located in Southeast Asia and in China. Second, they draw on chronological time, starting from ancestral emigration to Southeast Asia, to the Second World War, decolonization in their countries of residence, their re-migration to China, and subsequent Chinese modernization and political and social reforms. Third, there is a diverse set of social temporalities associated with the dominant temporality of modernization and national citizenship, and the discordant temporality of how they sought to recover their cultural identity as co-ethnics and patriotic comrades during different political events in China.

Throughout the mid- to late twentieth century, China emphasized co-ethnicity in its diaspora engagement. There were periods when the Chinese state retreated from diaspora engagement, but the Chinese abroad continued to feature prominently in state policies emphasizing the temporal and spatial ties that linked them with the ancestral land. Nonetheless, as China emerged from a period of isolationism, the state's approach toward diaspora engagement started to shift in other ways.

China's New Emigration and Contemporary Diaspora Strategies

From 1978 onward, China's Open Door Policy under Deng Xiaoping brought economic reforms and revived diaspora engagement policies. The Overseas Chinese Affairs Office (*Qiaoban*) was established in 1978 to replace the OCAC, and the state-supported non-governmental organization known as the All-China Federation of Returned Overseas Chinese (*Qiaolian*) was reinstated that same year, after having been suspended during the Cultural Revolution. In 1991 the special status of the returnees was formally institutionalized in the

Law of the People's Republic of China on the Protection of the Rights and Interests of Returned Overseas Chinese and the Family Members of Overseas
Chinese (*Guiqiao Qiaojuan Quanyi Baohu Fa*). The law was amended in 2000
and 2005 to enhance the welfare of returnees and their dependents in the areas of legal protection, political representation, housing and social welfare, education, and investment.[62] These marked a new phase of the Chinese state's
engagement with co-ethnics in places as diverse as Southeast Asia, Europe, and
North America.

As part of the reforms of the Open Door Policy, Deng Xiaoping established
special economic zones in areas bordering Hong Kong, Macau, and Taiwan.
The choice of these locations—namely Shenzhen, Zhuhai, Shantou, and
Xiamen—was by no means incidental; the zones were located near the ancestral hometowns of Chinese emigrants and diasporic descendants. Older generations of wealthy Chinese abroad were invited to invest in their ancestral
land, as the Chinese state sought to mobilize their knowledge of capitalist development. It portrayed the Chinese abroad as patriots rather than mere capitalist agents.[63] According to one estimate, over two-thirds of all foreign capital
coming into China came from the ethnic Chinese between 1979 and 1997.[64]
Such foreign investments predominantly came from the Chinese in Hong
Kong, Macau, Taiwan, and Southeast Asia.[65]

Chinese diasporic descendants in Southeast Asia are valued by the Chinese
state for their co-ethnic ties and as emblems of soft power, given China's strategic military interests in the region. Nonetheless, the Chinese state recognizes
that Chinese diasporic descendants are embedded in their countries of settlement and it treads a "delicate balance of power between diaspora and state."[66]
As Ma and Cartier established, the spatial attributes of the Chinese abroad are
diffused, the patterns of interaction evinced are multi-directional, and characterized by "multiple centers of origin and destination."[67] The Chinese living
in different parts of the world display diverse characteristics and hybridity, producing variegations of the Chinese diaspora.[68] Although culturalist explanations of Chinese investment from abroad present one way of understanding
China's spectacular development story, some scholars, such as Alan Smart and
Jinn-Yuh Hsu, eschew such explanations to argue that "dense social ties cannot normally substitute for the sophisticated managerial and technological
learning that is required to compete in a particular sector."[69] Rather, Smart and
Hsu highlight that the "deepening social division of labor ... creates opportunities for innovation in formerly peripheral regions."[70] This stratification of

labor evinced through the varied characteristics of the Chinese diaspora is a topic we will revisit in this book.

Pivotal also to the Chinese state's diaspora engagement policy is a group of emigrants known as the "new Chinese migrants" (*xinyimin*). In 1978, in addition to the Open Door Policy, China launched a Study Abroad Program to help bridge the scientific gap between China and the West.[71] The 1985 Law of the People's Republic of China on the Administration of the Exit and Entry of Citizens (*Zhonghua Renmin Gonghe Guo Churu Jing Guanli Fa*) liberalized the right of Chinese citizens to leave and return to the country.[72] But the Chinese state did not anticipate the number of student migrants who would choose to remain overseas. Initially the Chinese leadership curbed state funding for research studies in preference for short-term visiting fellowships, and it tightened visa restrictions to stem the brain drain, particularly following the Tiananmen massacre in 1989. By the 1990s the policy terrain shifted again and the Chinese state renewed efforts to entice return migration while maintaining that it supported freedom of mobility.[73]

The Chinese state identified science, education, and technology as sectors that the returnees could help develop. They were a source of human capital who had emotional attachments and national loyalties to China, so the state offered incentives to entice this group of elite emigrants to return.[74] Such policies focused narrowly on research and business development and aimed to address the difficulties that returnees faced in obtaining residency visas, settling matters of housing and schooling for family members as well as the costs and technical difficulties of starting up research or companies in China. Return under the post-1990s period was no longer seen as a one-way ticket home. The Chinese state harnessed global mobility, including temporary return, as an asset for the country.[75]

Returnees today are prominently represented in higher education and research, multinational corporations, and government leadership.[76] But the effectiveness of these programs in drawing back "the best" scientists and academics has been questioned. David Zweig and Yaohui Wang argue that the "100 Talents" program (*Bairen Jihua*), initiated by the Chinese Academy of Sciences to recruit academic returnees, brought back early-career scholars with only limited experience in designing and managing large research projects.[77] They add that of those who received doctorates in 2002 as many as 92 percent remained in the United States five years after graduation. Yun-chung Chen also observes from the case of Zhongguancun Science Park that the majority of returnees have neither strong transnational connections nor local connections with Chinese institutions.[78] Nonetheless, the initiatives to recruit highly skilled returnees have continued apace. Today as China develops new economic sectors in technology and finance or through ambitious infrastructure projects like the "New Silk Road," it continues to look to the Chinese abroad for foreign investments, knowledge transfers, and social networks. The migrant-receiving countries in which Chinese emigrants and diasporic descendants have settled similarly consider them an asset that can be mobilized as a bridge into the Chinese domestic market.

Conclusion

This chapter has described an earlier period of diaspora engagement in which the Chinese state extended membership to the Chinese abroad by invoking purportedly enduring co-ethnic or kinship ties. Diaspora engagement brings a different spatiotemporal dimension into the present (i.e., the "return of co-ethnics"). The extraterritorial reach of the state translated into re-territorializing tendencies enacted by the Chinese political elites, communist cadres, and the domestic Chinese. Even though Chinese diasporic descendants embodied Southeast Asian identities, the Chinese state glossed over such identity markers and labeled them returnees rather than refugees or immigrants.

The Chinese state sought to instill its version of genealogy and ethnic belonging, but the social histories of the refugee-returnees underlined the alterity they experienced culturally. Despite restrictive conditions in China's political and social climate at that time, they carved out connections with the Southeast Asian countries they had left, recalling times past and places missed. They recreated semblances of Southeast Asia through material culture, customs, and cuisine. The nonsynchronous temporality they brought from their memories of Southeast Asia disrupted China's synchronous national narratives. But they also valorized their "returnee" (*guiqiao*) status, which is closely associated with the overseas Chinese (*huaqiao*) identity that has been portrayed as an external wing of the Chinese nation. Among co-ethnics, notions of community, culture, and kinship are actively produced through self-conscious performances and practices of personhood.[79]

As time passed and China developed new economic ambitions, the co-ethnic solidarity of past diaspora engagement faded. Contemporary diaspora strategizing emphasizes the scientific skills and knowledge of the Chinese abroad. Return migration has new significance for China, but the value it seeks in returnees are the same skills and capital-bearing subjects courted by migrant-receiving countries. The next chapter examines the mutual imbrication of migrant-receiving and migrant-sending countries as they both develop an extraterritorial reach that changes state spaces. Emigration and immigration must be studied as contemporaneous events to comprehend the politics of return and citizenship more fully.

3 Citizenship Across the Life Course

Introduction

Preparing Chinese dumplings is a popular social activity among Mainland Chinese immigrants in Canada who miss the comfort food that they associate with China. There is a sense of camaraderie as they chop and mix the ingredients for the dumpling filling, followed by pleating the dumplings into the shape of a gold ingot, signifying prosperity. Such social gatherings carry an ironic twist, however, since they are also events where friends exchange stories of the difficulties they faced in Canada. The professional qualifications that had secured their immigration to Canada serve little purpose in the Canadian labor market: instead of employment in the accountancy, engineering, or information technology sectors, such immigrants end up working as cleaners, factory assembly-line workers, administrative assistants, or salespersons. Another common conversation topic concerns transnational family separation; as the difficulty of finding professional employment in Canada sets in, the husband typically returns to China for better work opportunities while his wife stays behind to fulfill the criteria to apply for Canadian citizenship status and to care for their child, who is attending school in Canada.

At such a social gathering in Vancouver, one of the immigrants told me his wife had returned to China to oversee the family business while he remained in Canada long enough to renew his permanent residency status. Immigrants like him, he said, find their time in Canada dull, as their careers take a backseat and they miss their social circles back in China. For the men, such circumstances result in a perceived decline in their social status. When I asked what he does in his spare time in Canada, his friends laughed and exclaimed,

"Gamble!" Those who have naturalized in Canada had to relinquish their Chinese citizenship, and returning to China means they would be required to apply for immigrant visas—with restrictions on their length of stay. They see Canada as the place where they would like to spend their post-retirement years; if they return to China it would be to seek a temporary respite from the emotional difficulties of adjusting to a new cultural context in Canada, and an opportunity for the careerists among them to reignite their ambitions to accumulate wealth for the future.

Patterns of re-migration are transforming the social relations of citizenship, and re-spatializing rights, obligations, and belonging.[1] Source and destination countries are also reversed during repeated re-migration across the life course. Analyzing contemporaneous migration directs us toward evaluating what it means to stake claims to different components of citizenship in more than one political community across a migrant's life course. This chapter examines the way that the Mainland Chinese migrants negotiate social reproduction concerns that extend across international borders, their multiple national affiliations, and aspirations for recognition and rights as they journey between China and Canada across the life course.[2] Those who hold citizenship status in one country but move to another country to seek permanent residency or another citizenship status exercise identity and subjectivity in ways that challenge the assumed conjoined relationship between national citizenship and territory.

David Ley and Audrey Kobayashi term the repeat migration journeys exhibited by migrants across the life course as "transnational sojourning,"[3] when the social dimensions of citizenship can exceed the political boundaries of national citizenship. Social reproduction and family formations extend across national borders at different life stages.[4] Such circuits are characterized by interdependent spatial and temporal imaginaries that should not be reduced to individual biographies, but are more suitably conceptualized as a set of additive familial projects across the life course. Transnational sojourning forges citizenship constellations that interlink how migrants understand and experience citizenship across different migration sites.[5]

Co-ethnic solidarity is an important feature of Chinese diaspora engagement, but such policies now target the overseas Chinese who can contribute to the scientific and economic development of China, an approach that assumes human and financial capital can be transferred across transnational contexts. AnnaLee Saxenian's seminal thesis on brain circulation and economic development has proven influential in driving state-led diaspora strategizing,[6] prompting migrant-sending states to use extraterritorial or external citizenship to capture the loyalty and contributions of diasporas.[7] Although the political economy of diaspora strategizing validates economic individualism and national agendas, gaps and tensions start to emerge once we recognize how the fluid dimensions of economic identities are reconfigured through transnational migration.

Immigrants negotiate expectations of them as new citizens or potential new citizens. There is a presumed correlation between economic identity and the privilege attached to social belonging and rights, but this relationship becomes subject to contestation when migrants traverse different destinations across their life course. As Geraldine Pratt posits in her study of Filipino migration to Canada, "not only [are the] citizenship rights [of migrants] fragmented and scattered across different nation-states—some political rights here, some economic rights there—[these happen] in ways that often weaken their claims to rights and entitlements in all places."[8] The Mainland Chinese skilled migrants (*jishu yimin*) discussed here experience a similar holding pattern as they journey between Canada and China to balance competing priorities of earning a respectable income and enhancing the well-being of the family.[9]

Prevailing norms on identity and subjectivity influence national debates on whether social groups that have been absent (thus deemed noncontributing members) from the national society deserve rights. An inside/outside binary remains even if migrant-sending states extend membership and recognition to citizens abroad.[10] Rainer Bauböck proposed the concept of external citizenship for assessing the citizenship recognition and rights that should be extended to *emigrants*.[11] Key to this conceptualization are the principles of biographical subjection and stakeholdership, which he argues can be used to weigh claims to external citizenship. When *immigrants* re-migrate and are absent from the migrant-receiving country for an extended period only to return later in life, this can also spark debate over their entitlement to rights in that country subsequently.

Transnational sojourning challenges expectations that those belonging to a political community will remain present in the territory (henceforth territorial presence) to consolidate their membership or fraternity to a national society. Principles of biographical subjection and stakeholdership are useful for assessing immigration and citizenship debates, which cannot be studied in isolation from the emigration context given today's transnational sojourning patterns. This discussion on Mainland Chinese re-migration draws on newspaper reports, original ethnographic research, and in-depth interviews that were conducted in Vancouver (Canada) and Beijing, Shanghai, and Guang-zhou (China).

The Emigration and Immigration Nexus: From China to Canada

Amid the hype over China's diaspora strategies, there are areas of neglect and tension that deserve critical scrutiny. The Chinese state's diaspora strate-gies target the migrant professionals who studied overseas (*haiwai xuezhe*), rather than the professionals who completed their education in China and then moved later, when they became accomplished professionals and could capital-ize on opportunities for skilled immigration to another country. Chinese pro-fessionals who desired a better living environment than what China could offer, or parents who aspired for their children to receive a Western education, found Canada an attractive destination. Mainland Chinese immigration to Canada peaked during the period from 2001 to 2006.[12] The 2001 and 2006 cen-suses record that immigration from China outstripped inflows to Canada from all other countries. The Mainland Chinese who qualified as skilled immigrants were considered competitive candidates under the points-based system that as-sessed their income level, age, and English language competency, among other attributes. Just as with the transnational Chinese students in Vanessa Fong's study, the professionals in my study sought the security of legal citizenship or permanent residency status abroad, along with the freedom and capabilities associated with citizenship in developed countries (*fazhan guojia*).[13]

However, life in Canada proved disappointing. Employers there did not rec-ognize the qualifications and professional experience of immigrants from China. Professionally trained engineers, accountants, and lawyers had to ob-tain additional training in Canada to re-qualify for employment in their areas of expertise. Using English, their second language, was challenging during both professional and social interactions, and immigrants experienced a disjunc-ture (*chayi*) in Canada as compared to the higher social status they were ac-customed to having in China. It became common for husbands, usually the breadwinners, to embark on return migration to find better-paying work in China, while their wives remained behind to fulfill the residency requirements for Canadian citizenship and to take care of their child's school-going needs.[14] Aihwa Ong found in her study of Chinese families in the United States that such flexible citizenship strategies resulted in families enduring long-distance separation for a prolonged period.[15] What makes the Canadian case distinct is that the Mainland Chinese families would usually undergo the separation only for a few years, deciding subsequently to relocate to China as a family unit to maintain physical closeness.

The Mainland Chinese migrants arrived in Canada after their counterparts from Hong Kong, who migrated before, or immediately following, the 1997 handover of the former British colony to China. They could observe the immigration and subsequent re-migration experiences of the Hong Kong migrants who underwent similar de-skilling and integration difficulties. Mainland Chinese families are cautious about living apart for a prolonged period because they have witnessed transnational family relationships suffer from strained marriages or parent-child relationships. It was more common for families to decide to return as a family unit to China once one of the family members secured Canadian citizenship status.[16]

In a climate where Canadian political leaders have called for a strong national identity and patriotism, the Canadian public has interpreted the re-migration of immigrants as a sign that they lack commitment to the national community. But a distinction can be made between Canadians who have natal ties to Canada and left during adulthood, and foreign-born immigrants, like the Mainland Chinese migrants, who stayed in Canada for a few years, and then re-migrated. Birthright citizenship privileges those who have acquired it by territorial descent or parentage.[17] It naturalizes the social membership of those with natal ties compared to foreign-born populations. Driving the re-migration of the Mainland Chinese migrants were the aforementioned de-skilling and integration difficulties, but critics of the pro-immigration policy in Canada argue that such migrants are opportunistic and their re-migration signals a lack of stakeholdership in the country. Migrant-receiving countries expect new immigrants to act "responsibly" by demonstrating efforts to integrate, accept the social norms prescribed, and contribute to the national community.[18]

Under the conservative government that won power in 2006, immigration schemes and citizenship requirements have been progressively tightened, moving away from the idea of admitting people based on the points-based criteria to admitting workers with pre-arranged job offers. Such changes sought to address a mismatch in the demand and supply of skilled migrants by requiring that potential applicants prove in advance that their credentials are recognized in Canada and acceptable to Canadian employers. Potential investor migrants were also hard hit by a sudden announcement in February 2014 that Canada would be canceling applications to the immigrant investor program. As many as 45,500 Mainland Chinese were affected by this unexpected change. Some had submitted applications as far back as 2009 and made personal arrangements to enroll their children in Canadian schools, buy property in Canada, or scale back their business operations in China in preparation for emigration.[19]

Accompanying the changes to immigration regulations were revisions to the Canadian Citizenship Act (Bill C-24). In 2014 a draft amendment was proposed in Parliament to increase the permanent residency requirements for citizenship.[20] It stipulated that permanent residents aged fourteen to sixty-four would have to meet official language requirements and pass a knowledge test to qualify for citizenship. Permanent residents abroad would be required to file tax returns and sign an undertaking to continue living in the country if they wanted to become citizens.[21] The proposed changes sought to clamp down on tax evasion and to reiterate the significance of residency in Canada as a sign of commitment to the national community.[22] On one level, citizenship tests are meant to assess an immigrant's understanding of the country; on another level, the migrant is expected to account for the time spent at each stage of immigration prior to naturalization and demonstrate physical presence. These translate into attributes, actions, and relationships that symbolize an immigrant's commitment to the country.[23] The changes to permanent residency, citizenship tests, and intent to continue to reside in Canada became law in June 2015, signaling an increasingly restrictive attitude toward immigration and expectations that immigrants would integrate, adopt Canadian identity, and fulfill their duties toward Canada.

The circumstances described above shape the subjectivities of the Mainland Chinese migrants. Prior to migration, they felt they had reached a pinnacle in their careers and sought new professional challenges abroad. They aspired to an environment different from what China could offer: the pollution in Chinese cities and the busy lifestyle, along with what they perceived as political uncertainty and subpar social welfare in China, prompted them to consider emigration. Canada proved to be an attractive destination, for cities like Vancouver, Toronto, and Montreal provided multicultural environments with Chinese populations and a range of urban amenities that made settling into a new country easier. As skilled professionals who earned high incomes in China, the Mainland Chinese migrants were considered desirable subjects by the Canadian immigration policy at the time of entry.

The apparent meeting of emigration aspirations and immigration opportunities suggested that they could leverage their economic identities to improve their social prospects. Reality proved otherwise, however, and over time return migration became part of the long-term transnational sojourning patterns. The migrants' move back to China should be considered re-migration rather than return migration, since the latter connotes a linear pattern of resettlement that is contrary to the repeated migration patterns evinced. While circular migration is a descriptor commonly invoked in studies of such migration trends elsewhere, it suggests an ease of entry and exit that no longer applied. Since China disallows dual citizenship, the Mainland Chinese migrants who naturalized abroad no longer had the right of return and were required to apply for immigrant visas. Under such circumstances, re-migration reverses emigration and immigration sites. Even though they were considered "returnees" on account of their biographical ties, such migrants are legally considered foreigners in China. Furthermore, their de-skilling experiences in Canada had an effect on their economic and social standing in China, and they became middling migrants (*zhongdeng yimin*), who had fallen behind their nonmigrant counterparts and were also considered less competitive than the younger generation entering the workforce.

Middling "Returnees" in China as Canada's Secondary Diaspora

China has been registering significant return migration rates among the overseas Chinese population who belong neither to the high-skilled category courted by China's diaspora strategies, nor are they considered low-skilled Chinese migrant labor protected by Chinese law. These "middling migrants" had immigrated to countries as diverse as Australia, Canada, New Zealand, and the United States, but chose to return to China subsequently.[24] The middling migrants (*zhongdeng yimin*) are also known as returnees in China (*huiliu zhongguo huaren*), but they are not privy to the incentives that have been highly publicized in China's diaspora strategies design. Those benefits are meant to attract highly skilled scientists, academics, and business investors to return to China. In comparison, middling returnees relocated independently and relied on personal networks to find employment and resolve resettlement difficulties in China. Some retained their Chinese citizenship status but many have naturalized abroad and are considered foreign nationals in China.[25]

The dual citizenship restriction in China means that those who naturalized abroad have automatically relinquished the right to Chinese citizenship, and with it their household registration status (*hukou*). The *hukou* system regulates rights to residency in a locality, employment opportunities in the public sector, and social provisions such as health care, pensions, and children's education.[26] Returnees who relinquished Chinese citizenship status are required to obtain employment or dependent visas and they are no longer entitled to the rights of Chinese citizenship or the benefits of *hukou* status. Chinese returnees who have foreign nationality status are classified under the wider category of foreigners (*waiji renyuan*); hence, it is difficult to discern the exact number of such returnees. However, it is sizable enough to warrant changes to visa regulations governing the stay of such returnees. For example, the Chinese authorities extended the permissible period of stay in China and made it easier for former Chinese nationals to apply for family-category visas.[27]

The middling returnees intend to re-migrate later in life, and their return to China is only temporary, but during this time they claim natal belonging to China and decry the disjuncture between their emotional attachment and their status as foreigners in China.[28] The overseas Chinese and returnees with foreign nationality status have been particularly vocal in lobbying for lifting the dual citizenship restriction.[29] They claim recognition and rights that are premised on ancestry, cultural affinity, and family relationships in China. These correspond to Bauböck's principles of biographical subjection and stakeholdership claims.[30] Their life circumstances mean they maintain a lifelong interest in the Chinese nation even if they no longer live there. In 2004 China implemented a "green card," or permanent residency scheme, which seemed to provide a midway solution for those who had naturalized abroad. By 2013, only around five thousand foreigners had successfully applied for permanent residency status in China[31] in view of the demanding criteria used to vet the human capital of potential applicants.[32] China's permanent residency scheme parallels the points-based system that the Mainland Chinese migrants had used to immigrate to a foreign country previously. Unless the dual citizenship restriction is withdrawn or the permanent residency scheme revised, the returnees remain in a state of uncertainty. They negotiate their economic identity and social reproduction priorities by navigating different national contexts at various stages of their lives.

There is another dimension to the re-migration journeys of the Mainland Chinese migrants from Canada. In China they are a potential audience of Canada's emerging diaspora strategies aimed at mobilizing "Canadians abroad." Although not nearly to the same degree as China's policymakers, Canadian policymakers and think tanks have started to consider the latent potential represented by the human capital of the Canadian diaspora, including the Chinese immigrants who re-migrated to Hong Kong and Mainland China. Canadian associations and Canada's consular missions in China organize activities to promote national identity and community among Canadians living in China. The Asia Pacific Foundation, an independent think tank, spearheaded research to identify the demographics of Canadians living abroad,[33] and given its geographical ambit, the foundation has a special interest in immigrants who re-migrated to Asian countries.[34] Another think tank, The Mowat Centre, published a report in 2011 arguing that Canada should mobilize immigrants as networks and institutionalize such networks to benefit the economy.[35] Both think tanks seek to influence policymaking and public attitudes toward the Canadian diaspora, consisting of Canadians born in Canada, the second generation born abroad, and immigrants who re-migrated from Canada. The last category includes international students or professionals who used to live in Canada, and Canadian permanent residents and naturalized Canadian citizens who live abroad.

On a muggy afternoon in Shanghai, hundreds of Canadians gathered at the Shanghai Centre to celebrate Canada Day, an event organized by the Shanghai Chamber of Commerce. At the center of the festivities was a red platform with a background banner featuring a cheerful beaver, popularly recognized as the mascot of Canada. The banner read "2009 Canada Day" and "Fête du Canada" (French for "Canada Day"). The Canadian flag flew high at the Shanghai Centre as red and white balloons dotted the landscape, symbolizing the colors of the Canadian flag. An area had even been roped off for an inflatable playground for young children. The Canadian diaspora represented at the event were mainly of Chinese ethnicity; many were Chinese-Canadian professionals working in China or Mainland Chinese immigrant-returnees who intend to re-migrate to Canada in the future. All along the pavement were stalls featuring Canadian businesses that had a presence in China, such as the Royal Bank of Canada and the Canadian Wheat Board, which attracted a line of visitors by offering beer samples made from Canadian wheat.

The other popular stall at the event belonged to the Canadian International School, where Chinese parents lingered over the promotional material and inquired about the syllabus and school fees. Among the onlookers was a Mainland Chinese couple that had accompanied me to this event. They had returned to China a few years earlier and brought with them their almost-three-year-old child. They told me they were considering schooling options in China that would ease their child's transition back in Canada when the family re-migrates there in the future. The local schools in China were reputed to be stressful for young children, and the students learn English only as a second language, which might make adjusting to life in Canada difficult for their child. Their first preference would be to send their child to the Canadian International School in Shanghai, but private education could prove costly for the parents. The other option would be for the wife to return to Canada first so that their child could be educated there, but that would mean separation again.

Mainland Chinese migrants such as those at the Canada Day celebration in Shanghai were considered part of the Chinese diaspora when they lived in Canada, but their sense of belonging to Canada has been enhanced since they re-migrated to China.[36] Their Canadian legal status and personal attachments in Canada position them as part of the "Canadian diaspora," a label that has gained currency in Canadian business and political circles. Despite experiencing de-skilling and integration difficulties in Canada, the Mainland Chinese migrants who returned temporarily to China expressed an emotional attachment to Canada. They had spent several years living in Canada, owned property, retained long-term legal status, and maintained an active interest in developments in the country even though they now live in China. Many supported Canada's liberal political context, social democracy, and multicultural characteristics. The anticipated transient nature of their stay in China reinforced their identification with Canada as a distant home to which they plan to return. They can be considered a secondary diaspora that identifies with and claims belonging to Canada as a second homeland in addition to their prior affiliation as a part of the Chinese diaspora.

But re-migration and formation of a secondary diaspora present new questions for projects concerned with immigrant integration and nation building. Even though the secondary diaspora acknowledged the migrant-receiving country as a homeland and site of future return, comparative recognition for immigrants' emotional ties and contributions to Canada while they are based overseas has been slow to gain state and societal support. To the migrant-receiving country, the secondary diaspora has been absent from the nation-state for a prolonged period or for recurring periods over an extended time. Angharad Closs Stephens and Vicki Squire point out that premising citizenship on rights and obligations "ties it to a designated legal and political space and/or to a preconstituted conception of the political subject."[37] Territorial absence lends to perceptions that immigrants who re-migrated have not demonstrated their economic contributions or deepened their stakeholdership and meaningful connections to the country. Considering the dialectics of presence and absence can help reveal the multiple hidden dimensions of the social realities that migrants face.[38] In weighing whether the secondary diaspora should have rights upon their return to the migrant-receiving country, periods of territorial presence or absence across the life course matter.

Transnational Sojourning and Citizenship Constellations

When migrants move in and out of more than one national territory repeatedly over the life course, it becomes challenging to premise the allocation of rights and duties on rigid conceptions of territorial presence in a political community. Rainer Bauböck and Virginie Guiraudon rightly observe:

> Norms of equality and relations of solidarity between aliens and citizens who share a daily experience of subjection to the same political authority cannot support equality between domestic citizens and citizens abroad. The configuration is also unstable because migrants change their citizenship relations with their countries of origin and destination over time when they become permanent residents or naturalized citizens, or when they return to a source country, and these relations will again change across generations as their children's legal and political ties to the countries will differ from those of their parents.[39]

Engin Isin has also called for critical investigation into the assumptions and projections of fraternity in conceptualizations of citizenship.[40] The Mainland Chinese migrants who identify as a secondary diaspora of Canada and express intentions to re-migrate again exemplify the shifting contours of political subjectivity and territorial ambiguity discussed by the scholars above.

One of the reasons the Mainland Chinese migrants chose Canada was because of its reputation for quality health care and universal social rights. Canadian political theorist Janine Brodie argues that it was only during the postwar period and since Canada's first citizenship act in 1947 that social governance became fused with the "cultural and symbolic infrastructure of a new pan-Canadian nationalism [and] social citizenship was progressively written onto Canadians' sense of themselves and their country."[41] She argues that social citizenship in Canada is characterized by programs that emphasize universality and social rights, but these have been de-emphasized since the late

1980s in line with neoliberal reforms that prioritize market logic and individualization.[42]

Critical observers in the Canadian public have suggested that skilled immigrants such as the Mainland Chinese did not contribute to the domestic economy as much as policymakers envisioned.[43] Underemployment by such immigrants negatively affected their tax contributions, which fell short of off-setting the social welfare benefits they were eligible to claim (e.g., in health care, language classes, re-skilling subsidies, and employment insurance). They came to be viewed as opportunistic migrants and a burden to the social welfare system. But their re-migration only serves to deepen the prejudice of the Canadian public toward immigrants like them. Mei, a female returnee, in Shanghai, expressed concerns over such perceptions when we met. She agreed to speak to me because of her personal frustrations with being caught between two worlds, Canada and China. She had studied in Canada from 2005 to 2008, and she became a Canadian permanent resident while her husband ran a business in China and traveled regularly to Canada. Once Mei secured Canadian permanent residency status she relocated with their child to China so the family could be together again. When we met in Shanghai she had been back for a year, and she told me she found readjusting to life in China difficult, especially finding local employment commensurate with her foreign qualifications and experience.

Mei told me she was considering naturalizing as a Canadian citizen. She explained, "If we do not naturalize in Canada it will be harder to retain our permanent residency (PR) status there. If we stay in China to care for our aging parents, we may fail to fulfill the three-years residency period [in Canada] that is required for renewing PR."[44] Mei's situation resonates with Coutin's argument that even if migrants have legal permanent residency status, they remain vulnerable to losing legal recognition in the migrant-receiving country.[45] Naturalizing in Canada would mean relinquishing her Chinese nationality status as required by China's nationality law. To delay that decision, she plans to re-migrate to Canada to fulfill the residency period for renewing her permanent residency first. Mei had other concerns about returning to Canada, however. She was visibly agitated as she asked rhetorically, "Will people in Canada welcome us even if we wanted to return? When we were students, the so-called local white Canadians did not invite us to join their activities. Even if we wanted to integrate what do we integrate into? The majority in Vancouver are now Chinese people!" Mei noted that her child's education would be a key consideration for re-migrating to Canada, but she was also prompted by the country's social welfare provisions. She explained, "The social welfare situation in China makes one want to have a backdoor. Despite reforms the improvements are slow. If I am employed in China the welfare protection is better but when I am retired it will be pegged to a lower level. This is a consideration for returning to Canada where social welfare will be better."

Scholarship on later-life migration has so far focused on return migration to the country of origin or re-migration to a third country as part of lifestyle migration.[46] It has not considered the re-migration of older adults to migrant-receiving countries that they left earlier during their life course. Access to social security and health and social care systems has been typically premised on a person's legal status in a polity (as permanent resident or citizen) and territorial presence across time. The re-migration of aging immigrant populations raises questions on whether foreign-born populations that became citizens through naturalization but left subsequently should have social rights in the country of immigration if they returned. Such migrants would have spent their economically productive years abroad rather than participating in the labor market or deepening community connections in the migrant-receiving country. Who should cover the costs of health care and geriatric care for aging immigrants? Should the country of immigration cover it if these returned migrants have not contributed economically during their younger days because they lived overseas?

The transferability of labor mobility across national contexts can be mired in difficulty due to the devaluation of professional skills and experience as well as language barriers in a foreign country. Even in the context of free mobility under the European Union, entitlement to social rights is contingent on the ability of the migrant or family members to show they are covered by sickness insurance and have sufficient financial resources rather than rely on the host state. Louise Ackers argues that "citizenship rights, under the free movement of persons provisions, radiate from the 'citizen-worker' positioned at the nucleus of the male breadwinning family."[47] By re-migrating from Canada, the Mainland Chinese migrants were seen as irresponsible, opportunistic, and ungrateful immigrants. Transnational sojourning was meant to enable them to balance competing economic and social reproduction concerns, but if the citizen-worker is the privileged subject of social rights, then their claims to social welfare protection are weakened in both China and Canada. Their plans to move back to Canada for retirement are at odds with the receiving society's

expectation that migrants should be physically present, contribute economically, and deepen stakeholdership in the political community. The presumed
relationship between labor productivity and the entitlement to national rights
becomes troubled once we consider transnational sojourning across the life
course.

Later-Life Migration and Citizenship Constellations

Transnational sojourning also has a bearing on the re-integration of foreign-
born populations when they return to the migrant-receiving country during
old age. Ackers highlighted the issues faced by older migrants when they move
to another country to receive care or to provide care for relatives.[48] The transition to a new social environment necessitates adjustment on the part of the
older migrant, unlike migrants who retire in their countries of origin and find
it easier to resettle into established social support networks. The limited English language competency of the Mainland Chinese migrants had hindered
their wider integration in Canada earlier in the life course. When they were in
Canada, their social networks consisted mainly of fellow Chinese migrants. But
the years they spent outside of Canada also lead to further erosion of those social support networks. When they re-migrate to Canada again during old age,
it will be even harder for them to establish resilient social networks. Geriatric
services also have to be tailored to their cultural needs. Australia, another multicultural country, has accommodated the aging needs of Chinese immigrants
from Hong Kong and China by providing geriatric services in Cantonese or
Mandarin, and provisioning nursing homes to suit their cultural needs. Canada has similar facilities for large immigrant communities, but demand already
outstrips supply. The re-migration of Mainland Chinese migrants to Canada
later in their life course is likely to enhance the demand for culturally tailored
geriatric services.

The discussion of care arrangements for older migrants in different national
contexts anticipates the issues brought by re-migration later in their life course.
As Glick Schiller argues, political borders do not delimit the social reproduction of migrants' life worlds in connection with the countries in which they
claim belonging, membership and rights.[49] A key contention would be whether
migrants such as the Mainland Chinese discussed here have contributed economically through participation in the national labor force. The repeated
border crossings they undertook, and by implication, their interrupted periods of residency in Canada, can be read as a sign of insufficiency when mea-

sured against the rights they claim. But we must also recognize the power relations at stake when migrants face structural inequalities, and global householding projects seem the most feasible, even if only temporary, solution to optimize the welfare of the family.[50]

Sociologist Ken Sun proposed the concept of "transnational healthcare seeking" to describe how aging returnees in Taiwan engage in cross-border health care.[51] To counteract perceptions that they take advantage of public medical services, the Taiwanese aging returnees he studied present themselves as respectable citizens who worked overseas to benefit the homeland. Similarly, the Mainland Chinese returnees in my study gave a range of reasons for leaving. Chen, a male returnee who has naturalized in Canada, recounted the difficult experiences that prompted him to re-migrate to China:

> I was in my thirties when I immigrated and my way of thinking was fixed. My English is all right [but] an immigrant has to have a ready mindset to fully integrate. . . . If you have [ambitions] it will prevent you from having a happy life there. As a newcomer you face communication barriers and cultural differences. There was also some discrimination towards new immigrants. . . . But overall, Canada has a good welfare system. . . . I heard that the Canadian government has reserves for the support of older people in the future. Canada is a country with abundant resources and it is a stable country. It can resolve social welfare issues. In contrast, China is a populous country and averaged out it has less resources per person. The political system is also unstable. These considerations influence our thinking about the future.

Migrants like Chen did not feel welcome while they lived in Canada, but they profess that re-migrating to the country would be a better outcome than spending their later life in China. The futures they envision are key considerations for re-migration later during the life course.

Wang, another male returnee in Shanghai, said he anticipates that when he re-migrates to Canada, it would not only be for the "fresh air or social welfare benefits." Rather, he intends to start a business to capitalize on his networks in China and Canada. He explained, "I want to use my dual affiliation to contribute in the financial and cultural domains. I still like Canada because it is better than China in terms of its abundant resources and welfare benefits. In the long term, I think I should leave China. It is too 'complicated' (*fuza*) compared to Canada." *Fuza* was a common refrain expressed by my respondents, referring to a range of social and cultural practices that one needs to adopt to succeed in China; these may include entertaining clients and superiors, or doing favors to pave one's career (or in other social domains). They believed that such time-consuming, expensive, and emotionally draining social practices would be less common in Canada.

Migrants incur emotional or psychological costs when they traverse nation-states to negotiate production and social reproduction concerns.[52] Despite being physically absent from the migrant-receiving country, they support the care needs and education of their children, who are Canadian citizens or permanent residents. Discussions of care as an integral component of governance and society have been limited thus far to national contexts.[53] A new social infrastructure of care and care ethics that extends across migration sites and across the life course is needed. Such a social infrastructure of care would introduce care structures and measures that recognize both the cross-national and intergenerational transfers that bring together migrant and nonmigrant populations, as well as encourage bilateral and multilateral policy initiatives to support the care needs of migrants who live in different national societies at various life stages.

Our discussion of the migration trajectories of the Mainland Chinese migrants provokes deeper reflection of how fraternity and the rights associated with national citizenship both demand territorial presence over an extended period. As a postcolonial state and multicultural nation, Canada has sought to deepen a sense of national identity and belonging among diverse cultural groups, including First Nations people, English and French-speaking settler populations, and a mosaic of immigrant groups. Of the Chinese population alone, current cohorts bear political and language identities that are distinct from earlier cohorts, such as those who feel affiliated with Taiwan or Hong Kong compared to those who claim affiliation to Mainland China. The latter group is further socially stratified depending on whether they left China before or after 1949, and whether they left when China was a developing nation or as part of the new rich and new middle classes who emigrated when the Chinese economy was booming.

The Mainland Chinese migrants discussed here belong to the last category. They emigrated from China with a sense of optimism and confidence, but after encountering de-skilling and integration difficulties in Canada, re-migration to China provided a temporary solution to rebuild their economic assets and self-esteem and enhance the welfare of the family in the way they thought best. As Fong puts it, there were "freedoms won and lost through transnational migration."[54] If they return to Canada later in the life stage as planned, it will be even harder for them to build social bridges and deepen their membership in the nation. Ethnic and language differences, the time they spent outside of Canada, and their claims to rights in older age are factors that will likely contribute to discussion of their status in the adopted homeland.

Conclusion

Transnationalism theory provides one way of understanding migrants' dual affiliations, but to advance understanding of what those affiliations mean for citizenship requires expanding the analytical lens to consider how migration sites are drawn into a citizenship constellation. In such citizenship constellations, identity, subjectivity, and access to rights are co-constituted across migration sites. The recognition and rights afforded to migrants are shaped by the citizenship norms and policies of both the countries of origin and settlement. Emigration aspirations of Mainland Chinese migrants were met by immigration opportunities, but re-migration to China was only temporary, as they planned to move back to Canada again later in life. While in China, the migrants identified as a secondary diaspora of Canada and saw it as a distant homeland.

As the economic identity of a migrant changes in one migration site, it impacts his or her economic status upon re-migrating to another migration site. Repeated re-migration or transnational sojourning also means the social dimensions of citizenship are likely to exceed the political boundary of national citizenship. The economic calculations of migration cannot be divorced from social reproduction concerns. Critically examining re-migration can advance analyses of migration and citizenship by showing how an inside/outside binary associated with citizenship remains in place even if certain features of citizenship are re spatialized. The Mainland Chinese migrants discussed here negotiate expectations of economic and social contributions in the different migration sites where they are embedded; yet their social membership and rights are called into question at both sites.

Across the life course, the perceived economic contributions of a migrant are correlated to national debates on whether this person deserves citizenship rights. New contestations over social membership and rights may arise when migrants who are naturalized citizens of a country decide to re-migrate to the country of immigration during their old age. Analyses of citizenship that have been narrowly premised on economic productivity and expectations of territorial presence need to take seriously how social reproduction and generational transfers extend across national borders. Studying the citizenship constellations that link how migrants experience citizenship across different migration sites provides new insights both for citizenship norms and practices.

4 Multiple Diasporas

Introduction

Settled by diaspora populations from past and recent immigration, Singapore is a fitting case for critically examining the postcolonial nation-building challenges that arise when immigration and emigration trends happen concurrently in a country. More than a third of the city-state's population is foreign-born, and the Singaporean state aspires to integrate recent immigrants into the political community. The immigrants it desires are those who qualify for entry through the skilled and investor migration programs. With growing numbers of Singaporeans now moving abroad, Singapore has also become a country that seeks to assert an extraterritorial reach over its emigrants. Membership to a national community is normally anchored in a territory and naturalized through the social compact of citizenship. Yet immigrants living in a territory can experience social exclusion through processes of Othering even if they are permanent residents or naturalized citizens of that country. The same country may engage in diaspora strategizing to extend extraterritorial membership to emigrants who continue to see it as their homeland, despite their absence from the national territory.[1]

This chapter examines how fraternity and alterity operate in contradictory ways under conditions of contemporaneous migration. Migration classifications distinguish migrants based on their educational qualifications, skills, income, nationality, age, or other identity attributes, but it is in the social interactions and cultural practices of everyday life that alterity is projected onto migrants most intimately. Lieba Faier describes these interactions as "cultural encounters" that produce identities relationally, including racialized identities.[2]

For Philip Kretsedemas, "migrant racialization is steeped in territorial imaginaries."[3] Introducing the concept of "territorial racism," he explains:

> *Territorial racism justifies discriminatory treatment by using racially coded, territorial distinctions to identify those who authentically belong to the territory and those who do not.* . . . [It] sensitizes people to how "their group" is distributed and organized in a given space in relation to other groups that are presumed to be racially and culturally different from theirs. As a result territorial distinctions become another way of expressing power relations through racialized categories.[4]

Qualifying that territorial racism builds on but is distinct from Etienne Balibar's "cultural racism,"[5] Kretsedemas adds that territorial racism "re-codes racial distinctions with a territorial language that is often expressed in a "colorblind" way (referring to nativist discourse)."[6] The concept of territorial racism converges with arguments on autochthony, referring to those who are "born of the soil."[7] For Kretsedemas, nativity is associated with the social construction of the modern nation-state whereas autochthony is associated with the indigenous identities of aboriginal or Amerindian populations.[8]

Deploying a different approach from Kretsedemas is Peter Geschiere, who differentiates indigeneity from autochthony.[9] For Geschiere, autochthony is employed in "more variable ways [such that] it is the free-floating profile of this term, combining apparent self-evidence with great ambiguity and variation in its meaning, that makes it of particular interest for unravelling the general conundrum of belonging in our globalizing world."[10] Autochthony refers to struggles over local belonging as entwined with global circuits. It stresses issues of belonging, provokes highly charged emotions, and is mobilized for different purposes. Yet, as Geschiere observes, "Despite its heavy appeal to the soil, autochthony turns out to be quite an empty notion in practice: it only expresses the claim to have come first."[11]

Territorial racism and autochthony provide useful insights, but both are inadequate for grappling with the complexities of alterity manifested when immigration politics play out alongside emigration pressures, or in multicultural societies that are populated by different cohorts of co-ethnic migrants. Existing scholarship on social inclusion and exclusion has focused on interethnic racial coding, but this glosses over the complexities of co-ethnic relations. Multiple diaspora populations, including co-ethnics from other lands, are converging and diverging in multicultural migration hubs like

Singapore. Each successive cohort advances its own claim to belonging and rights to the national territory, premised on what they consider an earlier period of migration. Social scientists need to develop new theoretical tools for analyzing both the dynamics of interethnic and co-ethnic relations, as well as concurrent immigration and emigration trends.

The relationship between fraternity and alterity—in the context of contemporaneous migration—remains to be unpacked systematically: alterity demands the rethinking of fraternity. How is each operationalized and legitimized in citizenship contestations? This chapter bridges theories on the social effects of time with analyses of cultural complexity to show how the principle of time is deployed to legitimize natal ties and territorial belonging (henceforth natal belonging).[12] The multidirectional migration flows evinced in Singapore exemplify how states and national societies invoke temporal framings to prioritize natal ties that are based on selected versions of territorial belonging, memory, and culture. Negotiations of fraternity and alterity are centered on temporal and spatial narratives that carve out differentiated domains of belonging and stakeholdership. The chapter draws on original ethnographic observations from field research in Singapore and China, and newspaper reports on immigration in Singapore and on Singaporean emigration.

Past and Present Diaspora Populations in Singapore

Singapore achieved independence in 1965 after a brief political merger with Malaysia (1963–1965) under the Federation of Malaysia. The years preceding the merger are remembered as a time when anticolonial groups contended for ideological influence and the right to govern the territory.[13] The period preceding and immediately following British decolonization saw the loyalty of immigrants who had settled in postcolonial states regularly questioned during inter-state negotiations.[14] Consequently, China implemented a dual citizenship restriction in 1955 during the Bandung Conference to assuage the concerns of those countries.[15] But the struggle of managing competing Chinese identity and loyalties to China as set against the urgent task of nation building continued into the immediate decolonization years for Southeast Asian countries, including Singapore.[16]

Upon gaining political independence, the Singaporean state systematically calibrated how ethnicity and state-society relations would be managed; leveraging migration has characterized Singapore's development strategy both under British colonial rule and during the post-independence period. Past immigration created a multicultural society of ethnic and dialect groups including a Chinese majority and Malay, Indian, and Eurasian[17] minority populations. This cultural diversity is managed under a state-directed approach popularly referred to as the CMIO (Chinese, Malay, Indian, and "Others") model, which enabled the Singaporean state to pacify the social anxieties of ethnic minorities who feared being pressured to assimilate into a Chinese majority population. Singapore's political leaders also found it important to assert a separate political identity from China, rather than be considered a vassal state of the larger country.

The Singaporean state introduced constitutional recognition for multiculturalism (officially known as multiracialism) and implemented policies to promote interethnic relations.[18] It enforced interethnic mixing through policy on public housing (where more than 80 percent of the population reside) and adopted English as the lingua franca for all Singaporeans regardless of their ethnic background. The Chinese, Malay, and Indians continue, however, to learn a "mother tongue" (or second language) associated with their respective ethnic groups. Diverse regional dialects were subsumed under an officially recognized mother tongue, such as Mandarin for the Chinese or Tamil for the Indians.[19] The CMIO model prioritizes the ethnic identities that are tied to earlier waves of immigration during the pre-independence or immediate post-independence period.[20] This model of multiculturalism lends itself to invoking nostalgia for social belonging that is premised on that period of immigration to Singapore despite newer migration flows today.

Since the 1990s, the Singaporean state has used migration as a tool to meet skills shortages and boost declining fertility rates. From 2000 to 2010, Singapore's permanent resident and nonresident immigrant population nearly doubled.[21] At its peak in 2008, 79,167 permanent residency applications were approved.[22] Cumulatively this means the permanent resident immigrant population in Singapore increased by more than a quarter-million in less than a decade (2008–2013). Whereas high-skilled and high net-worth foreigners are encouraged to settle permanently in Singapore, low-skilled workers have been given restrictive work visas to remain temporarily. Crucially, China serves as a key source country for both categories of new immigrants.[23]

China's rise as a global power has presented new business opportunities for Singapore but also renewed anxieties toward immigrant integration. The new subjects of Singapore's integration project are the Chinese migrants who left

China after 1979 (i.e., *xinyimin*). They immigrated to Singapore through the managed migration program said to favor Chinese migrants, who are considered culturally similar to the majority Chinese population.[24] For the Singaporean state, questions about the loyalty of the new Chinese immigrants are tied to integration concerns about social cohesion in Singapore, given China's growing geopolitical assertiveness. To ordinary Singaporeans, the new Chinese immigrants are considered distant co-ethnics who fall short of deserving to be included in the national community because of their foreign backgrounds.

As Sara Friedman argues, the threat of similarity among co-ethnics from different nationality backgrounds calls into question the presumed nature of citizenship.[25] This tension is reconciled by reiterating "normative identity categories organized around foreigner/native and diaspora/homeland distinctions."[26] Likewise, Singaporeans of diasporic descent are now generationally settled in the country and consider it their natal land. Those who resent the new immigrants equate belonging to the nation with the idea of birthplace, thus prioritizing birthright citizenship.[27] The figure of the "local" person is used to associate natal ties with belonging in Singapore in contrast to the figure of the "foreigner."[28] Helpful in unraveling the logic of alterity at work here is Ash Amin's argument on the temporalities of race.[29] Building on Arun Saldanha's concept of "phenotypical racism,"[30] Amin argues that both sensory responses and precognitive categorizations are used to judge human difference based on phenotype.[31] Phenotypical racism functions as a tool of everyday orientation transmitted from one generation to another. But how do we account for cultural stigma or discrimination that is not portrayed through accounts of phenotype?

Elizabeth Grosz provides further insights on how cultural complexity operates through temporal framings.[32] For Grosz, the social effects of time are such that "the present must be understood as elastic, capable of expanding itself to include from the past and immediate future it requires to remain in continuity with itself, to complete its present action."[33] Once the social effects of time are understood in this way, it becomes possible to argue that natal ties to a territory are premised on a temporal coding located in the past and which can be used to legitimize (or delegitimize) the right to belong in the present. In multicultural Singapore, color-coded and allegedly color-blind racism can coexist simultaneously through such dynamics of territorial and temporal belonging.

New Chinese Immigrants: Degrees of Alterity

New cohorts of Chinese immigrants have converged in Singapore in response to the city-state's demand for migrants with a range of skills. Since the new immigrants from China share the same ethnicity as the majority Chinese population in Singapore, policymakers had assumed that such co-ethnics would integrate easily. However, social divisions borne out of geography and time proved otherwise. The Singaporean-Chinese consider Singapore their natal land and invoke a Singaporean identity to differentiate themselves from the new Chinese immigrants (*xinyimin*). The latter are considered strangers that belong to other spaces, citizens from other states, even if they have naturalized in Singapore.[34] As Cathryn Clayton observes in a study of Macau, the term "new immigrant" refers "not simply to a Chinese person recently arrived in the territory but to a specific social position that involved a particular configuration of class, neighborhood, language, and perceived degree of alienation."[35]

The Singaporean-Chinese, or Chinese diasporic descendants (*huayi*), who now consider themselves "native" Singaporeans, distinguish themselves from the "new Chinese immigrants" in two ways: regional affiliations in the ancestral land and the period of migration. The new Chinese immigrants in Singapore come from a range of regions in China (including inland provinces), whereas the ancestors of the Singaporean-Chinese came primarily came from coastal regions such as Fujian, Guangdong, or Hainan Island. The former have formed new clan associations based on their regional affiliations in China or pan-regional associations that reach out to a wider constituency of new Chinese immigrants in Singapore. Their clan associations can be differentiated from the "pioneer clan associations" that were established in Singapore by the "coolie" Chinese migrants of the nineteenth and early twentieth centuries.[36]

Older Singaporeans characterize the new Chinese immigrants as descendants of abject co-ethnics. They recall their grandparents or parents in Singapore (then part of Malaya) sending food packages or remittances to relatives in China during the troubling times of the Great Leap Forward (1958–1961). Horrendous stories of human suffering also circulated back to Singapore during the Cultural Revolution (1966–1976).[37] Younger Singaporeans who do not have immediate memories of family ties in China see the new Chinese immigrants as persons who have questionable moral values in family life, business, and politics.[38] They believe that societal degeneration in China is tied to desperation over personal and family survival under communist rule and accelerated affluence after the country's successful economic reforms.[39]

The contrasting attitudes of older and younger Singaporeans exemplify how coding habits from the past can reach into the present to constitute the logics of cultural differentiation, despite the absence of phenotypical difference. Public feelings of aversion arise from personal and collective labeling conventions that have been inherited, learned, and absorbed, and those feelings are practiced in the specifics of an occasion.[40] What emerges is a new social category that is less about the "Mainland Chinese" and more about the sentiments binding locals together through a sense of native place that is denied to the newcomers.[41] In this way, Singaporeans participate implicitly in sovereignty projects that carve out "ever finer lines of inclusion and exclusion within and between populations."[42]

The new Chinese immigrants residing in Singapore are far from a homogeneous category. Apart from business investors and professionals who are eligible for long-term settlement, the population also comprises students, service workers, and low-skilled migrant workers on temporary visas. Different cohorts are further stratified by their time of arrival. An earlier cohort that settled in Singapore in the 1990s is known colloquially in Chinese-speaking social circles as the "old-new immigrants" (*lao xinyimin*, or *laoyimin* for short).[43] The *laoyimin* worked and lived in Singapore as skilled migrants holding employment passes, qualifying for permanent residency or citizenship application in this way. Distinct from them is a later cohort of new Chinese immigrants who arrived after the mid-2000s. During the 1990s, the salary requirement for employment passes was lower compared to the salary requirement for skilled migrants who applied for such visas a decade later.[44] From 2004 onward, migration policy in Singapore also started to court rich entrepreneurs and investor migrants. This group of new Chinese immigrants are colloquially called the "crass rich" (*tuhao*) or "new rich" (*xinfu*). Their ostentatious displays of wealth have drawn the ire of Singaporeans. Compounding those negative opinions are suspicions of ill-gotten wealth, a public perception compounded by controversial news such as the case of a tour guide from China who lived a life of luxury in Singapore by conning an elderly Singaporean widow of S$1.1 million.[45]

The *laoyimin* left China during the 1990s when it was still a newly developing country. Born before the 1970s, they see themselves as more "cultured" (*you wenhua*) than later Chinese emigrants. With opportunities for higher educa-tion scarce, they were considered the cream of the crop (*jingying*) when they entered top Chinese universities that would pave the way for them to emigrate as skilled professionals. Their emigration ambitions were met by immigration opportunities in Singapore, where skilled professionals were in demand to fill its domestic labor shortages. They rented rooms in affordable public housing and worked alongside local employees, thereby facilitating their incorporation into Singaporean society.

One of my interviewees was Cao, a male immigrant who came to Singa-pore during the 1990s on a student visa, qualified for permanent residency, and subsequently naturalized. He was an active member of a clan association es-tablished by the new Chinese immigrants and had ample opportunity to ob-serve the two cohorts. He said, "[*Laoyimin*] like us have lifestyles and habits that are different from the new Chinese immigrants who came recently. We [have] integrated into the local [society]. When we see the newer arrivals ex-hibit bad habits from China, we remind them to take note of their conduct. For instance they should tone down their volume when they speak." Cao's view resonates with the unease expressed by local Singaporean-Chinese toward the new Chinese immigrants who seem threateningly similar yet are considered shamefully dissimilar from them.

In the view of the *laoyimin*, the new Chinese immigrants who came after mid-2000 command higher salaries, own expensive private property, work in professions that leverage connections with businesses in China, and socialize in circles of other new Chinese immigrants only. This later cohort belongs to a generation similar to the post-1980s Chinese citizens described by Fong as "singletons"—the single children of China's 1979 one-child policy.[46] Their par-ents had great aspirations for them and concentrated family resources on the child's upward social mobility. Other new Chinese immigrants may not come from single-child families, but they command social status and respect in China on account of their newfound wealth (i.e., *xinfu*).

Exemplifying the qualitative distinctions projected on newer immigrants are the sentiments shared by Zhou, a female permanent resident who migrated to Singapore during the 1990s.[47] She said, "When I came here [on a skilled visa] I had nothing so I approached things in a down to earth manner, I did not feel that I was superior. However, this is different for the newly arrived immigrants, particularly the investor migrants. They are very rich and enjoy a very high standard of living. They are oblivious to the lives of [Singaporeans] from the middle or lower classes. These new immigrants do not work. They play golf or eat in restaurants. Their children attend international schools. It means they are out of touch with government schools and the majority of Singaporeans." The newer arrivals, accustomed to a life of privilege and too ambitious to accept life at a lower rung of the social ladder, find life in Singapore unsettling because they speak English poorly and have weaker social connections there. While their wealth may buy them luxuries, they remain social outcasts in Singaporean society.[48] Both the Singaporean-Chinese and the *laoyimin* expect the *xinyimin* to "improve" their behavior and change their mind-set to integrate into the host society.[49]

The *laoyimin* are multiply situated and invoke various affiliations, at times identifying with the generic category of "new Chinese immigrants" and at other times acknowledging the dissatisfaction of Singaporeans toward the new Chinese immigrants. Nonetheless, the *laoyimin* do not experience a seamless transition into life in Singapore since their "bodily habitus [as] expressed in their movements, dress, and speech" mark them as immigrants whose natal belonging lies in China rather than Singapore.[50] The social ordering of events and migration experiences discussed here reflect how the periodization of migration carves out domains of spatial belonging and stakeholdership, compounding degrees of alterity between co-ethnics.

Alterity and "Panicked Multiculturalism"

Deepening cultural complexity in migrant-receiving countries means we need to account for a paradoxical situation where "the excluded can be neither really accepted nor effectively eliminated, [and may be] even simply pushed into a space outside the community."[51] For Balibar, there are two logics at work in such societies, namely a logic commodifying individuals in the capitalist market, and a logic of racialization that projects a fantasy of purity, homogeneity, and unity in historical communities.[52] Balibar's insights are useful for analyzing the backlash toward immigration in multicultural Singapore. Under the managed-migration approach, immigrants in the skilled, entrepreneur, or investor categories embody the human capital and financial value to drive economic development. But Singaporeans aspiring to upward social mobility in the labor or housing market treat immigrants as competitors. The less skilled immigrants are not direct competitors, but they take up physical space, such as in transportation or leisure spaces, adding to congestion in a city-state that has a total land area of only 719 square kilometers.

For Balibar, the logic of racialization is perceptible when outsiders are transformed into enemies "by race."[53] But racialization in Singapore is characterized by the multiplication of diversity as new immigration produces different "orders of interaction" that defy the juxtaposition of fixed differences.[54] The tension between state-directed multicultural policies and the social realities of how diversity has multiplied through new immigration results in what Greg Noble terms "panicked multiculturalism—those spaces which have been subject to social anxieties because of perceived conflicts around ethnicity."[55] Such spaces of "panicked multiculturalism" are experienced in daily life in Singapore, from the local coffee shops where neighbors linger to chat, to the workplace where Singaporean colleagues gripe about the "foreign talent" competing with "locals," and even at home, where family and close friends gather over meals to catch up on news.

A seemingly ordinary dinner social I attended turned out to illuminate the social anxieties that locally born Singaporeans have toward the new Chinese immigrants. An innocuous discussion about Singaporean food prompted a Singaporean of Eurasian ethnicity in our party of three to recount an unhappy incident at the food center that afternoon. Expressing frustration, she told us she wanted to order a quintessential Singaporean noodle dish known as *char kuay teow,* but she had difficulty communicating with the hawker's assistant, who was from China. My friend only spoke English but the hawker's assistant only understood Mandarin. The Singaporean of Indian ethnicity in our company interjected, "The [new] Chinese immigrants are everywhere and they don't speak English. We are in Singapore and [Singaporean] English is the language of communication here." "They should learn to speak English," concurred the Eurasian friend. Clearly, the two non-Chinese friends felt it safe to criticize the use of Mandarin in my company even though I am a Mandarin speaker. They considered me a Singaporean of Chinese ethnicity, with "Chinese" as the secondary identity and "Singaporean" as the primary identity. Attributes normally associated with the Singaporean identity, such as birthplace (i.e., Singapore), language (i.e., Singaporean English or *Singlish*), and other social codes, are invoked contingently depending on the social company and nature of interactions. The ambiguity of those social codes means the only constant variable that differentiates a "local" Singaporean from a foreigner is the former's natal ties to Singapore.

The Singaporean-Chinese distinguish their identities from the new Chinese immigrants by prioritizing what they perceive as an overarching Singaporean identity, one that expresses national solidarity with the Malays, Indians, and Eurasians whose natal ties lie in Singapore. An event known as "Cook a Pot of Curry Day" in 2012 depicts such notions of Singaporean multiculturalism. A grassroots initiative, the event called for Singaporeans all over the island to cook curry on the same day to express solidarity with an Indian-Singaporean family whose neighbors, a family from Mainland China, had complained about the smell of curry spices cooked at such close proximity to their flat. At the height of the public furor, curry was touted as the national food of Singapore. "Cook a Pot of Curry Day" illustrates how the state-directed CMIO model of multiculturalism has been normalized in the Singaporean imagination. Such expressions of fraternity, nationhood, and citizenship are allegedly "color-blind" even if racial lines remain perceptible in other social interactions.[56]

At the core of the cultural contestations described above lies the question: "Who came first?" The answer, "We, Singaporeans," refers narrowly to the indigenous Malays and the diasporic descendants of immigrant ancestors who had contributed to the early nation building of Singapore. This version of Singaporean identity is multicultural while prioritizing the pioneer immigrant groups. Such trends are perceptible in other national contexts too. For example, Aguilar observes similar dynamics in Malaysia, where Malaysian-Malays (i.e., indigenous people) feel a closer affinity with long-settled Malaysian-Chinese and Indians (i.e., diasporic descendants) than with contemporary labor migrants and Muslim migrants (i.e., new immigrants).[57] He argues that "citizenship is being treated increasingly in [an] instrumentalist fashion even as national belonging is constantly being redefined in essentialist terms."[58] In such cases, the fraternity of the national community is borne out of a temporal ordering that privileges a particular historical period as the dominant narrative of nationhood.[59]

Presumably it is possible for immigrants who arrived after that period to achieve functional integration (e.g., labor market participation and educational attainment). But the emotional aspect of integration will always be elusive for newer immigrants because it belongs to a time past, borne out of a different temporal register that cannot be captured in the present. Immigration provides but one side of the story of how an earlier periodization of belonging can be used to legitimize fraternity. Emigration shows how this imaginary of fraternity is extended beyond the territory by state design.

Singaporean Emigration: Extending Fraternity Extraterritorially

Anxieties about emigration and immigration coexist in Singapore. Emigration decisions by Singaporeans are said to arise from an ancestral "migration culture," the state's design, and tensions over new immigration. During the 1970s and 1980s, Singaporean political leaders regarded emigration as a sign of disloyalty to the newly independent nation-state. But rising emigration rates and emphasis on the internationalization of the Singaporean economy altered such attitudes.[60] The transition was signaled tentatively initially in government speeches, and it was subsequently incorporated into the mission of a government agency, Contact Singapore, alongside its original mandate to recruit highly skilled foreigners for Singapore. Meanwhile, the state's pro-immigration scheme has gradually created a social rift in Singaporean society, as foreigners are seen as competitors for jobs and housing. Such complaints have prompted Singaporeans to emigrate for opportunities abroad: in a public survey conducted in 2011, more than a quarter of the people sampled indicated they had considered the possibility of emigrating.[61]

Anxious about the potential loss of young and highly skilled Singaporeans to other countries,[62] the Singaporean state has designed diaspora strategies to stay connected with overseas Singaporeans,[63] emphasizing the global professional skills that overseas Singaporeans can bring to the country's economic progress and their role in social reproduction for the nation. Legislation in 2004 made it easier for overseas Singaporeans to pass on citizenship to their children born abroad. But the passing of citizenship to Singaporeans abroad is restricted to the second generation born abroad; that is, a Singaporean citizen by descent can pass on citizenship to a child born overseas only if the parent has stayed in Singapore for a total of at least four years before the child's birth, or a total of at least one year out of the five years immediately before the child's birth. Singaporean citizenship thus represents an individual's ties to a Singaporean parent or grandparent who was born in Singapore.

The Overseas Singaporean Unit (OSU) was established in 2006 under the Prime Minister's Office to coordinate the work done by different government agencies to reach out to overseas Singaporeans where they are concentrated—particularly in Australia, China, the United Kingdom, and the United States. Australia appeals to Singaporeans who desire a slower pace of life or an overseas education at lower costs, while the United Kingdom and the United States are popular destinations for other Singaporean students and young professionals. The OSU's signature event is Singapore Day, an annual festival to celebrate Singaporean culture abroad and remind overseas Singaporeans of their homeland. One such event held in New York's Central Park during 2012 was estimated to have cost as much as S$4 million.[64] The organizers had sponsored the travel costs of Singaporean celebrities and food vendors to feature entertainment and cuisine that overseas Singaporeans missed. This lavish event was reported widely in the Singapore media, triggering discussions of whether the expenditure of taxpayer money had been worth it, since there was no guarantee that overseas Singaporeans would return to serve the homeland.

A stint abroad has become widely accepted and might even be considered a rite of passage for aspiring Singaporeans. China has emerged as a destination for many such Singaporeans, particularly the Singaporean-Chinese, who desire to distinguish themselves professionally through exposure to the Chinese market. Singaporean migration to China was prompted initially by bilateral government collaborations such as the Suzhou Industrial Park near Shanghai. Bilateral collaboration has continued in the form of Tianjin Eco-City in northeast China and another project planned for the southwestern city of Chongqing. But aspiring Singaporeans now seek opportunities in China independently of government-directed collaborations too. The Singaporean-Chinese who live and work in China consider it both a boon and a bane. A job posting in China brings exposure to a work culture different from Westernized Singapore, access to a consumer market of one billion people, potential career progression, and greater opportunity for business profits. It presents a career opportunity that is distinctive from traditional expatriate postings in London, New York, and San Francisco.

Yet living in China can also seem like a "hardship posting," sharpening the sense of difference that overseas Singaporeans have toward co-ethnics in the ancestral land (henceforth domestic Mainland Chinese). Overseas Singaporeans whom I met in China often expressed concerns over food safety in China, associating poor business practices with the allegedly questionable moral values of the domestic Mainland Chinese. Media reports of counterfeit powdered milk, "fake eggs," or food cooked in carcinogenic oil prompt highly paid Singaporeans in China to consume food only at high-end restaurants that they frequent regularly, where the food is perceived to be safer. Many also buy imported or organic food from "Western-style" supermarkets in China or bring their own food supplies from Singapore or Hong Kong during regular business commutes or through visiting friends and colleagues.

Such overseas Singaporeans also become aware that Chinese workers are willing to endure long working hours and subpar working conditions despite poor pay, if only to gain a foothold toward upward social mobility. A common refrain they express is "Singaporeans are not 'hungry' enough compared to the Mainland Chinese," a catch-all phrase that refers to the unwillingness of Singaporeans working in Singapore to accept lower salaries or endure difficult working conditions. Encounters with co-ethnics in China sharpen the awareness of overseas Singaporeans that Singapore's economic performance will lag if Singaporeans lack the energy to outshine their co-ethnics in the ancestral land.[65] Their social anxiety resonates with reminders by Singaporean political leaders that, from a geopolitical viewpoint, a robust economy is crucial if Singapore is to maintain independence from China, which may see the smaller city-state with a Chinese majority as an extension of itself. The entwining of sovereignty and economic concerns is reflected in the management of both Singaporean emigration and immigration to Singapore.

Re-migration and Citizenship Constellations

Public complaints about companies hiring more foreigners than Singaporeans has prompted the Singaporean state to encourage employers to groom "Singaporean talent" and attract returning Singaporeans to take on senior management roles. Both government speeches and news reports place new emphasis on training the "Singapore core"[66]—those who identify as Singaporean and feel anchored by a sense of natal belonging to the nation. This core is to be strengthened by skills training and career progression in key industries that have become progressively reliant on foreign labor, such as health care, academia, information communications, the maritime industry, and banking and finance.[67] Crucially, overseas Singaporeans are considered members of the Singapore core, potential subjects to be courted for talent grooming in these industries.

Liberalizing citizenship laws, allowing overseas voting, and organizing outreach events are all meant to signal that the Singaporean state recognizes the transnational affiliations of overseas Singaporeans but still cherishes the ties that they maintain with Singapore. Yet there remains the question of how the state should negotiate the duties expected of citizens abroad. The responsibilities of citizenship cannot be enforced upon external citizens in the same way as with citizens living within the state's political jurisdiction,[68] unless strong measures are taken by the state. For example, overseas Singaporean men are expected to return to fulfill their conscription duty when they turn sixteen years old (although youths are usually enlisted at age eighteen).[69] Those who refuse are compelled to relinquish Singaporean citizenship when they turn twenty-one years old or be considered national service defaulters, who face the possibility of incarceration or fine upon reentering Singapore.[70]

Reports of such cases have appeared in the Singapore media. In one incident, a Singapore-born youth who grew up in New Zealand and had dual citizenship (through parental descent) refused to return to Singapore for a pre-enlistment medical test as required by conscription duty. But Singaporean law prohibits giving up one's Singaporean citizenship until the person turns twenty-one years old. The young man's family appealed to the government to defer the pre-enlistment medical test until the young man reached the age of twenty-one and could renounce Singaporean citizenship. Those appeals were rejected. This case was widely reported in the media, with online commentators criticizing the young man for refusing to perform his national service and intending to renounce Singaporean citizenship. At the heart of the issue were anxieties over community and loyalty when considering the right of overseas Singaporeans to retain Singapore citizenship and access rights indefinitely, the dual citizenship restriction, and exemption of second-generation youth from national service. Even though the diaspora strategies of the Singaporean state are meant to extend fraternity to nationals abroad, migrant transnationalism in the first generation and extending into the second generation generates new dilemmas that the state has yet to resolve.

Even if the legal entanglements can be sidestepped, overseas Singaporeans who return to the country may face difficulty re-integrating into society. Overseas Singaporeans who return have encountered challenges that include differences in working styles, not switching to Singlish when communicating with other Singaporeans, and behaving differently from those who have not lived abroad.[71] Many returnees adapt eventually, but those who don't may choose to re-migrate again. Others re-migrate because of the lure of a foreign working experience or a lifestyle different from what Singapore can offer. Regardless, societal reception toward overseas Singaporeans who return has been less controversial than attitudes toward immigrants. Returnees are considered prodigal children returning to the fold who can adapt to Singaporean society more easily than immigrants because they were born and bred in Singapore, even if they have lived abroad for decades.

Comparing immigration and emigration trends in Singapore illuminates the intersecting concerns over the loyalty of both new immigrants and overseas Singaporeans. The convergence of a variety of immigrants in the city-state means there exist multiple diaspora populations that embody distinct cultures and national affiliations. To the Singaporean state and locally born Singaporeans, newer immigrants should be "integrated," but such immigrants are always a step away from fully belonging because their natal ties lie elsewhere. Singaporeans who have emigrated may not be physically present in the territory, but their natal belonging is naturalized and prioritized by the state and society. Nonetheless, the state regularly reminds them of their duties and seeks to enforce the ones it deems nonnegotiable given national security concerns. The Singaporean state maintains a public culture of anxiety over identity and security by invoking transversal axes of alterity. Under conditions of contemporaneous migration, it is not possible to apply a uniform concept of racism, cultural difference, or class exploitation.[72] Each axis of alterity demands careful investigation to recalibrate the always shifting parameters of citizenship inclusion or exclusion.

Conclusion

Studying immigration and emigration in tandem sets into sharp relief the contradictions of fraternity and temporal periodization on several levels. First, migrant-receiving countries negotiate immigration integration challenges while strategizing their own outreach toward emigrants to consolidate national identity. The Singaporean state institutionalizes immigration as a necessary pillar of nation building but undermines it in two ways: first, by deepening differentiations between citizenship, permanent residency, and migrancy; and second, by naturalizing natal ties, even toward emigrants. This chapter showed how processes of fraternity and alterity manifest in a trans-territorial context as the state treads an uneasy line of navigating immigration and emigration to optimize economic gains and political clout.

Studies of immigration tend to conflate race with cultural difference, whereas this discussion on Singapore has demonstrated how co-ethnics from another nationality can be portrayed as less deserving of fraternity. Natal belonging is naturalized for those considered "born of the soil," even if this has been socially constructed to privilege immigrants who arrived during an earlier period. Studies of urban diversity take as a starting point issues of co-presence during a snapshot in time, premised on chronological periodization. This is the nation-state's framing of time that marks milestones and achievements toward building fraternity and social cohesion. For the emigrant, absence during the present is compensated by territorial presence in the past and anticipated futures. For the immigrant, territorial presence in the present is inadequate as long as they have been absent in the past. In this rendering of time, fraternity to the territorial community is always elusive for the immigrant because presence in the past can never be captured in the present moment. Assumptions of natal ties and the periodization of migration thus flexibly legitimize the gradations of inclusion or exclusion that are extended to different migrant groups, including co-ethnics, within and outside of the national territory.

5 China at Home and Abroad

Introduction

"He's like you, a *huaqiao*, but from Malaysia," said my new acquaintance, Ahmed, as he introduced me to his friend. We exchanged a few words with the Malaysian-Chinese and continued on our way. Ahmed explained, "There are many like that who have returned to China." Further along the street, we paused again as he chanced upon another group of friends returning with cartons of beer in hand. "They are from Australia and Eastern Europe," he told me. That ten-minute stroll in Wuhan from the university hostel to the shuttle bus stop turned out to be a window into the multicultural face of changing China. Ahmed was an African-Muslim postgraduate who was studying in a Chinese university. He was from Egypt but had introduced me to the multi-ethnic and multinational character of changing China in fluent Beijing-accented Mandarin,[1] a feat I could not have mastered myself.

Emigration, immigration, and re-migration each capture a snapshot of China's interconnection with the world, but they come together to simultaneously shape nationhood and international relationships. Usually considered an emigration nation, China is facing immigration trends today that challenge its approach to migration governance and societal understandings of ethnicity. Chinese universities are fast internationalizing as they attract foreign students eager to acquire Chinese language skills and cultural knowledge or derive lessons from China's accelerated development. The universities are but a window into the growing cultural diversity found in China.[2] The student who introduced me to his multinational social circle is one of many Africans who are in China today for economic or educational reasons.

Historian Rebecca Karl argued that how China saw and portrayed itself globally during the late Qing period was linked to developments in the world.[3] The political episodes connecting China to the world at that time can be read as "a contemporaneous global space" that resulted in an epoch of domestic and foreign policy changes.[4] Drawing inspiration from Karl, this chapter proposes that studying the contemporaneous aspects of migration illuminates the connections through which domestic change and external processes are unfolding in China today. The approach considers different manifestations of migration that take place concurrently in a polity, while keeping in view the global historical conjunctures that forge trans-territorial connections.[5] Such processes direct attention to the "globe-spanning systems of power" that transform the way social, political, and economic life is organized and reproduced, affecting perceptions of self and society.[6]

Equating phenotypical difference with foreignness presents only a partial picture of how China is changing today. By juxtaposing the treatment of Chinese diasporic descendants with that of non-Chinese foreigners, this chapter illuminates how fraternity and alterity are exercised contingently in Chinese society. In a legal sense, Chinese diasporic descendants who are foreign nationals are considered immigrants in China, but in a cultural sense they are treated as co-ethnics who re-migrated to the ancestral land. Domestic ethnic relations are also changing as the Chinese state responds opportunistically to the emigration of ethnic minorities in China (henceforth ethnic minority emigrants).

Studying the interface of distinct yet interrelated migration trends allows us to conceptualize both inter-ethnic and co-ethnic relations in culturally diverse societies. Contemporaneous migration further illuminates three dimensions of alterity, namely alterity as phenotypical difference, as the diversification of co-ethnicity, and as spatial recalibration. This analytical approach reveals how fraternity and alterity operate within and across ethnic categories in transnational contexts. The chapter builds on findings from the preceding chapters and further draws on secondary research, visual sources, and original ethnographic research conducted in China, Myanmar, and at the China-Myanmar border.

China, Emigrant Nation: Worldview and Diffusion

Managing the diffusion of ideologies and mobilizing the resources of the Chinese abroad to advance nation building and promote China's role in the world has driven successive Chinese governments to assert an extraterritorial reach toward its diaspora.[7] Both historically and today, the Chinese state manages its relationship with the Chinese abroad with a delicate sense of balance on multiple fronts.[8] Chinese emigrants and diasporic descendants are seen by the Chinese state as interlocutors for China in their countries of residence.[9] The new Chinese immigrants (*xinyimin*) emigrating from China today also symbolize the soft power through which Chinese developmental models and values can be exported.[10] Notably, Chinese emigration and China's growing global prominence are both prompting new immigration to China. The Chinese worldview of *tianxia* informs understanding of the multidirectional migration patterns that reflect and impact China's domestic management of ethnic diversity and its external orientations.

Tianxia's distinctive worldview attributes centrality to China as the "Middle Kingdom," with a system of tributary states comprising the rest of the world. Such a worldview influences the way the Chinese state and (Han) Chinese society approach domestic ethnic relations and their relationship to the Chinese abroad.[11] Interpolating the ethnic stratification seen in Chinese society are also notions of orientalism and self-orientalism. Orientalism uses essentialized cultural characteristics to portray societies, rendering spatial difference as temporal difference. Orientalized societies are seen to have "no real contemporaneity, since their presents are but simple reproductions of their pasts."[12] The contemporary version of *tianxia* popularized by Chinese scholar Zhao Tingyang prescribes an internal hierarchy of social relations that extends to foreign policy orientations.[13] Several scholars have likened *tianxia* to Western notions of cosmopolitanism,[14] but such accounts have not engaged adequately with China's overtures to consolidate geographical and social difference under the guise of exporting Chinese developmental values through migration, foreign investments, and cultural diplomacy.

Offering a different viewpoint is Pál Nyíri, who highlights how the Chinese state's development goals emphasize the "civilizing role" of the overseas Chinese who contribute to improving the economic development and cultural quality of other countries.[15] The geographical worldview of *tianxia* also guides China's public and private development projects abroad, creating what Ong describes as lateral spaces that "stretch across continents and intersect processes of production and exploitation involving processes of ethnicization, carceral modes of labor discipline, and the dominance of market over territorial rights."[16] Chinese globalization connects not only goods and services, but also people. Once an emigration nation, China is becoming an immigration nation. The racial categorizations that shape its domestic ethnic management and external engagement with the world influence its treatment of immigrants and emigrants too.

Immigrant China: Restrictive Migration Management

The 2010 census stated that China had a foreign population of 593,832 people; this figure excluded foreigners in the Hong Kong and Macau Special Administrative Regions.[17] By 2015, the numbers had increased to 978,000.[18] These figures account for registered foreigners only and likely underestimate the actual number of foreigners in China. The foreign population in China spans skilled professionals and business investors, international students, marriage migrants, traders, and unskilled laborers. They come from countries in North America, Europe, Asia, Africa, the Middle East, and more. Among them are Chinese diasporic descendants, first-generation emigrants who naturalized abroad and then re-migrated, non-Chinese foreigners, and cross-border migrants. The diversity of immigrants with different visa situations and migration intentions presents unprecedented challenges that, as a nation more accustomed to emigration, China has not experienced previously.

China's management of immigration is piecemeal, characterized by "a large number of subsidiary orders, directives, rules, and circulars."[19] Immigration management involves multiple ministries and agencies representing different vested interests.[20] The government agency known as the Overseas Chinese Affairs Office (*Qiaoban*) and the government-affiliated All-China Federation of Returned Overseas Chinese (*Qiaolian*) operate at the federal and sub-national levels to oversee matters concerning emigrants (*huaqiao* or *waiji huaren*) and Chinese diasporic descendants (*huayi*). Entry (immigration) and exit (emigration) regulations were fairly relaxed from 1949 to 1957, when China welcomed the return of the Chinese abroad, including diasporic descendants. This liberal attitude waned against the backdrop of the Cultural Revolution and subsequent concerns over China's talent loss through emigration. Immigration slowed to a trickle: foreigners who came were students from countries that had shared ideological leanings with China or those from the developed world who wanted to learn the Chinese language and culture; expatriates who worked in approved businesses, journalism, or diplomacy; and foreign experts serving state agencies.[21]

Despite economic reforms in 1979, draconian restrictions remained over exit regulations for Chinese nationals. Successive legislative changes were enforced after 1986,[22] but it was only in 2001 that comprehensive reforms happened. The state streamlined exit procedures for citizens (2002–2004) and piloted a permanent residence program for immigrants in 2004.[23] China desires to attract business and skilled migrants, but stringent rules about the amount of investment, and the type of high-ranking job designations and employment institutions recognized by the state, limit the take-up rate for these categories of migration.[24] Meanwhile, management of family migration evolved to accommodate the overseas Chinese who returned after naturalizing abroad (known as *haiou* or seagulls). They apply for immigrant visas to re-migrate as "foreigners" of Chinese ethnicity (*waiji huaren*). Those married to spouses who retained Chinese nationality qualify for family reunification, but their temporary visas cause inconvenience and uncertainty. The Chinese state has gradually increased the types of family reunification allowed and the length of stay permitted, measures that take into account the returnees' ancestral ties, life biographies, and co-ethnicity. By comparison, the authorities treat the family migration of non-Chinese foreigners who are spouses or dependents of Chinese nationals less favorably. Their social ranking and visa entitlements depend on their ethnic and nationality backgrounds and socioeconomic status.[25]

So far, reforms to immigration in China have emphasized providing legal channels for desirable migrants who possess financial and human capital, while enforcing stricter regulation over low-skilled and undocumented migrants.[26] Despite the clarifications to China's migration and citizenship law, such reforms sidestep the qualitative changes brought about by immigration in China. Immigration precipitates new questions over the political or social rights of immigrants from plural backgrounds and the social status of the second generation growing up in China with foreign nationality status or who are children of mixed marriages. Concurrent with these immigration trends is the re-migration of Chinese emigrants and diasporic descendants to the ancestral land. How does China negotiate the changing boundaries of membership alongside ongoing debates over Chinese identity and the domestic ethnic diversity of the country? Everyday social relations and identities in China are crafted within transnational networks of power, and three features of alterity stand out when we study the contemporaneous aspects of migration.

Alterity as Phenotypical Difference

Fei Cheng Wu Rao is a dating game show that has achieved one of the highest television ratings in China; it represents in microcosm the Chinese fascination with the diversity of new immigration. The format features twenty-four bachelo-rettes who make a recurring weekly appearance to assess the dating potential of four to five bachelors in each episode. The female contestants use a buzzer to change the lighting color of their podiums to indicate interest or to reject a bachelor. The game show has showcased foreigners among the bevy of bache-lorettes and bachelors, including Chinese diasporic descendants and contes-tants of African, Caucasian, Korean, Thai, and Indonesian ethnicity. Through the question-and-answer segment or the banter of the game show hosts, a so-cial commentary emerges of Chinese attitudes toward marriage, values, and intercultural encounters.

In one episode, the male game show host described a female African con-testant from Guinea Bissau as "irresistible as chocolate" (referring to her phe-notype). In a different episode, a bachelor contestant from Namibia introduced himself by saying, "My [Chinese] teacher asked me why I am so dark; I replied I was tanned by the sun [in Africa] . . . but since coming to China I have be-come fairer!" He professed that he joined the show to court the aforementioned African female contestant. But she rejected him by stating that she preferred to date Chinese men, because highly educated African women like her "have seen the world and realize there are better men out there who can give them freedom and opportunity." Subsequent social media reports revealed that the female African contestant was an international student in a Chinese univer-sity and the niece of an African ambassador on posting in China.

Growing international relations and trade between China and African coun-tries has triggered new Chinese emigration to African countries and parallel Af-rican immigration to China. Chinese migrants in Africa work as petty traders and entrepreneurs, or investors and employees in infrastructure, natural re-source, and manufacturing projects.[27] Many of these projects are led by Chinese state-owned enterprises, but there are also private commercial investments. Chi-na's diplomatic engagement with African countries is prompted by domestic agendas related to the country's energy or production needs and demand for new consumer markets. China adopts a policy of non-interference to secure its eco-nomic interests in different African countries, supporting democracies and non-democracies alike.[28] In return for China's investment dollars, several African countries have granted economic concessions to Chinese state-owned enter-prises, creating what Ong describes as "zones of graduated sovereignty."[29]

Accompanying Chinese investment abroad is an outflow of Chinese mi-grants who belong to the "new Chinese diaspora" (i.e., distinct from the "old

Chinese diaspora" of the nineteenth and early twentieth centuries). This co-hort of migrants (*xinyimin*) embodies and projects newfound confidence in China's economic prospects and global political clout. Their presence in Africa has been mired by reports of discrimination and poor working practices among Chinese employers who hire African employees. Barry Sautman and Hairong Yan argue that the Western media's depiction of China has created negative international opinions of China.[30] Nevertheless, social interactions between the Chinese and Africans are characterized by mutual racial stereotypes. Chinese emigrants export not only Chinese values but also Chinese ethnocentrism,[31] under which "blacks are essentialized and racialized to perpetuate the negative image of Africa as the 'primitive' and 'inferior Other.'"[32] Such impressions filter back to China through communication with left-behind family and friends, return migration, news reports, or social media.

Africans are also migrating to China for trading, business, or educational purposes. Existing literature on African migration to China mainly considers the experiences of African traders, focusing on illegality and "low-end" globalization in Chinese trading cities.[33] But China's expanding presence in Africa has also directed an increasing number of African students to seek educational opportunities and learn from the Chinese developmental model.[34] In 2015, 49,792 Africans studied in China, out of a total of 397,635 international students.[35] They come from a range of countries in the African continent and represent the overlaps between trading and educational migration.[36] Student visas allow such migrants to keep an eye on family businesses in China while finding casual employment as trading brokers or translators for African businesses.[37]

For example, the African-Muslim postgraduate introduced at the start of this chapter studied in Wuhan, but during the semester break he would go to Guangzhou, Shenzhen, or Hong Kong to work as a translator in export companies set up by African traders. Ahmed had studied the Chinese language in Beijing for a year before moving to Wuhan to pursue a postgraduate degree in international relations. His goal was to become a diplomat and he worked hard to master the language. Lining one side of the wall in his hostel room were pages of Chinese text for memorizing. On another side hung a Chinese calligraphy scroll with the auspicious word "longevity" (*shou*) and next to it an Egyptian wall painting that symbolized his ties to his homeland. The first time we met, Ahmed invited me to lunch at the school canteen. As we waited for our food to be prepared, a Chinese student greeted Ahmed, who introduced me to his friend and commented, "This is one of my few Chinese friends." Turning to his friend, he asked rhetorically, "Why don't Chinese students mix with foreign students?" The Chinese student did not have a ready answer so Ahmed offered his viewpoint: "The Chinese students are shy and don't take the initiative." After his friend left, Ahmed added that the school administrators discouraged mingling between the Chinese and foreign students outside of class time because of anxieties that the Chinese would be adulterated by foreign values.

Most of the African students in China come from privileged socioeconomic backgrounds, since both financial and social resources are required for migration. They come to China, a land they know only through the media, Internet, or word of mouth before they arrive, with lofty dreams. They appreciate the amenities of urban life in China but are also disappointed by the social norms they encounter. In Wuhan, I met Nisha and Zoe, who were from Zimbabwe and Congo-Brazzaville respectively. As we chatted in a classroom, Nisha told me she was studying international trade and economics and Zoe studied medicine. They chose Wuhan on account of the university's good reputation. Initially shy, the two students warmed up as they shared their opinions about living in Wuhan. Gesturing to their hostel across the road, Nisha said, "It was nice in pictures on the Internet but the actual [place] was quite disgusting." To reinforce her point, Nisha extended her observations to Chinese urban life, "I don't like that Chinese people spit at food markets, shopping malls, everywhere they just spit on the ground." Listening attentively, Zoe added, "They are shocked to see foreign and black people too." Elaborating on their educational experience in China, Zoe said, "Sometimes if we don't understand something, we say, 'excuse me teacher, can you explain this.' If it is a student from Nepal or Europe he will answer. He will never answer if it is an African student who asks, he will ignore us. It is kind of racist."

Disappointment at the living conditions, social norms, and educational environment in China were common gripes among the African students I met. Both Nisha and Zoe plan to leave China after graduation because they do not want to continue learning "Chinese words" and they did not like "Chinese food." Such African students aspire to re-migrate to a third country that would be less likely to stigmatize cultural difference.[38] While in China, the Africans bear the brunt of a racial hierarchy in which they are dehumanized as *heigui* (black ghosts), inclined to crime and immoral behavior.[39] Yet the Chinese public is fascinated by their ostensible alterity. This is illustrated in the backhanded compliment paid to the female African contestant on *Fei Cheng Wu Rao*; her corporeal phenotype is rendered as both exotic and erotic through the metaphor, "as irresistible as dark chocolate." The flippant remark made by the male African contestant (i.e., becoming fairer) reflects Chinese stereotypes on social acceptability. As Saldhana observes, "Phenotype is capable of conjuring up a whole series of fears, desires, clichés, and antagonisms [. . .] phenotype does always matter somehow—to experience, imagination, and belonging, to interaction and the allocation of bodies."[40] Echoing the geographical worldview embedded in the political philosophy of *tianxia*, Africans in China are considered abject subjects whose black skin symbolizes the underdevelopment of their countries in the eyes of the Chinese public.[41]

Migration transforms *tianxia* from a treatise on China's international relations into intimate visceral encounters that both reflect and reinforce racial stratification. In the urban spaces of everyday life, African migrants can be treated as objects of curiosity by Chinese observers. A telling episode happened when I was with an African undergraduate who accompanied me to visit Hubu Xiang, a popular pedestrianized alley in Wuhan. The burly African student had studied in the local university for several years and offered to be my guide. In a sea of Chinese faces, he stood out from the crowd as he was nearly a head taller than most. Unexpectedly a Chinese man wearing a bucket hat and with a camera slung around his neck approached us from the front, snapped an unsolicited photograph of the African student, and walked away wearing a smug grin. Stoically, my guide said it was not the first time this had happened. Curious Chinese persons have touched his skin or hair without seeking his approval first.[42]

That evening, the taxi driver ferrying us back to the university questioned the African student incessantly about the country he came from and how his studies were funded, even though the student refused to answer those questions. Carrying on a monologue, the driver expressed with conviction that the African country in question was subpar compared to China. In the taxi driver's view, African countries need Chinese investment to develop their national infrastructure, industries, and overall *suzhi* ("quality," or human capital). As Ann Anagnost explains, "*suzhi*'s sense has been extended from a discourse of backwardness and development (the quality of the masses) to encompass the minute social distinctions defining 'a person of quality' in practices of consumption and the middle-class desire for social mobility."[43] To the Chinese taxi driver, the African student's black skin connoted the value associated with a country's developmental stage and personal *suzhi*.

The Chinese public sees the Africans in China as outsiders of poorer *suzhi* who cannot be successfully assimilated, even if they have lived in China for decades, speak the language fluently, and exhibit familiarity with Chinese culture.[44] Contrasted with the opening vignette of this book, where the taxi driver in Beijing had unreservedly associated my Chinese ethnicity with expectations of return and service to the ancestral land (*huiguo weiguo fuwu*), this encounter in Wuhan highlights how visible phenotype marks out a hierarchy of *suzhi* in Chinese society. The Chinese cultural imagination of *suzhi* denotes a relationship between value and phenotype. Nevertheless, this account of alterity as phenotypical difference does not explain the social difference experienced and articulated by "foreign" Chinese diasporic descendants now living in China. The discourse of *suzhi* creates axes of differentiation between co-ethnics too.

Alterity as the Diversification of Co-ethnicity

When China underwent economic reforms after 1979, government officials looked to Chinese diasporic descendants in Southeast Asia as co-ethnics who could facilitate foreign investment inflows from capitalist nations to China. Such links with co-ethnic capital continue apace, described by Ong as "the two-way flows of professional and business classes between China and overseas Chinese communities [which] create complex networks that amount to a de facto transborder integration of the socialist mainland with overseas Chinese capitalist citadels at the scientific, business, and personal levels."[45] Connections and networks like these are facilitated through the re-migration of Chinese diasporic descendants to the ancestral land. They come from Asia, North America, Europe, and beyond by way of company-sponsored postings, entrepreneurial ventures, educational stints, or retirement. The Chinese diasporic descendants converging in China today have foreign nationalities, identify with multiple sites of natal belonging, and embody a range of cultural identities. These attributes lend to the diversification of co-ethnic identity.

The re-migration and adaptation of Chinese diasporic descendants to the ancestral land is often the subject of caricature in popular culture. For instance, the dating game show *Fei Cheng Wu Rao* has featured several "American-Born Chinese" (ABC) bachelors. One such contestant professed his admiration for Chinese culture in his self-introduction video and expressed regret that he had not learned Mandarin properly as a Chinese person growing up in the United States. He added that he wanted to improve his Mandarin because China is "so formidable" (*lihai*). In another film production called *Shanghai Calling*, the protagonist is a blundering American-Chinese corporate lawyer posted to work in China by his employer.[46] As the show progresses, its plot centers on a series of cultural misunderstandings that lead to the protagonist's coming to understand and appreciate his ancestral culture and society. The story is set in the sophisticated glamor of Shanghai, thus accentuating his cosmopolitan capital as he deepens his familiarity with the ancestral land and its people.

Setting aside media depictions, academic research suggests that Chinese diasporic descendants negotiate more complex articulations of cultural superiority or inferiority.[47] Emigrant connections with China are not reducible to an essentialized version of Chinese identity and nationalism. Examples from Singapore, Taiwan, and Myanmar aptly illustrate a range of alterity manifestations that can be projected on co-ethnics. The geopolitical histories linking China to these three countries are distinct. Singapore, part of Malaya prior to 1965, served as a migration destination for Chinese laborers and aspiring youths, whereas Taiwan was birthed through the political separation of the Kuomintang from the communists. Chinese diasporic descendants in Myanmar trace their family histories to trade-led, labor, or conflict-induced migration.[48] The Burmese-Chinese are a minority population in Myanmar, unlike Chinese diasporic descendants in Singapore and Taiwan, who comprise the majority in those countries. The distinct geopolitical and development paths of the three countries produce cognitive taxonomies and hierarchies of difference that Chinese diasporic descendants use to distinguish themselves from co-ethnics who consider China their natal land (henceforth domestic Mainland Chinese), and vice versa.[49]

Consider, for example, the attitudes expressed by the Singaporean-Chinese in a study conducted by Brenda Yeoh and Katie Willis on Singaporeans living in China.[50] The Singaporean-Chinese regularly brought up what they consider the moral depravation of the domestic Mainland Chinese. One of the respondents, a Singaporean-Chinese woman, puts it this way: "The Cultural Revolution has done much harm to [China]. You can actually see it. Basically the country has lost its own character, lost its own culture, it doesn't have a soul. Many customs we keep so steadfastly in Southeast Asia are not practiced here."[51]

By referring to the impact of the Cultural Revolution (1966–1967), this comment invokes the past to legitimize the purity of the Chinese culture that has been preserved by members of the diaspora who were not subject to the Maoist policies that banned traditional customs, cultures, ideas, and habits.[52]

Territorial identification constructs a social identity that projects immorality on those considered abject, in the process conflating geographical borders with cognitive bordering.[53]

In a different study of Taiwanese migrants who re-migrated to China, Ping Lin found that although this group maintained a strong political and cultural affiliation to China, their interactions with domestic Mainland Chinese relatives enhanced attitudes of moral superiority on the part of both parties.[54] The Taiwanese respondents claimed that their Mainland Chinese relatives sought monetary benefits while the domestic Mainland Chinese countered that the Taiwanese were "arrogant and selfish."[55] Such cognitive borders are borne out of territorial location and temporally locate the abject co-ethnic as lagging behind.[56] The political and social orientations of Chinese diasporic descendants from Singapore and Taiwan lie with the countries they consider their natal land. They regard the Mainland Chinese as co-ethnics of a lower status because of geopolitical and developmental perceptions of the ancestral land. Diasporic moments can deepen identification with the ancestral land on some occasions or mutually accentuate co-ethnic differences on other occasions.[57]

The Chinese in Southeast Asia (especially Singapore) and Greater China (Taiwan and Hong Kong) were once seen as the bridge to capitalist experimentation for China.[58] Today China is eyeing another set of economies in the bordering countries of the Mekong region, deepening the transborder integration Ong had described.[59] Frontier economies in Cambodia, Laos, Myanmar, and Vietnam present economic opportunities for China in natural resource extraction (e.g., timber, oil, and gas), construction projects (e.g., dams, roads, bridges, and real estate), manufacturing (e.g., garment industry), agriculture (e.g. rice, cassava, and other cash crops), and import-export activity (e.g., electronics and textiles). As cultural exchanges and China's soft power grew in those countries, Chinese diasporic descendants in the Mekong countries have experienced re-sinicization.[60]

Chinese clan associations, schools, and chambers of commerce in the Mekong countries play crucial roles in nurturing business and cultural networks with their counterparts in China. These platforms facilitate the Chinese state's extraterritorial reach to instill patriotic identification among Chinese diasporic descendants. Chinese diasporic descendants in the Mekong countries are minority populations who maintain a delicate balance of integrating into their natal land while retaining features of Chinese identity and culture. Land travel to China for business purposes is common among those who live near the border, and those who commute by land are not considered immigrants; the Chinese refer to them as *kuajing minzu* (cross-border ethnic groups). Some stay for a few days, but others remain for longer periods undetected by the Chinese authorities. The porosity of border crossings means that co-ethnics from neighboring countries can move freely, find work, and live in Mainland China as long as they evade police checks.

As an example, when I visited the Chinese town of Ruili at the border China shares with Myanmar, I encountered such a group of young co-ethnics who identified themselves as Myanmar nationals of Chinese ethnicity; they were employed as waitresses in a restaurant, and none of the girls had rightful documentation to work in China. My host in Ruili, a Chinese businessman who made regular cross-border trips to Myanmar, had asked his wife to take me out that day. His wife gathered her friends and brought along her toddler and a younger Chinese lady who turned out to be the nanny. I learned later that the nanny was Burmese-Chinese; she spoke Mandarin fluently but retained an accent that can be described in the Mainland Chinese context as "unsophisticated," signaling a lower socioeconomic status and identifying her as a migrant from Myanmar.

While I was exploring the landscaped garden in the restaurant I chanced upon the Chinese waitresses from Myanmar, who were having their lunch break. One of the waitresses was especially chatty and told me it was not their first stint working as cross-border casual labor. Gradually the others joined in the conversation. They said they would stay for three to six months at a time and return to Myanmar once they had earned enough and then seek employment again in China a few months later. As co-ethnics who speak Mandarin and share the same phenotype as the (Han) Mainland Chinese, they find it easier to find jobs in China than the Burmese or other ethnic minorities from Myanmar such as the Kachin and Shan. Nonetheless, they expressed that being from a country considered poorer than China means the Mainland Chinese "look down" on them as co-ethnics of poorer *suzhi*—a comment that made me recall a remark made by the Chinese businessman who was my host in Ruili.

On the first day we met he shared a biographical account of his family history and his personal ties to Myanmar. He had moved to Ruili from Fujian province more than a decade earlier to capitalize on cross-border business opportunities with Myanmar. Before him, his grandfather had migrated from Fujian province to Yangon in Myanmar to make a living, subsequently setting up home there. In time, the grandfather decided to re-migrate to spend his golden years in China (*gaolao huanxiang*) and brought along my host's father.

The rest of the family remained in Yangon and has become a wealthy branch of the extended family (*da jiazu*). When my host was seventeen years old, he lived in Yangon for a few years, but he could not fit in. By way of illustration, he told me that since he grew up in China he was used to wearing covered shoes and trousers, but in Yangon both men and women would wear open-toed slippers with the *longgyi* (a roll of fabric wrapped and knotted around the waist securely). He couldn't get accustomed to that. Comparing covered shoes to open-toed slippers proved to be a metaphor: the covered shoes symbolized higher levels of development; they cost more and signaled attentiveness to decorum and style whereas open-toed slippers were inexpensive and shabby to the Mainland Chinese.

My host had subtly expressed his view that China was economically and culturally more advanced than Myanmar. In the time I spent with my host's family, I noticed that his wife and her friends would speak deprecatingly of the Burmese-Chinese who worked in Ruili. The wife described the nanny as a family friend whom she could trust to care for her child, but the nanny was provincial and lacked aspirations because she came from Myanmar. Although the emphasis that *tianxia* places on Chinese lineage suggests that the Chinese living abroad are considered ethnic kin who are culturally closer to China, such discourses of co-ethnic kinship are modulated by developmental hierarchies that are projected onto individual personhood. In the absence of phenotypical difference, alterity manifests through notions of national development, morality, socioeconomic status, and *suzhi*. Alterity projects can be flexibly mobilized to carve out domains of inclusion or exclusion. Likewise, definitions of the Chinese nation and diaspora are changing as a result of new emigration patterns by ethnic minorities in China.

Alterity as Spatial Recalibration

Diaspora engagement by the Chinese state has focused typically on Chinese emigrants and diasporic descendants of Han ethnicity, considered descendants of the Yellow Emperor. The Chinese nation, known as *zhonghua minzu*, consists of fifty-six ethnic groups living within the national territory, of which the Han are the majority ethnic group. Ethnic groups in China are known as *minzu*, which connotes "nationality" in the Chinese context but refers to a state-driven construction of ethnic identity.[61] Ethnic classification in China assumes cultural difference, and Han ethnocentrism naturalizes the alleged social inferiority of ethnic minority groups.[62]

Chris Vasantkumar argues that the "territorial and extraterritorial versions of Chinese-ness are not congruent" in this reading of nation and ethnicity.[63] The Chinese state's relationship to ethnic minority groups in China ranges from directing hostility and armed violence at separatists such as the Tibetans and Uyghurs to incentivizing other ethnic minority groups that are considered more cooperative toward Han Chinese leadership and its version of nation building.[64]

Despite interpretations of *tianxia* as a Chinese worldview that positions ethnic minorities at the periphery of nationhood, emigration and re-migration can serve to reconfigure statist projects of fraternity and alterity. In recent years, the Chinese state has started to turn its attention to two categories of emigrants of ethnic minority status. One category refers to persons with Chinese nationality status who have emigrated to study or work abroad.[65] The other category refers to diasporic descendants of ethnic minority backgrounds living abroad but whose ancestral hometowns are in China.[66] To project the unity of the nation, Chinese political leaders enfold such ethnic minorities abroad under the label of "Ethnic Minority Overseas Chinese" (*Shaoshu Minzu Huaqiao Huaren*).[67] The Chinese state has a twofold purpose for extending the fraternity connoted by the labels "Chinese diaspora" and "the overseas Chinese" to ethnic minority emigrants. First, capitalizing upon the social connections of ethnic minorities allows China to both reach into under-explored economic territories and extend its soft power through initiatives such as the "New Silk Road."[68] For example, the Hui Muslim who populate the Ningxia Hui Autonomous Region are treated as economic partners in the Chinese state's project to revamp the region as a free trade zone—a project that would enhance Sino–Arab economic cooperation in the global halal food trade and Muslim commodities. As Sino–Arab trade increases, more Hui Chinese Muslims sojourn to the Gulf countries and other Muslim countries for business and religious purposes. As Ho Wai Yip puts it, "The identity of the Hui Muslims has been approved inside China and they are 'good citizens' in the view of the Han majority. Likewise, they have been accepted outside China with their identity as China's 'cultural ambassadors' in the view of the Muslim world."[69]

Second, in regions like Tibet or Xinjiang, which are considered politically volatile, the Chinese state engages the ethnic minority emigrants from these places to minimize the spread of political ideologies that are opposed to Chinese communism and governance. Vasantkumar observes that the Chinese state aims to transform Tibetans overseas into "real Chinese citizens" through an extraterritorial reach that instills patriotism while they are abroad.[70] The Chinese state also seeks to nurture the emotional attachment of the second and third generations (i.e., diasporic descendants of ethnic minority backgrounds) to China as an ancestral land.[71] In this regard, roots tourism is promoted by the Chinese state as a way of enabling Chinese diasporic descendants of ethnic minority backgrounds to familiarize themselves with Chinese culture and see that their ethnic kin are benefiting from China's developmental projects.

As such, ethnic minority emigrants are emerging as new targets of the policy work done by the Overseas Chinese Affairs Office and the All-China Federation of Returned Overseas Chinese (*Qiaoban* and *Qiaolian*). New organizations with strong government links have also been established, such as the Overseas Chinese Ethnic Minorities Association in the United States (renamed the Global Chinese Ethnic Minorities and Religions Association in 2010), the Kyrgyzstan Overseas Chinese Association, and the Overseas Chinese Muslim Association in Malaysia.[72] These organizations aim to nurture the emotional connection of ethnic minorities with China from afar and consolidate national unity. When the ethnic minority emigrants return to China, they become subjects of re-integration initiatives by the *Qiaoban* and *Qiaolian* too.[73]

Although China now considers an overseas experience as cosmopolitan capital, the task of managing domestic ethnic difference continues unabated. Observing the alterity orientations among ethnic minority migrants, Barabantseva adds that they "find it difficult to reconcile the two social categories imposed on them by the Chinese state [and] to choose which of the two types of positive discrimination, either for ethnic minorities or overseas Chinese, would be more beneficial for them."[74] Only by journeying abroad and extending China's extraterritorial reach or by bolstering the image of ethnic unity can ethnic minority populations acquire greater legitimacy in the Chinese nation. Alterity within the nation is spatially recalibrated through diaspora strategizing that extends membership to ethnic minorities abroad, even if it is only to reinforce the state's version of history, identity, and nationhood.

Nevertheless, the "sojourn work" sponsored by the Chinese state raises questions for both China's new iteration of the "Chinese diaspora" and the diasporic descendants in countries that are pursuing nation building projects of their own.[75] Consider, for example, Barabantseva's account of an unnamed Chinese-Muslim Dungan visitor from Kazakhstan who had been invited on a sponsored visit to China.[76] Accordingly, the Dungan visitor praised the Chinese state's treatment of ethnic minorities and preservation of Hui heritage and religion. His visit invoked feelings of "return" even though he had not lived in China before. In this instance, roots tourism strengthened relations between diasporic descendants and the ancestral land. When the former's countries of settlement view those ancestral relations as an advantage for trade and economic partnerships, China's quest for ethnic unity across transnational contexts is a boon rather than a bane. However, research on the Chinese-Muslim Dungans in Kyrgyzstan suggests that the presence of new Chinese migrants (*xinyimin*) who represent China's economic interests in post-Soviet countries has caused tensions with the latter's domestic ethnic groups, which view China's role as one of economic exploitation.[77] The extraterritorial reach of the Chinese state toward diasporic descendants of ethnic minority backgrounds might be seen in a positive light if it complements the economic agendas of their countries of residence, or if framed negatively, then it is likelier viewed as competition to the domestic nation building objectives of those same countries.

Conclusion: Contemporaneous Migration and the Manifold Faces of Alterity

This chapter has deployed the analytical framework of contemporaneous migration to conceptualize the different ways in which alterity operates through both racial hierarchies and alterity orientations among co-ethnics. It considered these ways through the Chinese geographical worldview of *tianxia* on how social relations should be ordered. *Tianxia* regards the (Han) Chinese abroad as culturally proximate co-ethnics. Meanwhile, non-Chinese immigration to China together with the re-migration of diasporic descendants to the ancestral land is creating new challenges for how the Chinese state manages cultural diversity. Toward ethnic minority emigrants, the state's new diaspora strategizing seeks to reinforce nation building within the territory and enhance China's global competitiveness. The contemporaneous migration trends discussed in this chapter, interfacing African immigration with the re-migration of Chinese diasporic descendants and emigrant ethnic minorities, has drawn attention to three distinct but interrelated manifestations of alterity.

While *phenotypical difference* positions non-Chinese foreigners as subjects who cannot be assimilated, "foreign" Chinese diasporic descendants are considered co-ethnics deserving of re-integration into the ancestral land. Nonetheless, the chapter also describes circumstances through which we see a *diversification of co-ethnicity*, connoting the cognitive borders that distinguish co-ethnics from different natal lands. Modulating the worldview of *tianxia*, which conventionally privileges co-ethnicity, are cultural distinctions wrought by development hierarchies, socioeconomic status, and connotations of personal quality and morality (*suzhi*). Our discussion of the alterity contained within co-ethnicity also begins to direct attention to how alterity may be flexibly exercised in the context of spatial change (i.e., movement from one place to another). Supporting this argument is how China's approach toward domestic ethnic relations has been changing. The Chinese state seeks to leverage the ethnic minority emigrants for breaking into new frontier markets or to enroll them as nation-building partners, precipitating the *spatial recalibration* of alterity. The cosmopolitan capital they acquired from a stint abroad has the potential to reconfigure their social positioning within Chinese society, albeit only if their global mobility can be harnessed for the national interest.

Interfacing the above migration patterns highlights how the social ordering of ethnicity within a nation extends to global space through emigration and channels back into the management of immigration or re-migration to a country. Contemporaneous migration fosters China as an active site of global interconnections with the world, compelling it to reconsider its approach toward migration governance and diversity.

6   Contemporaneous Migration

Contemporaneous Migration in Perspective

Studying the multidirectional aspects of migration reveals how contemporaneous migration shapes the norms and practices of citizenship in a given site and across migration sites. By setting out the conditions under which Chinese emigration happened historically and during the contemporary period, what becomes clear are the impacts of Chinese migration on nation building in China and other migration sites. The analysis of Chinese emigration is enhanced by the incorporation of insights from migrant-receiving countries, namely Canada and Singapore, which are facing new emigration or re-migration trends among their own citizens. By analyzing shifts in migration patterns over time we also come to understand how China is becoming an immigration country. These arguments present new insights for researchers studying Chinese migration and diaspora. As an analytical approach, contemporaneous migration allows an examination of the citizenship constellations that are forged across migration sites, as certain themes that are key to this process surface: citizenship and territory, fraternity and alterity, and the co-constitution of time and space.

The developmental aspirations of both nation-states and migrants are central to shaping both state-level policies and personal migration decisions that underpin fundamental shifts in the practice of citizenship.[1] Chinese migration during the nineteenth and early twentieth centuries was prompted by the desire of Chinese migrants to fulfill personal ambitions and improve the life chances of their families. This capacity to aspire through sojourning abroad has continued into the present.[2] Development as discussed here is related to but not reducible to only economic calculations; rather it also concerns personal and family aspirations. Put differently, migration enables the pursuit of freedom and the capability to secure goals that a person deems important for happiness.[3] The ability of migrants to meet these goals is met by the migration policies designed by states in both migrant-sending and migrant-receiving countries. Migration does not happen in a societal vacuum; it comes up against existing migration and citizenship regimes, cognitive taxonomies, and hierarchies of difference, which lend to negotiation of the identity, rights, and duties associated with citizenship.

Citizenship and Territory: Constellations and Life Course Journeys

The policies of both migrant-sending and migrant-receiving countries mutually reconfigure the territorial premises and practices of citizenship, impacting the way that migrants and nonmigrants experience citizenship. Extraterritorial citizenship practices by migrant-sending states reshape state spaces, as well as the subjectivity of emigrants and diasporic descendants targeted by state-directed diaspora strategizing. But emigrants and diasporic descendants are simultaneously members of migrant-receiving countries, and they experience countervailing pressures to integrate into or express loyalty to the place of immigration. Studying how the norms and expectations of citizenship in one country become mutually entangled with those of another brings attention to citizenship constellations that impact the identity and subjectivity of migrants as they journey across different migration sites.[4]

A historical example of citizenship constellations can be found in the case of decolonizing Southeast Asian countries, which imposed assimilation expectations on Chinese emigrants and diasporic descendants, compelling their re-migration to China during the period from 1949 to 1979. Yet in the ancestral land they faced similar pressures to re-integrate into the societal norms demanded by domestic political and social transformation.

Contemporary re-migrants today, including diasporic descendants who were born and bred abroad, face similar experiences. They may have re-migrated to the ancestral land to capitalize on their ethnic ties as resources for work or business opportunities, or to escape immigrant assimilation or integration pressures in their country of birth.[5] While in the ancestral land, they experience demands for their re-integration as ethnic kin but they hover between the two worlds they inhabit, forging pathways for citizenship constellations.

Migrants juggle economic and social reproduction priorities during re-migration or transnational sojourning across their life course. Their economic identities can become reconstituted during migration due to their de-skilling experiences, thus placing under closer scrutiny the social contract of citizenship, wherein a person's economic contribution is weighed against one's right to social entitlements. Some de-skilled migrants opt for return migration to improve their earning power temporarily. In so doing, they balance their earnings against concerns about their children's education and their family's well-being, prompting re-migration across the life course. Studying such contemporaneous migration trends highlights how the social dimensions of citizenship exceed the political boundaries of citizenship.

Another example of citizenship constellations is the formation of "secondary diasporas," when migrants develop a secondary identity and sense of belonging to the migrant-receiving country which they left. Normally emigrants are identified or self-identify as the diaspora of their country of origin when they immigrate to another country. Through re-migration, former immigration sites become new emigration sites. Migrants who re-migrate end up negotiating the membership, rights, and duties of two or more countries that consider them its diaspora population. This book considered the example of Mainland Chinese migrants who identify as Canada's secondary diaspora in China. Its theoretical insights can be applied to analyze the re-migration of other groups, such as South Asian immigrants in Canada, who moved back to their countries of origin after obtaining Canadian permanent residency or citizenship. They also form a secondary diaspora affiliated to Canada while they are abroad.

Canada is but one example of a migrant-receiving country experiencing such re-migration trends. Similar dynamics can be found in Australia, New Zealand, the United Kingdom, and the United States, which have seen significant re-migration trends among immigrants. Such immigrants become secondary diasporas of those countries in sites of return. Studying transnational sojourning across the life course offers insights on future contestations over the social rights of migrants who return to immigration countries during their old age. A life course perspective is necessary to fully comprehend how migrants negotiate membership, rights, and duties in a trans-territorial context during various junctures of their life course.

The insights from this book are also useful for analyzing emigration countries such as India, Sri Lanka, or Pakistan as ancestral lands from which long-standing emigration originates. These countries are experiencing the re-migration of diasporic descendants from North America, Europe, and elsewhere in Asia, alongside new immigration from neighboring countries in South, Southeast, and Central Asia. Just as with China, an analysis that juxtaposes diverse migration trends across time and in connection to other migration sites will need to account for geopolitical considerations, sub-regional affiliations, and identity politics that cut across domains of ethnicity, religion, nationality, socioeconomic status, and notions of morality and personhood.

Fraternity and Alterity: From Ethnicity to Periodization and Recalibration

Migration scholars have argued that social categorizations serve to differentiate the "migrant" from "nonmigrant" or "citizen." The corollary of alterity are practices of fraternity that establish notions of membership, rights, and duties as captured in the concept of citizenship. Ethnicity is one such cognitive taxonomy that nation-states and national societies use to set majority populations apart from minority populations, and migrants from nonmigrants and citizens.[6] Ethnicity is usually conflated with phenotypical difference that is associated with the assumed cultural homogeneity of a social group, and it serves as one way of socially ranking migrants within the nation-state. Social exclusion based on alterity as phenotypical difference exists, but there are permutations of social difference or alterity that cannot be fully captured through the lens of ethnicity, particularly as exercised on co-ethnics.

The Chinese case of prioritizing co-ethnicity may be distinctive, but tropes of co-ethnic privilege are seen elsewhere too. Migrant-sending countries, including ancestral lands, reach into the past to extend fraternity to emigrants and diasporic descendants. Examples include Japan and Korea in the Asia-Pacific; Greece, Ireland, Germany, and Sweden in Europe; Russia, Poland, Slovakia, Slovenia, Romania, Ukraine, and Latvia of the former Soviet Union; and Israel in the Middle East.[7] Juxtaposing state discourses and policies of co-ethnic privilege with the lived realities of co-ethnics who have re-migrated brings attention to the multiple ways in which alterity manifests through embodiment, cultural habitus, and temporal devices that situate the co-ethnic "returnee" as always belonging to a different time and space. They inhabit a discordant social imaginary that detracts from assumptions of kinship and alleged national norms but producing also the diversification of co-ethnicity.

In migration hubs where different cohorts of co-ethnics converge, negotiations of fraternity and alterity are intertwined with the receiving society's perception of the developmental stage of the migrant's country of origin and how these reflect purported moral values and quality of personhood (*suzhi*). The way these social and cultural attributes function in social situations is contingent on a person's intersecting axes of identity, the context of the social interaction, and the people involved. Crucially, it is also the flexibility or contingency afforded within tropes of fraternity or alterity that allows for the spatial recalibration of alterity across trans-territorial contexts.

Several of the countries mentioned above are simultaneously experiencing migration transitions and facing new immigration that challenge the ideology of ethnic homogeneity. The challenges faced by migrant-receiving countries that have evolved into multicultural societies reveal other dimensions of fraternity and alterity dynamics that are deserving of further study. Apart from ethnicity and socioeconomic status, the period of immigration also factors into the degree of inclusion or exclusion extended to them as potential citizens or new citizens. Periodization of migration socially ranks cohorts of migrants and accords priority to those with natal ties to the country. The multicultural ethos of a country and its fraternity can thus be maintained while still asserting degrees of social exclusion toward newer arrivals. This kind of temporal logics also makes it possible to extend the fraternity of the national community to emigrants with natal ties to a country (through diaspora strategies), and their children born abroad, even if such persons are absent from the national territory. Privilege associated with the periodization of migration exists in different forms. For example, in the United Kingdom, an ancestry visa allows preferential entry to migrants from Commonwealth countries who can prove that one of their grandparents was born in the country (i.e., re-migration of diasporic descendants). Yet increasingly restrictive criteria are placed on immigrants whose ancestral ties lie outside of the United Kingdom, even if they have been present in the national territory for an extended period.

The dynamics of fraternity and alterity manifested in a trans-territorial context, as found in the countries studied in this book, can be usefully contextualized to study other migration contexts that are juggling both immigration and emigration agendas. An example is Malaysia, which is facing a range of new immigration from neighboring countries in Asia and Muslim countries in the Middle East. At the same time, it is developing diaspora strategies to reach out to Malaysians abroad. But its diaspora strategies allegedly reproduce existing racial divisions in the country that are related to the *bumiputra* policy that privileges Malays.[8] Against the backdrop of colonial pasts and contemporary globalization, multidirectional migration exchanges add to the cultural complexity of societies. Rather than assuming and adopting ethnic difference as the analytical framework for research, an approach that recognizes the transversal aspects of fraternity and alterity makes clear the necessity of multiply tackling the tensions that exist between co-ethnics alongside long-standing and new interethnic tensions.

Co-constitution of Spatiality and Temporality

Analyzing the multidirectionality of migration reveals how time functions as a Janus-faced device that legitimizes or delegitimizes membership and belonging, working alongside spatial metaphors of presence or absence from a national territory.[9] Thus a chief concern of this book has been to systematically unpack the *spatiality of temporality*—how spatial constructs feature in narratives of temporal structure and social time—and the *temporality of spatiality*—how time matters in the organization of space and flows of people across space.

For the former, crucial to the maneuver of time are spatial narratives that emphasize the extraterritorial ties of the migrant-sending country to emigrants and diasporic descendants. Such migrant-sending countries reach into the past to extend spatial belonging beyond the national territory in the present. For the latter, when migrants re-migrate and spend different stages of their life course in different countries (i.e., transnational sojourning), their absence from a national territory can count against their later fraternity with a national society, including their ability to receive social rights and protection from that country. Other members of that national society may question the patriotism of transnational sojourners and contest the extent of their economic or social contributions to the country. This spatiotemporal tactic emphasizes how notions of territorial presence or absence from a country matter in determining fraternity or alterity over time.

Juxtaposing migrants' changing mobility patterns across time and in connection to events and experiences in other migration sites brings to view how migration governance constructs vastly different experiences of time and the production of space within and beyond a territory. Periodization of migration establishes temporal hierarchies and claims over space within or beyond a territory. Migrants invoke temporal and spatial narratives to assert their stakeholdership to one or more countries. Their claims to belonging, recognition, rights, and duties are both situated in a particular space and time and extend across sites and scales. Migration over the life course and citizenship constellations involve an interplay between spatial and temporal dimensions, namely the co-constitution of spatiality and temporality.

The insights offered by this book have relevance beyond the Chinese context. Multidirectional migration exchanges are likely to grow in magnitude and complexity globally given intensifying regional economic integration in the Asia-Pacific (e.g., ASEAN and the Trans-Pacific Partnership), Africa (e.g., African Economic Community), Europe (e.g., European Economic Area Agreement), the Gulf countries (e.g., Gulf Cooperation Council), North America (e.g., NAFTA), and more. Migration exchanges with countries outside of regional blocs will also continue, deepening citizenship constellations across migration sites and complicating the features of fraternity and alterity in both countries of emigration and immigration. More investigations into the spatiotemporal connections of migration and citizenship remain to be conducted in other migration contexts and across migration sites (see last section on methods).

Chinese Diaspora and Migration in/of China

To date, researchers have considered Chinese labor, educational, and skilled migration; the presence of new Chinese immigrants in the frontier economies of Southeast Asia and Africa; and the emigration of ethnic minorities from China.[10] Bringing together the interconnected aspects of such migration trends alongside a study of the new immigration patterns found in China today provides new insights on how the Chinese state and society approaches ethnic diversity within China and toward co-ethnic relationships abroad. As an analytical approach, contemporaneous migration presents new research directions for overseas Chinese studies or research pertaining to the "Chinese diaspora." First, it directs attention to China's relationship with diasporic descendants, without assuming such generational ties are restricted to those of Han Chinese ethnicity. Rather, China is according recognition to diasporic descendants of ethnic minority backgrounds who are citizens of another country. Just as with the Han Chinese diasporic descendants settled abroad, China's diaspora outreach to those of ethnic minority backgrounds abroad can create complications for how they are perceived in their countries of residence, which are developing nation-building projects of their own. New citizenship constellations are being forged as a result of China's diaspora strategizing to multiple diaspora populations it considers its own, and this is an area that remains to be investigated more fully in academic research.

Second, contemporaneous migration puts the spotlight on membership recognition, allocation of rights, and expectations of duties among the different social groups that are connected to China within and outside of its national territory. The (Han) overseas Chinese and the Chinese diaspora have been enrolled in the nation-building project of the Chinese state for decades. The Chinese state is now extending membership and privileges to emigrants and diasporic descendants that it considers an extension of the Chinese nation abroad. Meanwhile, new research on immigration in China has started to probe the barriers to membership and restricted rights of immigrants in the country, including the social status of children in interethnic marriages and those of foreign nationality who are growing up in China. Future comparative analysis of the gradations in membership and rights afforded to these different migrant groups will provide valuable insights into the changing social contract of citizenship in China as it adapts to new migration trends. Another area worthy of investigation pertains to the social lives and transnational ties of the second generation from interethnic marriages in China, or those who have foreign nationality status but remain connected to China through their parents' natal ties.

China's Worldview of *Tianxia* vis-à-vis Cosmopolitanism

The Chinese worldview of *tianxia* brings together the domestic and foreign dimensions of how China sees itself and its engagement with the world through spatial organization and social ordering—and is thus intimately tied to the country's various migration streams. Eminent historian Wang Gungwu explains that *tianxia* connotes a vision in which Chinese civilization carries superior moral authority and serves as a unifying factor for those who live within China's borders, even as China recognizes the rules of equality and sovereignty under an international system of nation-states.[11] With its connotations of dealing with Otherness and international relations, *tianxia* is often likened to iterations of Western cosmopolitanism.[12] But integrating analyses of territorial and extraterritorial state power with the ethnic stratification contained within *tianxia* provides a cautionary note against conflating *tianxia* with cosmopolitanism and underlines that it is equally capable of deploying cultural logics of fraternity and alterity to serve the national interest.[13]

As an example, ethnic minorities have been treated as subjects of alterity within the Chinese nation, but new forms of fraternity are being extended by the Chinese state to ethnic minority emigrants because of their newfound cosmopolitan capital from abroad. Their economic and cultural connections to new developmental frontiers are seen as assets for expanding the Chinese economy externally. Ethnic minority emigrants who are conciliatory toward the leadership role of the Chinese state are regarded as potential ambassadors who can disseminate the benefits of supporting national unity to their ethnic communities. Diasporic descendants of ethnic minorities who are settled in a foreign country are also enrolled in the Chinese state's enlarged version of extraterritorial kinship. Even though the alterity of ethnic minorities is reconfigured through emigration to a more respectable social status, it serves only to buttress the Chinese state's unilateral version of history, identity, and nationhood.

Contemporaneous migration contributes to alternative readings of cosmopolitanism by defying the teleological imperative in two ways: First, it signals the different manifestations of migration that simultaneously shape a nation's self-image and its interconnections with the world. Rather than upholding parochial national narratives, contemporaneous migration brings to view domains of mutuality forged through circulatory histories,[14] interconnections, and citizenship constellations. Second, contemporaneous migration is attentive to the alterity found within both cultural similarity and dissimilarity. Such an approach recognizes the personhood of those who are different without presuming that those differences must be eliminated.[15] This allows for a cosmopolitan ethic through which there is "an existential engagement with one's tradition and the constellation of traditions that constitute the world."[16] Such an ethic is always political but creates potential for recognizing the domains of mutuality that can advance cosmopolitan sociability.

Contemporaneous Migration as Method

Contemporaneous migration as an analytical framework carries methodological implications that are worth drawing out. Portrayals of the migration flows connecting China to the world and the world to China might be construed as an accidental design of chance encounters developed through multisited study and the extended case approach.[17] But as AbdouMaliq Simone argues, "A single entry point . . . simply is not adequate in order to have access to many critical urban processes."[18] Studying the diverse perspectives and points of connection between multifaceted migration flows is all the more challenging, as migration connects social groups, cultures, rural and urban areas, and countries across the globe. How does one study contemporaneous migration? At its core, contemporaneous migration is about the vantage point adopted by the researcher.

Migration processes can be found within a migration site and across migration sites. Re-migration is also reversing source and destination countries as emigration or immigration sites. Rather than isolating one migration trend for analysis, studying immigration through the lens of emigration, and vice versa, can fruitfully reframe citizenship debates in both contexts. Each provides a mirror to critically reflect on the discourses, policies, actions, and events that would be otherwise normalized if such migration processes were studied in isolation. The approach of contemporaneous migration is therefore attentive to the multiple migration routes that migrants undertake across migration sites. It challenges the assumptions of a researcher about which is the migrant-sending or migrant-receiving country, and which is the home culture or destination culture. The researcher develops an enhanced awareness of the way meanings of home and what is foreign or familiar change across a migrant's life course (see Chapters 2 and 3). The methods to uncover such migration processes are manifold depending on the people involved, the social interactions, the context of the situation, and the routes to be traced.

Another approach for studying contemporaneous migration would be to consider how emigration and immigration processes, normally considered separately, take place concurrently within a migration site at any given time. With such an approach, it is useful to identify an analytical connection such as the focus on Chinese migration employed in this book, or identifying a site as the hub of migration inflows and outflows (see Chapters 4 and 5 for examples that study Singapore and China as hubs). The research approach adopted here is one that *interfaces* the migration routes and experiences of different social groups within a site and in connection to another part of the world. This approach also allows the researcher to consider how nonmigrants and the different social groups identified for study perceive migration processes. Crucially, the two research approaches discussed above are not mutually exclusive and can in fact complement one another.

Contemporaneous migration provides a different approach for considering the multidirectional population exchanges that characterize our world today, and the multifarious ways in which such migration impacts citizenship within and across migration sites. Emigration, immigration, and re-migration are migration trends that profoundly affect how states, migrants, and nonmigrants experience social transformation, for better or worse.

Notes

Chapter 1: Migration and Citizenship

1. The phrase *huiguo weiguo fuwu* contains a double alliteration (*guo*), which puts the nation-state at center stage of the idea of return and the idea of service.

2. Linda Basch, Nina Glick Schiller, and Cristina Szanton Blanc, *Nations Unbound: Transnational Projects, Postcolonial Predicaments, and Deterritorialized Nation-States* (New York: Gordon and Breach, 1994); Thomas Faist, *The Volume and Dynamics of International Migration and Transnational Social Spaces* (Oxford: Oxford University Press, 2000).

3. Rainer Bauböck, "Studying Citizenship Constellations," *Journal of Ethnic and Migration Studies* 36, no. 5 (May 2010): 847–859.

4. Susan Bibler Coutin, *Nations of Emigrants: Shifting Boundaries of Citizenship in El Salvador and the United States* (Ithaca, NY: Cornell University Press, 2007); Filomeno V. Aguilar, *Migration Revolution: Philippine Nationhood and Class Relations in a Globalized Age* (Singapore and Kyoto: NUS Press and Kyoto University Press, 2014).

5. Coutin, *Nations of Emigrants*, p. 4.

6. Anastasia Christou and Russell King, *Counter-Diaspora: The Greek Second Generation Returns "Home"* (Cambridge, MA: Harvard University Press, 2015).

7. Roger David Waldinger, *The Cross-Border Connection: Immigrants, Emigrants and Their Homelands* (Cambridge, MA: Harvard University Press, 2015).

8. For examples on Korea, see Eleana Jean Kim, *Adopted Territory: Transnational Korean Adoptees and the Politics of Belonging* (Durham, NC: Duke University Press, 2010); Caren Freeman, *Making and Faking Kinship: Marriage and Labor Migration Between China and South Korea* (Ithaca, NY: Cornell University Press, 2011). On Japan, see Takeyuki Tsuda, ed., *Diasporic Homecomings: Ethnic Return Migration in Comparative Perspective* (Stanford, CA: Stanford University Press, 2009). On Taiwan,

see Sara Friedman, *Exceptional States: Chinese Immigrants and Taiwanese Sovereignty* (Oakland: University of California Press, 2015). On Macau, see Cathryn H. Clayton, *Sovereignty at the Edge: Macau and the Question of Chineseness* (Cambridge, MA: Harvard University Press, 2009). On Hong Kong, see Nicole DeJong Newendorp, *Uneasy Reunions: Immigration, Citizenship, and Family Life in Post-1997 Hong Kong* (Stanford, CA: Stanford University Press, 2008).

9. This approach is inspired by critical theorists of time who argue that periodization should be examined as rhetorical strategies and that juxtaposing the state's periodization with the lived experiences of migrants (i.e., social time) can restore "diverse forms of co-presence" that are denied in national discourses. See Michael J. Shapiro, "National Times and Other Times: Re-Thinking Citizenship," *Cultural Studies* 14, no. 1 (2000): 79–98, quotation from p. 79. See also Prasenjit Duara, *Rescuing History from the Nation: Questioning Narratives of Modern China* (Chicago: University of Chicago Press, 1995); Saulo B. Cwerner, "The Times of Migration," *Journal of Ethnic and Migration Studies* 27, no. 1 (January 2001): 7–36; Espen Hammer, *Philosophy and Temporality from Kant to Critical Theory* (Cambridge: Cambridge University Press, 2011).

10. For example, Hong Kong laws prevent Filipino labor migrants from gaining long-term legal residency, while co-ethnic immigrants from Mainland China are also excluded by the Hong Kong public, who believe that they have different historical and political backgrounds that would deter their integration. See Nicole Constable, *Born Out of Place: Migrant Mothers and the Politics of International Labor* (Berkeley: University of California Press, 2014); Newendorp, *Uneasy Reunions*. Clayton observes similar trends in Macau but adds that what differentiates the Macanese Chinese from the Mainland Chinese is the former's claim to a sense of "native place." Clayton, *Sovereignty at the Edge*, p. 220.

11. For examples, see Rosa Mas Giralt and Adrian J. Bailey, "Transnational Familyhood and the Liquid Life Paths of South Americans in the UK," *Global Networks* 10, no. 3 (2010): 383–400; Ken Chih-Yan Sun, "Transnational Healthcare Seeking: How Ageing Taiwanese Return Migrants View Homeland Public Benefits," *Global Networks* 14, no. 4 (2014): 533–550.

12. Coutin, *Nations of Emigrants*, p. 9; Saskia Sassen, *Territory, Authority, Rights from Medieval to Global Assemblages* (Princeton, NJ: Princeton University Press, 2006).

13. Arif Dirlik, "Intimate Others: [Private] Nations and Diasporas in an Age of Globalization," *Inter-Asia Cultural Studies* 5, no. 3 (2004): 491–502.

14. Avtar Brah, *Cartographies of Diaspora: Contesting Identities* (New York: Routledge, 1998).

15. Gungwu Wang, *China and the Chinese Overseas* (Singapore: Times Academic Press, 1991); Leo Suryadinata, "Ethnic Chinese in Southeast Asia: Overseas Chinese,

Chinese Overseas or Southeast Asians?," in *The Ethnic Chinese as Southeast Asians*, ed. Leo Suryadinata (Singapore: World Scientific Publishing, 1997), pp. 1–24; Adam M. McKeown, *Melancholy Order: Asian Migration and the Globalization of Borders* (New York: Columbia University Press, 2008).

16. See Chapter 2, note 4.

17. For a historical review of how each of these governments engaged Chinese emigrants and diasporic descendants, see Els van Dongen, "Behind the Ties That Bind: Diaspora-Making and Nation-Building in China and India in Historical Perspective, 1850s–2010s," *Asian Studies Review* 41, no. 1 (2017): 1–19.

18. Rebecca E. Karl, *Staging the World: Chinese Nationalism at the Turn of the Twentieth Century* (Durham, NC: Duke University Press, 2002).

19. Mette Thunø, "Reaching Out and Incorporating Chinese Overseas: The Trans-Territorial Scope of the PRC by the End of the 20th Century," *The China Quarterly* 168 (December 2001): 910–929; Elena Barabantseva, *Overseas Chinese, Ethnic Minorities and Nationalism: De-centering China* (New York: Routledge, 2011); Hong Liu and Els van Dongen, "China's Diaspora Policies as a New Mode of Transnational Governance," *Journal of Contemporary China* 25, no. 102 (2016): 805–821; Shelly Chan, "The Case for Diaspora: A Temporal Approach to the Chinese Experience," *Journal of Asian Studies* 74, no. 1 (2015): 107–128.

20. Pál Nyíri, "Chinese Investors, Labour Discipline and Developmental Cosmopolitanism: Chinese Investors in Cambodia," *Development and Change* 44, no. 6 (2013): 1387–1405.

21. Nina Glick Schiller, "Transnational Social Fields and Imperialism: Bringing a Theory of Power to Transnational Studies," *Anthropological Theory* 5, no. 4 (2005): 439–461.

22. Karl, *Staging the World*.

23. McKeown critiques the Eurocentric focus of scholarship on the history of globalization or the international state system, which locates the origin and diffusion of such processes in Europe, rather than studying the "mutual entanglement" with flows and borders elsewhere in the world. McKeown, *Melancholy Order*, p. 5.

24. Ibid.; Eng Seng Ho, *The Graves of Tarim: Genealogy and Mobility Across the Indian Ocean* (Berkeley: University of California Press, 2006); Prasenjit Duara, *The Crisis of Global Modernity: Asian Traditions and a Sustainable Future* (Cambridge: Cambridge University Press, 2015).

25. Robert D. Sack, "Human Territoriality: A Theory," *Annals of the Association of American Geographers* 73, no. 1 (March 1983): 55–74, quotation from p. 55; Stuart Elden, *Terror and Territory: The Spatial Extent of Sovereignty* (Minneapolis: University of Minnesota Press, 2009); Joe Painter, "Rethinking Territory," *Antipode* 42, no. 5 (2010): 1090–1118.

26. For example, see Austen L. Parrish, "Reclaiming International Law from Extraterritoriality" (Indiana University Maurer School of Law Paper 894, 2009), accessed on February 5, 2015, from http://www.repository.law.indiana.edu/facpub/894; Ananya Roy, "The 21st-Century Metropolis: New Geographies of Theory," *Regional Studies* 43, no. 6 (July 2009): 819–830; Susan Bibler Coutin, "Confined Within: National Territories as Zones of Confinement," *Political Geography* 29 (2010): 200–208.

27. Elaine Lynn-Ee Ho, "'Claiming' the Diaspora: Sending State Strategies, Elite Mobility and the Spatialities of Citizenship," *Progress in Human Geography* 35, no. 6 (December 2011): 757–772.

28. Sandro Mezzadra and Brett Nielson, *Border as Method, or, the Multiplication of Labor* (Durham, NC: Duke University Press, 2013), p. 8.

29. In the Chinese language, multiple and overlapping notions of the political subject exist, ranging from people (*renmin*) to nationals (*guomin*) and citizens (*gongmin or shimin*). The etymology and evolution of citizenship in China impact governance, nationalism, and civil society relations in the country today. Under dynastic rule, the emperor was considered the sovereign. Chinese reformers of the late Qing period integrated European, Japanese, and Marxist features of citizenship with Chinese historical traditions and political philosophy. See Michael Keane, "Redefining Chinese Citizenship," *Economy and Society* 30, no. 1 (2001): 1–17; Joshua A. Fogel and Peter G. Zarrow, eds., *Imagining The People: Chinese Intellectuals and the Concept of Citizenship, 1890–1920* (Armonk, NY: M. E. Sharpe, 1997); Merle Goldman and Elizabeth J. Perry, eds., *Changing Meanings of Citizenship in Modern China* (Cambridge, MA: Harvard University Press, 2002); Małgorzata Jakimów, "Chinese Citizenship 'After Orientalism': Academic Narratives on Internal Migrants in China," *Citizenship Studies* 169, no. 5–6 (August 2012): 657–671.

30. Newendorp, *Uneasy Reunions*; Clayton, *Sovereignty at the Edge*.

31. Peter Harris, "The Origins of Modern Citizenship in China," *Asia Pacific Viewpoint* 43, no. 2 (August 2002): 181–203.

32. Tingyang Zhao, "Rethinking Empire from a Chinese Concept 'All-Under-Heaven' (Tian-Xia)," *Social Identities* 12, no. 1 (January 2006): 29–41; Tingyang Zhao, *Tianxia Tixi: Shijie Zhidu Zhexue Daolun* [The *tianxia* system: An introduction to the philosophy of a world institution] (Beijing: Zhongguo Renmin Daxue Chuban She, 2011).

33. Gerard Delanty and Baogang He, "Cosmopolitan Perspectives on European and Asian Transnationalism," *International Sociology* 23, no. 3 (May 2008): 323–344; Shan Chun, "On Chinese Cosmopolitanism (Tian Xia)," *Culture Mandala: The Bulletin of the Centre for East-West Cultural and Economic Studies* 8, no. 2 (December 2009): 20–29; Jilin Xu, "Tianxia Zhuyi/Yixia Zhi Bian Ji Qizai Jindai De Bianyi" [Cosmopolitanism, the debate of the civilized and the uncivilized, and their variations in modern times], *Journal of East China Normal University* 44, no. 6 (2012): 66–76; Sang-Jin Han, Young-Hee Shim, and Young-Do Park, "Cosmopolitan Sociology and Confucian

Worldview: Beck's Theory in East Asia," *Theory, Culture & Society* 33, no. 7–8 (2016): 281–290.

34. Pheng Cheah, "Cosmopolitanism," *Theory, Culture and Society* 23, no. 2–3 (May 2006): 486–496.

35. Marilyn Fischer, "A Pragmatist Cosmopolitan Moment: Reconfiguring Nussbaum's Cosmopolitan Concentric Circles." *Journal of Speculative Philosophy* 21, no. 3 (2007): 151–165.

36. Ibid, p. 157.

37. Nina Glick Schiller, "Situating Identities: Towards an Identities Studies Without Binaries of Difference," *Identities* 19, no. 4 (July 2012): 520–532.

38. William A. Callahan, "Chinese Visions of World Order: Post-Hegemonic or a New Hegemony?," *International Studies Review* 10, no. 4 (December 2008): 749–761.

39. Frank Dikötter, *The Discourse of Race in Modern China* (London: Hurst, 1992), p. 6.

40. Barry Sautman, "Anti-Black Racism in Post-Mao China," *The China Quarterly* 138 (June 1994): 413–437; Michael J. Sullivan, "The 1988–89 Nanjing Anti-African Protests: Racial Nationalism or National Racism?," *The China Quarterly* 138 (June 1994): 438–457.

41. Dikötter, *The Discourse of Race in Modern China*, p. 86.

42. Thomas S. Mullaney, *Coming to Terms with the Nation: Ethnic Classification in Modern China* (Berkeley: University of California Press, 2011).

43. Elena Barabantseva, "Who Are 'Overseas Chinese Ethnic Minorities?' China's Search for Transnational Ethnic Unity," *Modern China* 38, no. 1 (January 2012): 78–109; Dru C. Gladney, "Representing Nationality in China: Refiguring Majority/Minority Identities," *Journal of Asian Studies* 53, no. 1 (February 1994): 92–123.

44. Chris Vasantkumar, "What Is This 'Chinese' in Overseas Chinese? Sojourn Work and the Place of China's Minority Nationalities in Extraterritorial Chinese-ness," *Journal of Asian Studies* 71, no. 2 (2012): 423–446; Barabantseva, "Who Are 'Overseas Chinese Ethnic Minorities?'"

45. Sautman, "Anti-Black Racism in Post-Mao China."

46. Dikötter, *The Discourse of Race in Modern China*, p. 12.

47. Ibid., p. 8.

48. Ibid., p. 194.

49. Sautman, "Anti-Black Racism in Post-Mao China."

50. For example, see Heidi Østbø Haugen, "Nigerians in China: A Second State of Immobility," *International Migration* 50, no. 2 (2012): 65–80; Tabea Bork-Hüffer and Yuan Yuan-Ihle, "The Management of Foreigners in China: Changes to the Migration Law and Regulations During the Late Hu-Wen and Early Xi-Li Eras and Their Potential Effects," *International Journal of China Studies* 5, no. 3 (December 2014): 571–597.

51. Xi Cheng, "The 'Distinctiveness' of the Overseas Chinese as Perceived in the People's Republic of China," in *Beyond Chinatown: New Chinese Migration and the Global Expansion of China*, ed. Mette Thunø (Copenhagen: NIAS Press, 2007), pp. 49–64; Karsten Giese, "Perceptions, Practices and Adaptations: Understanding Chinese– African Interactions in Africa," *Journal of Current Chinese Affairs* 43, no. 1 (2014): 3–8.

52. An immigration incorporation bias can remain perceptible even when emigration societies are brought into the picture. For example, see Peter Kivisto, "Theorizing Transnational Immigration: A Critical Review of Current Efforts," *Ethnic and Racial Studies* 24, no. 4 (2001): 549–577; Waldinger, *The Cross-Border Connection*.

53. Interest in diaspora-centered development is rooted in migration and development (MAD) agendas that consider transnational migrants as agents of economic and social development in their countries of origin. Enthusiasm for diaspora-centered development is perceptible at the national state, sub-national state, and international levels. Emphasis is placed on knowledge, networks, social capital, and capacity building for developing economies. See Hélène Pellerin and Beverley Mullings, "The 'Diaspora Option,' Migration and the Changing Political Economy of Development," *Review of International Political Economy* 20, no. 1 (2013): 89–120; Maureen Hickey, Elaine Lynn-Ee Ho, and Brenda S. A. Yeoh, "Introduction to the Special Section on Establishing State-Led 'Diaspora Strategies' in Asia: Migration-as-Development Reinvented?," *Singapore Journal of Tropical Geography* 36, no. 2 (July 2015): 139–146; Mark Boyle and Elaine Lynn-Ee Ho, "Sovereign Power, Biopower, and the Reach of the West in an Age of Diaspora-Centred Development," *Antipode* 49, no. 3 (June 2017): 577–596.

54. Mark Boyle and Rob Kitchin, "Diaspora-Centred Development: Current Practice, Critical Commentaries, and Research Priorities," in *Global Diasporas and Development: Socioeconomic, Cultural, and Policy Perspectives*, ed. Sadananda Sahoo and B. K. Pattanaik (New Delhi: Springer, 2014), pp. 17–37.

55. Coutin, *Nations of Emigrants*; David Fitzgerald, *A Nation of Emigrants: How Mexico Manages Its Migration* (Berkeley: University of California Press, 2009); Ho, "'Claiming' the Diaspora"; Dace Dzenovska, "The Great Departure: Rethinking National(ist) Common Sense," *Journal of Ethnic and Migration Studies* 39, no. 2 (2013): 201–218; Breda Gray, "'Generation Emigration': The Politics of (Trans)national Social Reproduction in Twenty-First-Century Ireland," *Irish Studies Review* 21, no. 1 (2013): 20–36.

56. Kim Barry, "Home and Away: The Construction of Citizenship in an Emigration Context," *New York University Law Review* 81, no. 1 (April 2006): 11–59; Michael Collyer, "A Geography of Extra-Territorial Citizenship: Explanations of External Voting," *Migration Studies* 2, no. 1 (March 2014): 55–72; Michael Peter Smith, "Transnationalism, the State, and the Extraterritorial Citizen," *Politics and Society* 31, no. 4 (December 2003): 467–502.

57. Smith, "Transnationalism, the State, and the Extraterritorial Citizen"; Coutin, *Nations of Emigrants*; Fitzgerald, *A Nation of Emigrants*; Rainer Bauböck, "The Rights and Duties of External Citizenship," *Citizenship Studies* 13, no. 5 (October 2009): 475–499.

58. Robert C. Smith, "Migrant Membership as an Instituted Process: Transnationalization, the State and the Extra-Territorial Conduct of Mexican Politics," *International Migration Review* 37, no. 2 (Summer 2003): 297–343; Bauböck, "The Rights and Duties of External Citizenship."

59. Smith, "Migrant Membership as an Instituted Process," p. 302.

60. For example, see Smith, "Transnationalism, the State, and the Extraterritorial Citizen"; Fitzgerald, *A Nation of Emigrants*; Alan Gamlen, "The Emigration State and the Modern Geopolitical Imagination," *Political Geography* 27, no. 8 (2008): 840–856; Alexandra Delano, *Mexico and Its Diaspora in the United States: Policies of Emigration Since 1848* (New York: Cambridge University Press, 2011); Waldinger, *The Cross-Border Connection*.

61. Coutin, *Nations of Emigrants*, p. 4.

62. Bauböck, "The Rights and Duties of External Citizenship," p. 477.

63. Bauböck, "Studying Citizenship Constellations." An example of how sending state policies can impact immigration integration can be seen in the United States–Mexico case. For example, Alexandra Delano, "Immigrant Integration vs. Transnational Ties? The Role of the Sending State," *Social Research: An International Quarterly* 77, no. 1 (2010): 237–268.

64. Laurence J. C. Ma and Carolyn Cartier, eds., *The Chinese Diaspora: Space, Place, Mobility, and Identity, Why of Where* (Lanham, MD: Rowman and Littlefield, 2003), p. 19.

65. Catherine Dauvergne, *The New Politics of Immigration and the End of Settler Societies* (New York: Cambridge University Press, 2016), p. 4.

66. Jane M. Jacobs, *Edge of Empire: Postcolonialism and the City* (London: Routledge, 1996).

67. Mezzadra and Nielson, *Border as Method*, p. 4.

68. Freeman, *Making and Faking Kinship*, p. 238. Also see Kim, *Adopted Territory*.

69. Newendorp, *Uneasy Reunions*, pp. 17–18.

70. Renato Rosaldo, "Cultural Citizenship in San Jose, California," *Political and Legal Anthropology Review* 17, no. 2 (November 1994): 57–63, quotation from p. 57.

71. Lieba Faier, *Intimate Encounters: Filipina Women and the Remaking of Rural Japan* (Berkeley: University of California Press, 2009), p. 10.

72. Dauvergne, *The New Politics of Immigration and the End of Settler Societies*, p. 15.

73. For example, see Hairong Yan, "Neoliberal Governmentality and Neohumanism: Organizing Suzhi/Value Flow Through Labor Recruitment Networks," *Cultural*

Anthropology 18, no. 4 (2003): 493–523; Ann Anagnost, "The Corporeal Politics of Quality (*Suzhi*)," *Public Culture* 16, no. 2 (Spring 2004): 189–208.

74. Chris Vasantkumar, "Unmade in China: Reassembling the Ethnic on the Gansu–Tibetan Border," *Ethnos* 79, no. 2 (May 2014): 261–286, quotation from p. 265.

75. For example, see Li Zhang, *Strangers in the City: Reconfigurations of Space, Power, and Social Networks Within China's Floating Population* (Stanford, CA: Stanford University Press, 1998); Della Davin, *Internal Migration in Contemporary China* (New York: St. Martin's Press, 1999); Yan, "Neoliberal Governmentality and Neohumanism"; Pál Nyíri, *Mobility and Cultural Authority in Contemporary China* (Seattle: University of Washington Press, 2010). See also Elaine Lynn-Ee Ho, "Transnational Identities, Multiculturalism or Assimilation? China's 'Refugee-Returnees' and Generational Transitions," *Modern Asian Studies* 49, no. 2 (March 2015): 525–545; Elaine Lynn-Ee Ho, "Incongruent Migration Categorisations and Competing Citizenship Claims: 'Return' and Hypermigration in Transnational Migration Circuits," *Journal of Ethnic and Migration Studies* 42, no. 14 (November 2016): 2379–2394.

76. Glick Schiller, "Situating Identities."

Chapter 2: Chinese Re-migration

1. Anastasia Christou and Russell King, *Counter-Diaspora: The Greek Second Generation Returns "Home"* (Cambridge, MA: Harvard University Press, 2015).

2. Eng Seng Ho, *The Graves of Tarim: Genealogy and Mobility Across the Indian Ocean* (Berkeley: University of California Press, 2006); Dennis Conway and Robert B. Potter, "Return of the Next Generations: Transnational Migration and Development in the 21st Century," in *Return Migration of the Next Generations: 21st Century Transnational Mobility*, ed. Dennis Conway and Robert B. Potter (Farnham, UK: Ashgate, 2009), pp. 1–16.

3. Research on counter-diasporic migration has also been termed "diasporic ethnic return" or the "return of the next generations." See Takeyuki Tsuda, ed., *Diasporic Homecomings: Ethnic Return Migration in Comparative Perspective* (Stanford, CA: Stanford University Press, 2009); Conway and Potter, "Return of the Next Generations."

4. Prior to 1979 it was known as the Overseas Chinese Affairs Commission (OCAC, or *Huaqiao Shiwu Weiyuanhui*). Established in 1949, the OCAC fell into disrepute (and closed in 1970) during the events leading up to and during the Cultural Revolution (1966–1976). The renaming of the bureau to *Qiaoban*, or the Overseas Chinese Affairs Office, in 1978 sought to give it a new image to refresh its mandate over the Chinese abroad (*qiaowu*).

5. For discussion of China's earlier diaspora engagement initiatives, see Chinghwang Yen, *Coolies and Mandarins: China's Protection of Overseas Chinese During the Late Ch'ing Period (1985–1911)* (Singapore: Singapore University Press, 1985); Adam M.

McKeown, *Melancholy Order: Asian Migration and the Globalization of Borders* (New York: Columbia University Press, 2008); Els van Dongen, "Behind the Ties That Bind: Diaspora-Making and Nation-Building in China and India in Historical Perspective, 1850s–2010s," *Asian Studies Review* 41, no. 1 (2017): 1–19.

6. The political struggles of decolonization and new nation building that affected the Chinese abroad extended to countries such as the Philippines, Cambodia, and Burma. Even Thailand, which was not colonized, implemented assimilation policies. The extent of localization depended on the policies of each country, the educational orientation of the Chinese settled abroad, their nationality status, period of migration, and social class. See Leo Suryadinata, *The Ethnic Chinese as Southeast Asians* (Singapore: World Scientific Publishing, 1997); Michael B. Hooker, ed., *Law and the Chinese in Southeast Asia* (Singapore: Institute of Southeast Asian Studies, 2002).

7. Between the eighteenth and twentieth centuries, British-ruled Malaya encompassed the Malay states under indirect British rule and the Straits Settlements (including Singapore). The Malayan Union was established in 1948 and replaced by the Federation of Malaya in 1948; it gained full independence in 1957 (Singapore was not part of these entities). In 1963, the Malay states under the Federation of Malaya merged with Singapore, North Borneo, and Sarawak to form a combined political unit known as Malaysia. In 1965 Singapore separated from Malaysia and became an independent state. See Michael Hill and Kwen Fee Lian, *The Politics of Nation Building and Citizenship in Singapore* (London: Routledge, 1995).

8. Dan Shao provides a compelling account of how the nationality status of the Chinese abroad was a subject of contention between the Republic of China (ROC) in Taiwan, the People's Republic of China (PRC), and the countries in which the Chinese abroad had settled. The ROC and PRC both subscribed to the principle of *jus sanguinis*, or the inheritance of nationality by bloodline. After 1949 the ROC continued to insist that the Chinese abroad who did not formally renounce their nationality status through its Department of the Interior would still be considered citizens of the ROC. The PRC officially ended recognition of dual nationality only in 1958 even though in the period preceding that it had been encouraging Chinese nationals abroad to naturalize and integrate in their countries of settlement. See Dan Shao, "Chinese by Definition: Nationality Law, Jus Sanguinis, and State Succession, 1909–1980," *Twentieth-Century China* 35, no. 1 (November 2009): 4–28; Stephen Fitzgerald, *China and the Overseas Chinese* (London: Cambridge University Press, 1972).

9. For examples on Japan, see Tsuda, *Diasporic Homecomings*. On Korea, see Eleana Jean Kim, *Adopted Territory: Transnational Korean Adoptees and the Politics of Belonging* (Durham, NC: Duke University Press, 2010); and Caren Freeman, *Making and Faking Kinship: Marriage and Labor Migration Between China and South Korea* (Ithaca, NY: Cornell University Press, 2011). On Hong Kong, see Nicole DeJong Newendorp, *Uneasy Reunions: Immigration, Citizenship, and Family Life in Post-1997*

Hong Kong (Stanford, CA: Stanford University Press, 2008). On Macau, see Cathryn H. Clayton, *Sovereignty at the Edge: Macau and the Question of Chineseness* (Cambridge, MA: Harvard University Press, 2009). On Taiwan, see Sara Friedman, *Exceptional States: Chinese Immigrants and Taiwanese Sovereignty* (Oakland: University of California Press, 2015).

10. The scientific diaspora refers to knowledge workers that a migrant-sending country has identified as part of its own population abroad.

11. Prasenjit Duara, *The Crisis of Global Modernity: Asian Traditions and a Sustainable Future* (Cambridge: Cambridge University Press, 2015).

12. For examples, see Gungwu Wang, *Chinese Overseas: From Earthbound China to the Quest for Autonomy* (Cambridge, MA: Harvard University Press, 2000); Leo Suryadinata, "China's Citizenship Law and the Chinese in Southeast Asia," in *Law and the Chinese in Southeast Asia*, ed. Michael B. Hooker (Singapore: Institute of Southeast Asia Studies, 2002), pp. 169–202.

13. See Chapter 5 for the changing meanings attached to the labels "overseas Chinese" and "Chinese diaspora." Whereas earlier diaspora engagement by the Chinese state focused on the Chinese abroad of Han Chinese ethnicity, today it is evolving to include the overseas Chinese of ethnic minority backgrounds for geo-strategic reasons.

14. Prasenjit Duara, *Rescuing History from the Nation: Questioning Narratives of Modern China* (Chicago: University of Chicago Press, 1995), p. 5.

15. Philip A. Kuhn, *Chinese Among Other: Emigration in Modern Times* (Singapore: NUS Press, 2008).

16. McKeown, *Melancholy Order*, p. 82.

17. Chinese emigrants were portrayed as traitors and deserters during the Qing dynasty until the late Qing period (especially after the 1860 Beijing Treaty) when they became seen as "coolies," or labor migrants, changing hostile attitudes to sympathy for their indentured status or the poor living conditions and menial labor that they endured. See Ching-hwang Yen, *Studies in Modern Overseas Chinese History* (Singapore: Times Academic Press, 1995); Yen, *Coolies and Mandarins*; Kuhn, *Chinese Among Other*; McKeown, *Melancholy Order*; Shao, "Chinese by Definition"; van Dongen, "Behind the Ties that Bind."

18. Kuhn notes that these included the Convention to Regulate the Engagement of Chinese Emigrants by British and French Subjects (1866) and the Burlingame Treaty (1868) signed with the United States. Kuhn, *Chinese Among Other*, pp. 137–138. For detailed accounts, see Yen, *Coolies and Mandarins*, and Yen, *Studies in Modern Overseas Chinese History*.

19. The Qing government issued the first Chinese nationality law in 1909. Following the collapse of the Qing dynasty in 1911, the newly established republican government issued another nationality law. Modifications were made to the 1909 law in 1914 and 1915. Then in 1929 the nationalist government (which became the government of

the Republic of China in Taiwan) issued another version during its reign (1925–1948). The People's Republic of China, which came to power in 1949, issued its version of the nationality law in 1980. A constant feature of these changes to China's nationality law is the reference to *jus sanguinis* (*xuetong zhuyi*), or inheritance of nationality by blood-line, even though the reference to "bloodline" is ambiguous in a multiethnic society like China. Shao notes for example that the Qing rulers were Manchus but Chinese society was dominated by the Han Chinese and characterized by Han ethnocen-trism. The topic of Han Chinese ethnocentrism will be revisited in Chapter 5. See Suryadinata, "China's Citizenship Law and the Chinese in Southeast Asia"; Shao, "Chinese by Definition."

20. Carine Pina-Guerassimoff and Eric Guerassimoff, "The 'Overseas Chinese': The State and Emigration from the 1890s through the 1990s," in *Citizenship and Those Who Leave: The Politics of Emigration and Expatriation*, ed. Nancy L. Green and François Weil (Urbana: University of Illinois Press, 2007), pp. 245–264.

21. Glen Peterson, "Socialist China and the Huaqiao: The Transition to Socialism in the Overseas Chinese Areas of Rural Guangdong, 1949–1956," *Modern China* 14, no. 3 (July 1988): 309–335.

22. Since 1955, talks concerning a dual nationality restriction had been conducted with decolonizing or newly decolonized nations in Southeast Asia which expressed con-cerns toward the allegedly divided loyalties of the Chinese in their countries. See Mette Thunø, "Reaching Out and Incorporating Chinese Overseas: The Trans-Territorial Scope of the PRC by the End of the 20th Century," *The China Quarterly* 168 (Decem-ber 2001): 910–929; Michael R. Godley, "The Sojourners: Returned Overseas Chinese in the People's Republic of China," *Pacific Affairs* 62, no. 3 (Autumn 1989): 330–352; Hong Liu, "An Emerging China and Diasporic Chinese: Historicity, State, and International Relations," *Journal of Contemporary China* 20, no. 72 (November 2011): 813–832; Hong Liu and Els van Dongen, "China's Diaspora Policies as a New Mode of Transnational Governance," *Journal of Contemporary China* 25, no. 102 (2016): 805–821; Xi Cheng, "The 'Distinctiveness' of the Overseas Chinese as Perceived in the People's Republic of China," in *Beyond Chinatown: New Chinese Migration and the Global Expansion of China*, ed. Mette Thunø (Copenhagen: NIAS Press, 2007), pp. 49–64.

23. Duara, *Rescuing History from the Nation*.

24. At the same time, the communist political leadership sought to demonstrate its solidarity with Southeast Asian countries in support of anti-imperialism in Asia and downplay their suspicions that China was using the Chinese abroad to spread com-munist ideology. See Stephen Fitzgerald, "China and the Overseas Chinese: Perceptions and Policies," *The China Quarterly* 44 (October–December 1970): 1–37; Peterson, "So-cialist China and the Huaqiao."

25. Espen Hammer, *Philosophy and Temporality from Kant to Critical Theory* (Cambridge: Cambridge University Press, 2011), p. 28.

26. Clayton, *Sovereignty at the Edge*, p. 14.

27. Kim, *Adopted Territory*; Freeman, *Making and Faking Kinship*.

28. Fitzgerald, "China and the Overseas Chinese."

29. Godley, "The Sojourners," p. 330.

30. Shelly Chan, "The Disobedient Diaspora: Overseas Chinese Students in Mao's China, 1958–66," *Journal of Chinese Overseas* 10, no. 2 (2014): 220–238.

31. China did so to assure Southeast Asian governments that it did not intend to use the Chinese abroad to spread communist ideology. Signs of the CCP detaching itself from the Chinese abroad were perceptible from as early as 1957. See Godley, "The Sojourners."

32. Fitzgerald, "China and the Overseas Chinese," p. 28. Also see Stephen Fitzgerald, "Overseas Chinese Affairs and the Cultural Revolution," *The China Quarterly* 40 (October–December 1969): 103–126.

33. By the end of 1958, an estimated quarter-million of the Chinese living abroad had "returned" to China. An estimated ninety-four thousand Indonesian-Chinese arrived in China by ship during 1960 alone following the 1959 retail ban, and another twenty thousand to thirty thousand in 1961. In the late 1970s, more than two hundred thousand Vietnamese Chinese crossed the land border or came by sea to China. See Godley, "The Sojourners," p. 332, citing *Xin Wen She*, September 11, 1959, and *Zhongguo Qingnian*, September 15, 1959; Fitzgerald, "Overseas Chinese Affairs and the Cultural Revolution"; Xiaorong Han, "Spoiled Guests or Dedicated Patriots? The Chinese in North Vietnam, 1954–1978," *International Journal of Asian Studies* 6, no. 1 (2009): 1–36.

34. The Chinese from British-ruled Malaya were deported for their pro-communism activities while the Chinese from Indonesia and later Vietnam had endured consecutive episodes of anti-Chinese discrimination in the newly decolonized nation-states.

35. Godley, "The Sojourners," p. 331.

36. Fitzgerald, "China and the Overseas Chinese," p. 2.

37. William A. Callahan, "Beyond Cosmopolitanism and Nationalism: Diasporic Chinese and Neo-Nationalism in China and Thailand," *International Organization* 57, no. 3 (Summer 2003): 481–517, from p. 492, citing Wang, *Chinese Overseas*, p. 47.

38. *Hukou* refers to the rural and urban household registration system in China which is tied to the ability of a person to qualify for Chinese citizenship. Without being assigned *hukou* status, the refugee-returnees were not eligible for Chinese nationality status, thus rendering them stateless persons. Pockets of stateless Vietnamese-Chinese remain in the state-owned farms today.

39. Duara, *Rescuing History from the Nation*, p. 65.

40. Etienne Balibar, "Difference, Otherness, Exclusion," *Parallax* 11, no. 1 (2005): 19–34.

41. Ibid., p. 34.

42. Kim, *Adopted Territory*, p. 99.

43. Batik is a fabric pattern associated with Indonesian culture.

44. Formally known as the Returned Overseas Chinese Farms.

45. For Thailand, see Callahan, "Beyond Cosmopolitanism and Nationalism." For Myanmar, see Elaine Lynn-Ee Ho and Lynette J. Chua, "Law and 'Race' in the Citizenship Spaces of Myanmar: Spatial Strategies and the Political Subjectivity of the Burmese Chinese," *Ethnic and Racial Studies* 39, no. 5 (2016): 896–916.

46. Xiaorong Han, "From Resettlement to Rights Protection: The Collective Actions of the Refugees from Vietnam in China Since the Late 1970s," *Journal of Chinese Overseas* 10, no. 2 (2014): 197–219.

47. Prior to the harsh treatment toward Chinese with foreign connections during the Cultural Revolution, the Chinese abroad were valued by the Chinese political leadership for their contributions to China such as represented by remittances, investments, infrastructure development, knowledge sharing, or philanthropy.

48. Also see Godley, "The Sojourners."

49. Former Chairman Mao Zedong implemented agrarian reform and collectivization that resulted in the central planning of food production and distribution across China. But the Agrarian Reform Law (1950) specified that there be "due consideration for the interests of overseas Chinese" during land reform. See Peterson, "Socialist China and the Huaqiao," p. 332.

50. Also see Glen Peterson, *Overseas Chinese in the People's Republic of China* (New York: Routledge, 2012).

51. Chee-Beng Tan, "Indonesian Chinese in Hong Kong: Re-Migration, Re-Establishment of Livelihood and Belonging," *Asian Ethnicity* 12, no. 1 (February 2011): 101–119.

52. Peterson, *Overseas Chinese in the People's Republic of China*, p. 56.

53. Also see Chee-Beng Tan for an account of life on another state-owned farm in Fujian province. The farm contains a majority of Indonesian returnees and Tan documents how they continue to recreate Balinese cultural customs in their life in China. Chee-Beng Tan, "Reterritorialization of a Balinese Chinese Community in Quanzhou, Fujian," *Modern Asian Studies* 44, no. 3 (May 2010): 547–566.

54. Ho, *The Graves of Tarim*; Conway and Potter, "Return of the Next Generations"; Tsuda, *Diasporic Homecomings*.

55. Clayton, *Sovereignty at the Edge*, p. 110.

56. Balibar, "Difference, Otherness, Exclusion," p. 24; Sandro Mezzadra and Brett Nielson, *Border as Method, or, the Multiplication of Labor* (Durham, NC: Duke University Press, 2013).

57. Godley, "The Sojourners."

58. Peterson, *Overseas Chinese in the People's Republic of China*, pp. 116–117.

59. Peterson, *Overseas Chinese in the People's Republic of China*.

60. John Frow, "A Politics of Stolen Time," in *TimeSpace: Geographies of Temporality*, ed. Jon May and Nigel Thrift (London: Routledge, 2001), pp. 73–88, quotation from p. 73.

61. Ibid., p. 82.

62. Guofu Liu, *The Right to Leave and Return and Chinese Migration Law* (Boston: Martinus Nijhoff, 2007).

63. Callahan, "Beyond Cosmopolitanism and Nationalism"; Peterson, *Overseas Chinese in the People's Republic of China*.

64. David C. Kang, *China Rising: Peace, Power, and Order in East Asia* (New York: Columbia University Press, 2007).

65. Alan Smart and Jinn-Yuh Hsu, "The Chinese Diaspora, Foreign Investment and Economic Development in China," *The Review of International Affairs* 3, no. 4 (Summer 2004): 544–566.

66. Liu, "An Emerging China and Diasporic Chinese," p. 832.

67. Laurence J. C. Ma and Carolyn Cartier, eds., *The Chinese Diaspora: Space, Place, Mobility, and Identity, Why of Where* (Lanham, MD: Rowman and Littlefield, 2003), p. 19.

68. Ien Ang, "Together-in-Difference: Beyond Diaspora, into Hybridity," *Asian Studies Review* 27, no. 2 (June 2003): 141–154; Elaine Lynn-Ee Ho and Fangyu Foo, "Debating Integration in Singapore, Deepening the Variegations of the Chinese Diaspora," in *Contemporary Chinese Diasporas*, ed. Min Zhou (Singapore: Palgrave Macmillan, 2017), pp. 105–126.

69. Smart and Hsu, "The Chinese Diaspora, Foreign Investment and Economic Development in China," p. 553. Also see Michael Jacobsen, "Navigating Between Disaggregating Nation States and Entrenching Processes of Globalisation: Reconceptualising the Chinese Diaspora in Southeast Asia," *Journal of Contemporary China* 18, no. 58 (January 2009): 69–91.

70. Smart and Hsu, "The Chinese Diaspora, Foreign Investment and Economic Development in China," p. 553.

71. David Zweig and Huiyao Wang, "Can China Bring Back the Best? The Communist Party Organises China's Search for Talent," *The China Quarterly* 215 (September 2013): 590–615.

72. Liu, *The Right to Leave and Return and Chinese Migration Law*.

73. Xiang Biao, "Emigration from China: A Sending Country Perspective," *International Migration* 41, no. 3 (2003): 21–48; Elena Barabantseva, "Trans-nationalising Chineseness: Overseas Chinese Policies of the PRC's Central Government," *Asien* 96 (July 2005): 7–28.

74. The most prestigious was the "100 Talents" program (*Bairen Jihua*), which became enlarged to the "1000 Talents" program (*Qianren Jihua*) in 2008. Other promi-

nent programs for returning academics and scientists are the "Distinguished Young Scholars" program and the "Cheung Kong Scholar" award.

75. Barabantseva, "Trans-nationalising Chineseness"; Liu, "An Emerging China and Diasporic Chinese"; Biao, "Emigration from China."

76. Frank N. Pieke, "Immigrant China," *Modern China* 38, no. 1 (2012): 40–77.

77. Zweig and Wang, "Can China Bring Back the Best?"

78. Yun-Chung Chen, "The Limits of Brain Circulation: Chinese Returnees and Technological Development in Beijing," *Pacific Affairs* 81, no. 2 (Summer 2008): 195–215.

79. Freeman, *Making and Faking Kinship*; Kim, *Adopted Territory*.

Chapter 3: Citizenship Across the Life Course

1. Daiva Stasiulis, "The Migration-Citizenship Nexus," in *Recasting the Social in Citizenship*, ed. Engin F. Isin (Toronto: University of Toronto Press, 2008), p. 140.

2. I use "Mainland Chinese migrants" as a term to capture the emigration, immigration, and re-migration profiles of the research participants who move between China and Canada. The discussion troubles categorizations such as the "overseas Chinese," "Chinese diaspora," or "Chinese abroad." Where the term "returnees" is used, it refers specifically to their re-migration to the natal land, albeit for a temporary period only, as they plan to re-migrate again to Canada. The adjective "Mainland Chinese" is adopted to differentiate them from the Hong Kong migrants in Canada whom other researchers have studied. See Audrey Kobayashi and Valerie Preston, "Transnationalism Through the Life Course: Hong Kong Immigrants to Canada," *Asia-Pacific Viewpoint* 48, no. 2 (August 2007): 151–167; Valerie Preston, Audrey Kobayashi, and Guida Man, "Transnationalism, Gender, and Civic Participation: Canadian Case Studies of Hong Kong Immigrants," *Environment and Planning A* 38, no. 9 (2006): 1633–1651; Johanna L. Waters, *Education, Migration, and Cultural Capital in the Chinese Diaspora: Transnational Students Between Hong Kong and Canada* (Amherst, NY: Cambria Press, 2008); Janet Salaff, Angela Shik, and Arent Greve, "Like Sons and Daughters of Hong Kong: The Return of the Young Generation," *The China Review* 8, no. 1 (Spring 2008): 31–57; David Ley, *Millionaire Migrants: Trans-Pacific Life Lines* (Oxford: Wiley-Blackwell, 2010).

3. David Ley and Audrey Kobayashi, "Back to Hong Kong: Return Migration or Transnational Sojourn?," *Global Networks* 5, no. 2 (2005): 111–127.

4. Rosa Mas Giralt and Adrian J. Bailey, "Transnational Familyhood and the Liquid Life Paths of South Americans in the UK," *Global Networks* 10, no. 3 (2010): 383–400.

5. Bauböck's later writing on citizenship constellations is distinct from his earlier work that argues for a model of transnational citizenship requiring an overarching set of rights and duties that spans two or more countries. See Rainer Bauböck, "Studying

Citizenship Constellations," *Journal of Ethnic and Migration Studies* 36, no. 5 (May 2010): 847–859; Rainer Bauböck, *Transnational Citizenship: Membership and Rights in International Migration* (Aldershot, UK: Edward Elgar, 1994). Holding dual or multiple citizenships can enable migrants to seek citizenship rights in more than one country. However, this is contingent on dual citizenship being recognized by the countries concerned. The legal acceptance of dual citizenship does not preclude contestations over whether those with dual or multiple citizenships deserve the privileges of both statuses.

6. AnnaLee Saxenian, *The New Argonauts: Regional Advantage in a Global Economy* (Cambridge, MA: Harvard University Press, 2006).

7. Susan Bibler Coutin, *Nations of Emigrants: Shifting Boundaries of Citizenship in El Salvador and the United States* (Ithaca, NY: Cornell University Press, 2007); Rainer Bauböck, "The Rights and Duties of External Citizenship," *Citizenship Studies* 13, no. 5 (October 2009): 475–499; Elaine Lynn-Ee Ho, "'Claiming' the Diaspora: Sending State Strategies, Elite Mobility and the Spatialities of Citizenship," *Progress in Human Geography* 35, no. 6 (December 2011): 757–772.

8. Geraldine Pratt, *Families Apart: Migrant Mothers and the Conflicts of Labor and Love* (Minneapolis: University of Minnesota Press, 2012), p. 4.

9. The integration challenges faced by the skilled migrants (*jishu yimin*) in Canada overlap with but are also distinct from the wealthy investor migrants (*touzi yimin*). The latter have greater wealth to carry them through a period of low income in Canada and an accelerated route to citizenship in Canada as allowed under the country's investor migrant scheme. Nonetheless, post-immigration life in Canada is difficult for the investor migrants too. David Ley has documented the experiences of investor migrants who immigrated from Hong Kong to Canada. See Ley, *Millionaire Migrants*.

10. Laurie A. Brand, "Arab Uprisings and the Changing Frontiers of Transnational Citizenship: Voting from Abroad in Political Transitions," *Political Geography* 41 (July 2014): 54–63; Michael Collyer, "A Geography of Extra-Territorial Citizenship: Explanations of External Voting," *Migration Studies* 2, no. 1 (March 2014): 55–72.

11. Bauböck, "The Rights and Duties of External Citizenship."

12. Statistics Canada, *Place of Birth for the Immigrant Population by Period of Immigration, 2006 Counts and Percentage Distribution, for Canada, Provinces and Territories—20% Sample Data*, last modified on March 27, 2009, accessed on January 26, 2016, from https://www12.statcan.gc.ca/census-recensement/2006/dp-pd/hlt /97-557/T404-eng.cfm?Lang=E&T=404&GH=4&GF=1&SC=1&S=1&O=D.

13. Vanessa L. Fong, *Paradise Redefined: Transnational Chinese Students and the Quest for Flexible Citizenship in the Developed World* (Stanford, CA: Stanford University Press, 2011).

14. For similar trends on Hong Kong migrants in Canada, see Johanna L. Waters, *Education, Migration, and Cultural Capital in the Chinese Diaspora: Transnational Students Between Hong Kong and Canada* (Amherst, NY: Cambria Press, 2008).

15. Aihwa Ong, *Flexible Citizenship: The Cultural Logics of Transnationality* (Durham, NC: Duke University Press, 1999).

16. Since China enforces dual citizenship restriction, naturalizing abroad meant the migrant automatically forfeits his or her right to Chinese nationality.

17. Ayelet Shachar, *The Birthright Lottery: Citizenship and Global Inequality* (Cambridge, MA: Harvard University Press, 2009); Engin F. Isin, "Citizens Without Nations," *Environment and Planning D: Society and Space* 30, no. 3 (2012): 450–467.

18. Nicole DeJong Newendorp, *Uneasy Reunions: Immigration, Citizenship, and Family Life in Post-1997 Hong Kong* (Stanford, CA: Stanford University Press, 2008).

19. Ian Young, "Canada Scraps Millionaire Visa Scheme, 'Dumps 46,000 Chinese Applications,'" *South China Morning Post*, February 12, 2014, accessed on January 24, 2017, from http://www.scmp.com/news/world/article/1426368/canada-scraps-millionaire -visa-scheme-dumps-46000-chinese-applications.

20. Parliament of Canada, *Second Session, Forty-First Parliament, 62–63 Elizabeth II, 2013–2014 House of Commons Canada Bill C-24*, June 4, 2014, accessed on June 23, 2016, from http://www.parl.gc.ca/HousePublications/Publication.aspx?Language=E& Mode=1&DocId=6646338.

21. Ian Young, "Canada Floats New Citizenship Rules that Could Affect Thousands of Chinese," *South China Morning Post*, February 7, 2014, accessed on January 24, 2017, from http://www.scmp.com/news/china/article/1423485/canada-floats-new-citizenship -rules-could-affect-thousands-chinese.

22. Shortly after the Liberal Party was elected in November 2015 it proposed a bill in February 2016 to lift several restrictive conditions stipulated under Bill C-24, such as expressing an intention to remain in the country and reducing the residency requirement for both permanent residency renewal and citizenship applications. However, both the citizenship test and the English or French language proficiency test remain.

23. Coutin, *Nations of Emigrants*, p. 114; Sara Friedman, *Exceptional States: Chinese Immigrants and Taiwanese Sovereignty* (Oakland: University of California Press, 2015), pp. 12–13.

24. David Conradson and Alan Latham, "Transnational Urbanism: Attending to Everyday Practices and Mobilities," *Journal of Ethnic and Migration Studies* 31, no. 2 (March 2005): 227–233.

25. They are known as *haiou*, which means seagulls.

26. Kam Wing Chan, "China's Urbanisation 2020: A New Blueprint and Direction," *Eurasian Geography and Economics* 55, no. 1 (2014): 1–9; Li Zhang, "Economic

Migration and Urban Citizenship in China: The Role of Points Systems," *Population and Development Review* 38, no. 3 (September 2012): 503–533.

27. Overseas Chinese Affairs Office of the State Council, *Guanyu Waiji Huaren Qianzheng, Juliu Ji Yongjiu Juming Liu De Zhengce Jing* [Policy concerning the visa and permanent residency status of the Chinese who have foreign nationality status], August 17, 2015, accessed on June 23, 2016, from http://www.gqb.gov.cn/news/2015/0817/36451.shtml.

28. On the disjuncture between legal status, emotional ties, and social connections that migrants experience, also see Saskia Sassen, *Territory, Authority, Rights: From Medieval to Global Assemblages* (Princeton, NJ: Princeton University Press, 2006); Coutin, *Nations of Emigrants*; Lynn A. Staeheli, Patricia Ehrkamp, Helga Leitner, and Caroline R. Nagel, "Dreaming the Ordinary: Daily Life and the Complex Geographies of Citizenship," *Progress in Human Geography* 36, no. 5 (2012): 628–644. Such studies focus on undocumented migrants. The Mainland Chinese migrants discussed here have legal status but experience different forms of dissonance too, providing a different angle into such debates.

29. Hong Liu, "An Emerging China and Diasporic Chinese: Historicity, State, and International Relations," *Journal of Contemporary China* 20, no. 72 (November 2011): 813–832; David Zweig and Huiyao Wang, "Can China Bring Back the Best? The Communist Party Organises China's Search for Talent," *The China Quarterly* 215 (September 2013): 590–615.

30. Bauböck, "The Rights and Duties of External Citizenship."

31. Yan Zhang, "Green Card Threshold Lowered," *China Daily*, June 9, 2015, accessed on January 24, 2017, from http://www.chinadaily.com.cn/china/2015-06/09/content_20944896.htm.

32. Guofu Liu, "Changing Chinese Migration Law: From Restriction to Relaxation." *Journal of International Migration and Integration* 10, no. 3 (2009): 311–333; Frank N. Pieke, "Immigrant China," *Modern China* 38, no. 1 (2012): 40–77.

33. For example, Don J. DeVoretz, "Canada's Secret Province: 2.8 Million Canadians Abroad" (Canadians Abroad Project Paper Series #09-5, Asia Pacific Foundation of Canada, Vancouver, BC, October 2009); Kenny Zhang, "Canadians Abroad: Foreigners with Canadian Passports or the New Canadian Diaspora?" (Working Paper Series #09-2, Asia Pacific Foundation of Canada, Vancouver, BC, 2009).

34. Kenny Zhang, "Chinese in Canada and Canadians in China: The Human Platform for Relationships Between China and Canada," in *The China Challenge: Sino–Canadian Relations in the 21st Century*, ed. Huhua Cao and Vivienne Poy (Ottawa: University of Ottawa Press, 2011), pp. 158–182.

35. Maurice Bitran and Serene Tan, "Diaspora Nation: An Inquiry into the Economic Potential of Diaspora Networks in Canada," Mowat Centre for Policy Innova-

tion, Toronto, September 2013, accessed on November 13, 2017, from https://mowatcentre
.ca/diaspora-nation/.

36. Also see Shibao Guo, "Toward Recognitive Justice: Emerging Trends and Challenges in Transnational Migration and Lifelong Learning," *International Journal of Lifelong Education* 29, no. 2 (March–April 2010): 149–167.

37. Angharad Closs Stephens and Vicki Squire, "Politics Through a Web: Citizenship and Community Unbound," *Environment and Planning D: Society and Space* 30, no. 3 (2012): 551–567, quotation from p. 555.

38. Coutin, *Nations of Emigrants*.

39. Rainer Bauböck and Virginie Guiraudon, "Introduction: Realignments of Citizenship: Reassessing Rights in the Age of Plural Memberships and Multi-Level Governance," *Citizenship Studies* 13, no. 5 (October 2009): 439–450, quotation from p. 443.

40. Isin, "Citizens Without Nations," p. 16.

41. Janine Brodie, "The Social in Social Citizenship," in *Recasting the Social in Citizenship*, ed. Engin F. Isin (Toronto: University of Toronto Press, 2008), pp. 20–43.

42. Ibid., pp. 39–41.

43. For example, Patrick Grady and Herbert Grubel, "Immigration and the Welfare State Revisited: Fiscal Transfers to Immigrants in Canada" (Vancouver, BC: Fraser Institute, May 31, 2015), accessed on June 28, 2016, from http://ssrn.com/abstract=2612456.

44. The residency requirement in Canada has since been reduced to two out of five years. However, the criteria for permanent residency and citizenship has also become more stringent.

45. Coutin, *Nations of Emigrants*.

46. Russell King, Anthony M. Warnes, and Allan M. Williams, "International Retirement Migration in Europe," *International Journal of Population Geography* 4, no. 2 (1998): 91–111; Alistair Hunter, "Theory and Practice of Return Migration at Retirement: The Case of Migrant Worker Hostel Residents in France," *Population, Space and Place* 17, no. 2 (2011): 179–192; Leng Leng Thang, Sachiko Sone, and Mika Toyota, "Freedom Found? The Later-Life Transnational Migration of Japanese Women to Western Australia and Thailand," *Asia and Pacific Migration Journal* 21, no. 2 (2012): 239–261; John Percival, *Return Migration in Later Life: International Perspectives* (Bristol, UK: Policy Press, 2013).

47. Louise Ackers, "Citizenship, Migration and the Valuation of Care in the European Union," *Journal of Ethnic and Migration Studies* 30, no. 2 (2004): 373–396, quotation from p. 390.

48. Ibid.

49. Nina Glick Schiller, "Explanatory Frameworks in Transnational Migration Studies: The Missing Multi-Scalar Global Perspective," *Ethnic and Racial Studies* 38, no. 13 (2015): 2275–2282, quotation from p. 2277.

50. Mike Douglass, "Global Householding in Pacific Asia," *International Development Planning Review* 28, no. 4 (2006): 421–446.

51. Ken Chih-Yan Sun, "Transnational Healthcare Seeking: How Ageing Taiwanese Return Migrants View Homeland Public Benefits," *Global Networks* 14, no. 4 (2014): 534.

52. Eleonore Kofman, "Rethinking Care Through Social Reproduction: Articulating Circuits of Migration," *Social Politics: International Studies in Gender, State & Society* 19, no. 1 (Spring 2012): 142–162.

53. For example, Selma Sevenhuijsen, "The Place of Care: The Relevance of the Feminist Ethic of Care for Social Policy," *Feminist Theory* 4, no. 2 (2003): 179–197; Joan C. Tronto, *Caring Democracy: Markets, Equality, and Justice* (New York: New York University Press, 2013).

54. Fong, *Paradise Redefined*, p. 142.

Chapter 4: Multiple Diasporas

1. Also see Susan Bibler Coutin, *Nations of Emigrants: Shifting Boundaries of Citizenship in El Salvador and the United States* (Ithaca, NY: Cornell University Press, 2007).

2. Lieba Faier, *Intimate Encounters: Filipina Women and the Remaking of Rural Japan* (Berkeley: University of California Press, 2009), p. 1.

3. Philip Kretsedemas, *Migrants and Race in the US: Territorial Racism and the Alien/Outside* (New York: Routledge, 2014), p. 44.

4. Ibid., p. 44; emphasis in the original.

5. Etienne Balibar, "Is There a Neo-Racism?," in *Race, Nation, Class: Ambiguous Identities*, ed. Etienne Balibar and Immanuel Wallerstein (London: Verso, 1991), pp. 17–28.

6. Kretsedemas, *Migrants and Race in the US*, p. 46.

7. Peter Geschiere, *The Perils of Belonging: Autochthony, Citizenship, and Exclusion in Africa and Europe* (Chicago: University of Chicago Press, 2009), p. 2.

8. Kretsedemas, *Migrants and Race in the US*.

9. Geschiere, *The Perils of Belonging*.

10. Ibid., p. 6.

11. Ibid., p. 28.

12. Elizabeth A. Grosz, *The Nick of Time: Politics, Evolution, and the Untimely* (Durham, NC: Duke University Press, 2004); Etienne Balibar, "Difference, Otherness, Exclusion," *Parallax* 11, no. 1 (2005): 19–34; Etienne Balibar, *Equaliberty: Political Essays* (Durham, NC: Duke University Press, 2014); Faier, *Intimate Encounters*; Greg Noble, "'Bumping into Alterity': Transacting Cultural Complexities," *Continuum* 25, no. 6 (December 2011): 827–840; Greg Noble, "Cosmopolitan Habits: The Capacities

and Habitats of Intercultural Conviviality," *Body & Society* 19, no. 2–3 (2013): 162–185; Ash Amin, *Land of Strangers* (Cambridge: Polity Press, 2012).

13. As discussed in Chapter 2, supporters or those suspected of supporting the Malayan communist party were forcibly expelled by the British colonialists and sent to China.

14. Itty Abraham, *How India Became Territorial: Foreign Policy, Diaspora, Geopolitics* (Stanford, CA: Stanford University Press, 2014).

15. Xi Cheng, "The 'Distinctiveness' of the Overseas Chinese as Perceived in the People's Republic of China," in *Beyond Chinatown: New Chinese Migration and the Global Expansion of China*, ed. Mette Thunø (Copenhagen: NIAS Press, 2007), pp. 49–64.

16. Gungwu Wang, "The Chinese as Immigrants and Settlers," in *Management of Success: The Moulding of Modern Singapore*, ed. Kernial Singh Sandhu and Paul Wheatley (Singapore: Institute of Southeast Asian Studies, 1989), pp. 552–562.

17. Eurasians are persons of mixed Caucasian and Asian ancestry; they use English as their language of communication, and they are categorized as "Others" in the CMIO model of ethnic relations. *Kristang* (a creole language bearing Portuguese and Malay influences) is considered by some to be their "mother tongue" but this is not offered in the educational curriculum.

18. Michael Hill and Kwen Fee Lian, *The Politics of Nation Building and Citizenship in Singapore* (London: Routledge, 1995).

19. Beng Huat Chua, *Communitarian Ideology and Democracy in Singapore* (London: Routledge, 1995).

20. A survey of attitudes toward ethnicity in Singapore, conducted in 2017 by the Institute of Policy Studies, indicated that the majority of those polled would accept new citizens from Chinese, Malay, Indian, and Eurasian countries as "truly Singaporean." Inadvertently, this finding reflects the hegemony of the CMIO categorizations, prioritizing the ethnic groups associated with earlier waves of immigration to Singapore. See Mathew Mathews, Leonard Lim, Shanthini Selvarajan, and Nicole Cheung, "CNA-IPS Survey on Ethnic Attitudes in Singapore" (IPS Working Papers No. 28, Institute of Policy Studies, Singapore, November 2017), p. 5, accessed on January 13, 2017, http:// lkyspp2.nus.edu.sg/ips/wp-content/uploads/sites/2/2017/11/IPS-Working-Paper-28 _081117.pdf.

21. Department of Statistics Singapore, *Population Trends 2015*, 2015, accessed on November 6, 2015, from http://www.singstat.gov.sg/publications/publications-and -papers/population-and-population-structure/population-trends.

22. National Population and Talent Division (NPTD), Singapore Department of Statistics, Ministry of Home Affairs and Immigration and Checkpoints Authority, *2014 Population Brief*, September 2014, accessed on January 13, 2017, from http://population .sg/population-in-brief/files/population-in-brief-2014.pdf.

23. Chinese immigrants gain entry to Singapore through the skilled immigration and Global Investor programs established in 2004 or as low-skilled foreign labor for the construction and service sectors. Aggregate figures on the magnitude of immigration, type of visas, and permanent residency or citizenship applications and approvals are data publicly released by the Singaporean state. However, data on the ethnicity or nationality backgrounds of immigrants are not released to the public.

24. Similar tensions are observable between the Singapore-born "Indians" (i.e., diasporic descendants from South Asia) and new immigrants from South Asia. The new immigrants have different regional affiliations from the Indian immigrants who migrated to Singapore during the nineteenth and early twentieth centuries. Just as with the plural identities of the Chinese population residing in Singapore, the Indian population speaks a variety of Indian languages and comes from a range of socioeconomic, educational, professional, and nationality backgrounds.

25. Sara Friedman, *Exceptional States: Chinese Immigrants and Taiwanese Sovereignty* (Oakland: University of California Press, 2015), pp. 20–21.

26. Ibid., p. 10. On Taiwan see Friedman, *Exceptional State*, and on Hong Kong see Nicole DeJong Newendorp, *Uneasy Reunions: Immigration, Citizenship, and Family Life in Post-1997 Hong Kong* (Stanford, CA: Stanford University Press, 2008).

27. Ayelet Shachar, *The Birthright Lottery: Citizenship and Global Inequality* (Cambridge, MA: Harvard University Press, 2009).

28. As Noel Salazar explains, "figures" function as concept-metaphors that capture lived experiences of a particular kind. Salazar builds on Barker et al.'s approach that studies figures as sites of ideological formations and contestations. See Noel B. Salazar, "Key Figures of Mobility: An Introduction," *Social Anthropology* 25, no. 1 (2017): 5–12; Joshua Barker, Erik Harms, and Johan Lindquist, eds., *Figures of Southeast Asian Modernity* (Honolulu: University of Hawai'i Press, 2014).

29. Amin, *Land of Strangers*.

30. Arun Saldanha, "Reontologising Race: The Machinic Geography of Phenotype," *Environment and Planning D: Society and Space* 24, no. 1 (2006): 9–24.

31. Amin, *Land of Strangers*.

32. Grosz, *The Nick of Time*.

33. Ibid., p. 177.

34. Etienne Balibar, "Strangers as Enemies: Further Reflections on the Aporias of Transnational Citizenship" (Globalisation Working Papers 06/04, Institute on Globalization and the Human Condition, Hamilton, ON, May 2006).

35. Cathryn H. Clayton, *Sovereignty at the Edge: Macau and the Question of Chineseness* (Cambridge, MA: Harvard University Press, 2009), p. 218.

36. The Chinese state engages both types of clan associations through diaspora strategies. See also Jean Michel Montsion, "Chinese Ethnicities in Neoliberal Singapore? State Designs and Dialect(ical) Struggles of Community Associations," *Ethnic*

and Racial Studies 37, no. 9 (2014): 1486–1504. It invokes historical ties and focuses on developing contemporary cultural and business links with the pioneer clan associations and diasporic descendants. The clan associations established by new Chinese immigrants are treated as a constituency with stronger emotional ties to China as the natal land.

37. These events are discussed in Chapter 2.

38. In an earlier study of Singaporeans in China, Brenda Yeoh and Katie Willis also discuss the negative perceptions that such overseas Singaporeans have of the domestic Chinese. Brenda S. A. Yeoh and Katie Willis, "Singapore Unlimited: Configuring Social Identity in the Regionalisation Process," Transnational Communities Programme, University of Oxford, 1998, accessed on December 28, 2016, from http://www.transcomm.ox.ac.uk/working%20papers/nottitc.pdf.

39. Hong Kong and Taiwanese Chinese immigrants have also settled in Singapore, but the new Chinese immigrants from China are treated more strongly as social outcasts.

40. Amin, *Land of Strangers*, p. 5.

41. Clayton, *Sovereignty at the Edge*.

42. Friedman, *Exceptional State*, p. 18.

43. The term *laoyimin* (translated as "old immigrant") refers to a person who immigrated to a country prior to another cohort of immigrants. The term as applied to describe Chinese immigration varies from country to country, and the periodization of migration is deployed loosely depending on its usage in a social context. In Singapore, the new Chinese immigrants (*xinyimin*) use it to refer to those who came to Singapore from 1979 till the late 1990s.

44. Starting on January 1, 2017, the employment pass for skilled migrants requires a minimum monthly salary of S$3600 (equivalent to US$2500). In 1998, when the tiered work-pass scheme was introduced, the minimum monthly salary was S$2000 (equivalent to US$1200 at that time). There are currently three categories of employment passes: "Q" for lower-income applicants and "P1" or "P2" for higher-income applicants. Only those who earn more than S$5000 per month have the right to apply for dependent visas for their family members. Migrants employed to do low-skilled work in Singapore are known as "work permit holders" and they do not have the right to apply for permanent residency, citizenship, or family reunification schemes.

45. K. C. Vijayan, "The Extent of Yang Yin's Manipulation," *The Straits Times*, August 30, 2015, accessed on January 24, 2017, from http://www.straitstimes.com /singapore/courts-crime/the-extent-of-yang-yins-manipulation.

46. Vanessa L. Fong, *Paradise Redefined: Transnational Chinese Students and the Quest for Flexible Citizenship in the Developed World* (Stanford, CA: Stanford University Press, 2011), p. 71. The one-child policy was a family planning policy introduced in 1979 to reduce population growth. It entailed draconian measures and incentives to

deter Chinese families from having large families. The policy was retracted in 2015 as China transitioned into an aging society.

47. Renato Rosaldo, "Cultural Citizenship and Educational Democracy," *Cultural Anthropology* 9, no. 3 (August 1994): 402–411.

48. See Chapter 3 for similar accounts of the Mainland Chinese immigrants in Canada.

49. See Newendorp, *Uneasy Reunions*, on similarities with the new Mainland Chinese immigrants in Hong Kong.

50. Friedman, *Exceptional State*, p. 19.

51. Balibar, *Equaliberty*, p. 201.

52. Ibid.

53. Ibid.

54. Noble, "Cosmopolitan Habits," p. 177.

55. Ibid., p. 163.

56. The normalization of the "CMIO" model in Singapore does not preclude the existence of interethnic tensions in everyday life. As Michael Barr and Jevon Low observe, the multiculturalism model in Singapore can also be interpreted as a mode of assimilation that normalizes Chinese hegemony. See Michael D. Barr and Jevon Low, "Assimilation as Multiracialism: The Case of Singapore's Malays," *Asian Ethnicity* 6, no. 3 (October 2005): 161–182.

57. Filomeno V. Aguilar, *Migration Revolution: Philippine Nationhood and Class Relations in a Globalized Age* (Singapore and Kyoto: NUS Press and Kyoto University Press, 2014), p. 202.

58. Ibid., p. 229.

59. Dauvergne presents a similar account of immigrant hierarchy in her study of the "settler society" (nations built through periods of extensive migration), but her analysis focuses on the multicultural societies of Canada, Australia, and the United States. See Catherine Dauvergne, *The New Politics of Immigration and the End of Settler Societies* (New York: Cambridge University Press, 2016).

60. Mui Teng Yap, "Brain Drain or Links to the World: Views on Emigrants from Singapore," *Asian and Pacific Migration Journal* 3, no. 2–3 (1994): 411–429.

61. The policy researchers surveyed more than two thousand Singaporeans between the ages of nineteen and thirty. See Debbie Soon and Chan-Hoong Leong, "A Study on Emigration Attitudes of Young Singaporeans" (IPS Working Papers No. 19, Institute of Policy Studies, March 2011), accessed on November 13, 2017, from http://lkyspp.nus.edu.sg/ips/publications/working-papers?y=2011.

62. The Singaporean political leadership is concerned that emigration would impact Singapore's future demographic composition, labor force regeneration, and political leadership renewal.

63. Other than the changes to citizenship law, overseas voting was introduced in 2001 and implemented during the general elections of 2006.

64. Jermyn Chow and Amanda Tan, "New York to Draw 4,000 on S'pore Day," *The Straits Times*, April 7, 2012, accessed on January 24, 2017, from http://articles.stclassifieds.sg/travel-and-holiday/new-york-to-draw-4000-on-spore-day/a/60632.

65. An illustrative account of the professional challenges that the Singaporean-Chinese face doing business with their co-ethnics in China can be found in an anonymous autobiography written by one such young Singaporean who worked in China. Titled "Young China Hand" (*zhongguo shou*, meaning an expert on bridging cultural differences in China), the book (even if dramatized for literary effect) resonates with the stories of professional aspirations and culture shock shared with me by Singaporeans who are working or had worked in China before.

66. For example, Fiona Chan, "Creating a More Welcoming Home for All Singaporeans," *The Straits Times*, March 11, 2015, accessed on January 24, 2017, from http://news.asiaone.com/news/singapore/creating-more-welcoming-home-all-singaporeans.

67. Wei Han Wong, "New Panel to Advise MAS on Strategies," *The Straits Times*, July 29, 2015, accessed on January 24, 2017, from http://www.straitstimes.com/business/new-panel-to-advise-mas-on-strategies; Pearl Lee, "Improved Support for Postgrads," *The Straits Times*, August 6, 2015, accessed on January 24, 2017, from http://www.straitstimes.com/singapore/education/improved-support-for-postgrads; Keng Fatt Loh, "Engage Public on Singapore's Maritime Future," *The Straits Times*, November 22, 2015, accessed on January 24, 2017, from http://www.straitstimes.com/singapore/engage-public-on-singapores-maritime-future; Salma Khalik, "Quality of Healthcare 'Not Tied to Workforce Numbers,'" *The Straits Times*, March 2, 2016, accessed on January 24, 2017, from http://www.straitstimes.com/singapore/quality-of-healthcare-not-tied-to-workforce-numbers; Irene Tham, "$120m to Help Arm S'poreans with IT Skills as Demand Rises," *The Straits Times*, April 12, 2016, accessed on January 24, 2017, from http://www.straitstimes.com/singapore/120m-to-help-arm-sporeans-with-it-skills-as-demand-rises.

68. Rainer Bauböck, "The Rights and Duties of External Citizenship," *Citizenship Studies* 13, no. 5 (October 2009): 475–499.

69. Male Singaporean citizens (including those who obtained citizenship by descent) and second-generation permanent residents are required by law to serve two years of national service.

70. The same penalties are enforced for second-generation permanent residents (PRs) who obtained the status through parental descent. They are required to renounce their PR status if they decide not to fulfill their national service duty in Singapore.

71. For example, Melissa Kwok, "Return of the Native," *The Straits Times*, October 23, 2011, accessed on January 24, 2017, from http://sglinks.com/pages/1796908 -return-native-singaporean-home-feels-foreign.

72. Balibar, *Equaliberty*, p. 203.

Chapter 5: China at Home and Abroad

1. Mandarin (*Putonghua*, also known as Standard Chinese) is the official language in China, enabling a shared communication medium in a country where multiple regional dialects exist. A person's intonation of Mandarin can vary by locality. The Beijing dialect is popularly considered the origin of Mandarin.

2. Academic attention normally focuses on the Chinese metropolises of Beijing, Shanghai, and Guangzhou, where foreigners converge for business, work, educational, or marriage purposes. But there exists a range of immigrants in different parts of China. They include "Western" expatriates in Xiamen of Fujian province; "Western" foreign teachers in Shenyang, Liaoning province; African and Indian traders in Yiwu, Zhejiang; Japanese professionals and business personnel in Dalian of Liaoning province; and foreign spouses of interracial marriages in China. For example, Zhigang Li, Laurence J. C. Ma, and Desheng Xue, "An African Enclave in China: The Making of a New Transnational Urban Space," *Eurasian Geography and Economics* 50, no. 6 (2009): 699–719; James Farrer, "From 'Passports' to 'Joint Ventures': Intermarriage Between Chinese Nationals and Western Expatriates Residing in Shanghai," *Asian Studies Review* 32, no. 1 (2008): 7–29; Phiona Stanley, "Superheroes in Shanghai: Constructing Transnational Western Men's Identities," *Gender, Place & Culture* 19, no. 2 (2012): 213–231; Angela Lehman, *Transnational Lives in China: Expatriates in a Globalizing City* (Basingstoke, UK: Palgrave Macmillan, 2014); Eric S. Henry, "Emissaries of the Modern: The Foreign Teacher in Urban China," *City & Society* 25, no. 2 (2013): 216–234; Ka-kin Cheuk, "China," in *Brill's Encyclopedia of Hinduism*, ed. Knut A. Jacobsen, Helene Basu, Angelika Malinar, and Vasudha Narayanan (Leiden, The Netherlands: Brill, 2013), pp. 213–216; Enyu Ma and Adams Bodomo, "We Are What We Eat: Food in the Process of Community Formation and Identity Shaping Among African Traders in Guangzhou and Yiwu," *African Diaspora* 5, no. 1 (2012): 3–26; Kumiko Kawashima, "Service Outsourcing and Labour Mobility in a Digital Age: Transnational Linkages Between Japan and Dalian, China," *Global Networks* 17, no. 4 (2017): 483–499; Pan Wang, *Love and Marriage in Globalizing China* (New York: Routledge, 2014).

3. Rebecca E. Karl, *Staging the World: Chinese Nationalism at the Turn of the Twentieth Century* (Durham, NC: Duke University Press, 2002).

4. Ibid., p. 11.

5. Nina Glick Schiller, "Explanatory Frameworks in Transnational Migration Studies: The Missing Multi-Scalar Global Perspective," *Ethnic and Racial Studies* 38, no. 13 (2015): 2275–2282.

6. Ibid., p. 2280.

7. Chapter 1 identified three key cohorts of Chinese migrants that factor into China's diaspora strategizing: first, the "old diaspora" and Chinese diasporic descendants with foreign nationality status; second, overseas Chinese from the "new diaspora" who have naturalized abroad; and third, overseas Chinese from the "new diaspora" who retain Chinese nationality.

8. See Liu and van Dongen on the "Five Overseas Chinese Structures" that characterize Chinese diaspora engagement on multiple levels of governance, integrating the public and private sectors. Hong Liu and Els van Dongen, "China's Diaspora Policies as a New Mode of Transnational Governance," *Journal of Contemporary China* 25, no. 102 (2016): 805–821.

9. Hong Liu, "An Emerging China and Diasporic Chinese: Historicity, State, and International Relations," *Journal of Contemporary China* 20, no. 72 (November 2011): 813–832.

10. Pál Nyíri, "Chinese Investors, Labour Discipline and Developmental Cosmopolitanism: Chinese Investors in Cambodia," *Development and Change* 44, no. 6 (2013): 1387–1405.

11. Refer to Chapter 1 for discussion of *tianxia* (all-under-heaven).

12. Arif Dirlik, "Chinese History and the Question of Orientalism," *History and Theory* 35, no. 4 (December 1996): 96–118, quotation from p. 98, citing Johannes Fabian, *Time and the Other: How Anthropology Makes Its Object* (New York: Columbia University Press, 1983).

13. Tingyang Zhao, "Rethinking Empire from a Chinese Concept 'All-Under-Heaven' (Tian-Xia)," *Social Identities* 12, no. 1 (January 2006): 29–41; Tingyang Zhao, *Tianxia Tixi: Shijie Zhidu Zhexue Daolun* [The *tianxia* system: An introduction to the philosophy of a world institution] (Beijing: Zhongguo Renmin Daxue Chuban She, 2011); Shan Chun, "On Chinese Cosmopolitanism (Tian Xia)," *Culture Mandala: The Bulletin of the Centre for East-West Cultural and Economic Studies* 8, no. 2 (December 2009): 20–29; Jilin Xu, "Tianxia Zhuyi/Yixia Zhi Bian Ji Qizai Jindai De Bianyi" [Cosmopolitanism, the debate of the civilized and the uncivilized, and their variations in modern times], *Journal of East China Normal University* 44, no. 6 (2012): 66–76; Sang-Jin Han, Young-Hee Shim, and Young-Do Park, "Cosmopolitan Sociology and Confucian Worldview: Beck's Theory in East Asia," *Theory, Culture & Society* 33, no. 7–8 (2016): 281–290.

14. Gerard Delanty and Baogang He, "Cosmopolitan Perspectives on European and Asian Transnationalism," *International Sociology* 23, no. 3 (May 2008): 323–344.

15. Pál Nyíri, "The Yellow Man's Burden: Chinese Migrants on a Civilizing Mission," *The China Journal* 56 (July 2006): 83–106.

16. Aihwa Ong, "Mutations in Citizenship," *Theory, Culture & Society* 23, no. 2–3 (2006): 499–505.

17. National Bureau of Statistics of China, *Major Figures on Residents from Hong Kong, Macao and Taiwan and Foreigners Covered by 2010 Population Census*, April 29, 2011, accessed on December 28, 2016, from http://www.stats.gov.cn/english/NewsEvents /201104/t20110429_26451.html.

18. The same report cites that China had 508,000 international migrants during 2000, excluding those from Hong Kong. United Nations (UN) Department of Economic and Social Affairs, Population Division, *International Migration Report 2015: Highlights*, 2016, accessed on January 3, 2017, from http://www.un.org/en/development /desa/population/migration/publications/migrationreport/docs/MigrationReport2015 _Highlights.pdf.

19. Guofu Liu, "Changing Chinese Migration Law: From Restriction to Relaxation," *Journal of International Migration and Integration* 10, no. 3 (2009): 311–333, quotation from p. 317.

20. They include the Ministry of Foreign Affairs, the Ministry of Public Security, the Ministry of Education, the Ministry of Human Resources and Social Security, the Ministry of Commerce, and the subdivisions or subnational agencies of these ministries.

21. Frank N. Pieke, "Emerging Markets and Migration Policy: China," The Emerging Markets and Migration Policy Publication Series, Center for Migrations and Citizenship, Paris, July 2014, accessed on January 3, 2017, from http://www.ifri.org/sites /default/files/atoms/files/ifri_migrationpolicychina_2.pdf.

22. For example, the Law on the Control of Exit and Entry of Citizens 1985 and the Law on the Control of Entry and Exit of Aliens 1985. These were followed by subsequent migration reforms in 1992, 1996, and 2000.

23. Liu, "Changing Chinese Migration Law."

24. Yan Zhang, "Green Card Threshold Lowered," *China Daily*, June 9, 2015, accessed on January 24, 2017, from http://www.chinadaily.com.cn/china/2015-06/09 /content_20944896.htm.

25. Wang, *Love and Marriage in Globalizing China*.

26. Tabia Bork-Hüffer and Yuan Yuan-Ihle, "The Management of Foreigners in China: Changes to the Migration Law and Regulations During the Late Hu-Wen and Early Xi-Li Eras and Their Potential Effects," *International Journal of China Studies* 5, no. 3 (December 2014): 571–597; Sheng Ding and Rey Koslowski, "Chinese Soft Power and Immigration Reform: Can Beijing's Approach to Pursuing Global Talent and Maintaining Domestic Stability Succeed?," *Journal of Chinese Political Science* 22, no. 1 (2017): 97–116.

27. See the journal special issue edited by Karsten Giese, "Perceptions, Practices and Adaptations: Understanding Chinese–African Interactions in Africa," *Journal of Current Chinese Affairs* 43, no. 1 (2014): 3–8.

28. Richard Aidoo and Steve Hess, "Non-Interference 2.0: China's Evolving Foreign Policy Towards a Changing Africa," *Journal of Current Chinese Affairs* 44, no. 1 (2015): 107–139.

29. Ong, "Mutations in Citizenship."

30. Barry Sautman and Hairong Yan, "African Perspectives on China–Africa Links," *The China Quarterly* 199 (September 2009): 728–759.

31. Nyíri, "The Yellow Man's Burden."

32. Ying Hong Cheng, "From Campus Racism to Cyber Racism: Discourse of Race and Chinese Nationalism," *The China Quarterly* 207 (September 2011): 561–579. But several studies are careful to underscore African agency, conviviality, or cooperation that characterize relations between Chinese migrants and Africans. See Codrin Arsene, "Chinese Employers and Their Ugandan Workers: Tensions, Frictions and Cooperation in an African City," *Journal of Current Chinese Affairs* 43, no. 1 (2014): 139–176; Giles Mohan and Ben Lampert, "Negotiating China: Reinserting African Agency into China–Africa Relations," *African Affairs* 112, no. 446 (2013): 92–110; Cheryl M. T. Schmitz, "Significant Others: Security and Suspicion in Chinese–Angolan Encounters," *Journal of Chinese Current Affairs* 43, no. 1 (2014): 41–69.

33. For examples see Bork-Hüffer and Yuan-Ihle, "The Management of Foreigners in China"; Ma and Bodomo, "We Are What We Eat."

34. Most fund their studies independently but some are scholarship recipients. Scholarships offered by the Chinese state to African students date back to the 1950s, when China sought to secure alliances with African countries against Western imperialism. See Sandra Gillespie, *South–South Transfer: A Study of Sino–African Exchanges* (New York: Routledge, 2001).

35. Ministry of Education of the People's Republic of China, *Nian Quanguo Laihua Liuxuesheng Shuju Fabu* [Statistical report on the number of international students in China 2015], April 14, 2016, accessed on January 3, 2017, from http://www.moe.edu .cn/jyb_xwfb/gzdt_gzdt/s5987/201604/t20160414_238263.html/. Another news report published in *China Daily* states that 27,052 African students studied in China in 2012. Clearly there has been an upward trend in African student enrollment in China. See Wangshu Luo, "African Students Get Real-Life Experience," *China Daily*, March 29, 2013, accessed on January 24, 2017, from http://www.chinadaily.com.cn/china/2013-03 /25/content_16344269.htm.

36. The students recruited in this study self-identified as "African" and came from Benin, Burkina Faso, Congo-Brazzaville, Egypt, Ethiopia, Gabol, Ghana, Guinea, Ivory Coast, Madagascar, Mauritius, Nigeria, Saudi Arabia, Senegal, Seychelles, Somalia, Sudan, Tanzania, Togo, and Zimbabwe. The label "African" glosses over the heterogeneity of the migrants represented in China (e.g., nationality, Anglophone or Francophone,

religious affiliations, and socioeconomic status differences). But this referent contextualizes their migration in geopolitical and economic discourses of China–Africa relations.

37. See Elaine Lynn-Ee Ho, "The Geo-Social and Global Geographies of Power: Urban Aspirations of 'Worlding' African Students in China," *Geopolitics* 22, no. 1 (2017): 15–33.

38. Tim Bunnell, Jamie Gillen, and Elaine Lynn-Ee Ho, "The Prospect of Elsewhere: Engaging the Future Through Aspirations in Asia," *Annals of the Association of American Geographers* 108, no. 1 (2018): 35–51.

39. For example, Heidi Østbø Haugen, "Nigerians in China: A Second State of Immobility," *International Migration* 50, no. 2 (2012): 65–80; Bork-Hüffer and Yuan-Ihle, "The Management of Foreigners in China"; Shanshan Lan, "State Regulation of Undocumented African Migrants in China: A Multi-Scalar Analysis," *Journal of Asian and African Studies* 50, no. 3 (2015): 289–304.

40. Arun Saldanha, "Reontologising Race: The Machinic Geography of Phenotype," *Environment and Planning D: Society and Space* 24, no. 1 (2006): 11.

41. In contrast, "White" foreigners stand out as occidental emblems of development and internationalization, such as featured in advertising, teaching, architecture, company field trips, and other everyday interactions. Henry, "Emissaries of the Modern," p. 230.

42. Anecdotal accounts of the African informants suggest that such incidents were commonplace. However, a few thought that the Chinese who behaved in such a manner were from regions or rural areas where international migrants of a different phenotype were less common. They believed that as China transitions into an immigrant society, the Chinese would become more accustomed to phenotypical difference.

43. Ann Anagnost, "The Corporeal Politics of Quality (*Suzhi*)," *Public Culture* 16, no. 2 (Spring 2004): 190.

44. Zhou, Shenasi, and Xu's study of Chinese-African encounters in Chinese cities shows how unfavorable perceptions can improve over time through positive social encounters. Roberto Castillo adds that precarity contributes to building solidarity and support networks among the African migrants. Nonetheless, social prejudice remains an issue. Min Zhou, Shabnam Shenasi, and Tao Xu, "Chinese Attitudes Toward African Migrants in Guangzhou, China," *International Journal of Sociology* 46, no. 2 (2016): 141–161; Roberto Castillo, "'Homing' Guangzhou: Emplacement, Belonging and Precarity Among Africans in China," *International Journal of Cultural Studies* 19, no. 3 (2016): 287–306.

45. Aihwa Ong, *Neoliberalism as Exception: Mutations in Citizenship and Sovereignty* (Durham, NC: Duke University Press, 2006), p. 1377.

46. The film star is of Korean rather than Chinese ethnicity.

47. Nicole DeJong Newendorp, *Uneasy Reunions: Immigration, Citizenship, and Family Life in Post-1997 Hong Kong* (Stanford, CA: Stanford University Press, 2008); Cathryn H. Clayton, *Sovereignty at the Edge: Macau and the Question of Chineseness*

(Cambridge, MA: Harvard University Press, 2009); Sara Friedman, *Exceptional States: Chinese Immigrants and Taiwanese Sovereignty* (Oakland: University of California Press, 2015).

48. Trade and labor migrants moved to Burma from China or via Southeast Asia by land or coastal routes. Another group of migrants are the Kuomintang insurgents who fled by land to neighboring Burma after being defeated by the communists in 1949. See Wen-Chien Chang, *Beyond Borders: Stories of Yunnanese Chinese Migrants of Burma* (Ithaca, NY: Cornell University Press, 2014); Elaine Lynn-Ee Ho and Lynette J. Chua, "Law and 'Race' in the Citizenship Spaces of Myanmar: Spatial Strategies and the Political Subjectivity of the Burmese Chinese," *Ethnic and Racial Studies* 39, no. 5 (2016): 896–916; Jayde Lin Roberts, *Mapping Chinese Rangoon: Place and Nation Among the Sino-Burmese* (Seattle: University of Washington Press, 2016).

49. This chapter will not discuss the co-ethnic tensions in Hong Kong or Macau as these are now considered Special Administrative Regions of China (i.e., part of its geopolitical unit). A different migration administrative framework is used to regulate the entry of Chinese diasporic descendants who are considered immigrants of foreign nationality status.

50. Brenda S. A. Yeoh and Katie Willis, "Singapore Unlimited: Configuring Social Identity in the Regionalisation Process," Transnational Communities Programme, University of Oxford, 1998, accessed on December 28, 2016, from http://www.transcomm.ox.ac.uk/working%20papers/nottitc.pdf.

51. Ibid., p. 17.

52. Chapter 4 also discussed the cognitive bordering processes and moral framings that the Singaporean-Chinese deploy to differentiate themselves from the new Chinese immigrants (*xinyimin*) in Singapore or the domestic Mainland Chinese they met in China.

53. Sandro Mezzadra and Brett Nielson, *Border as Method, or, the Multiplication of Labor* (Durham, NC: Duke University Press, 2013).

54. Ping Lin, "Chinese Diaspora 'At Home': Mainlander Taiwanese in Dongguan and Shanghai," *The China Review* 11, no. 2 (Fall 2011): 43–64.

55. Ibid., p. 55.

56. Dirlik, "Chinese History and the Question of Orientalism."

57. Shelly Chan, "The Case for Diaspora: A Temporal Approach to the Chinese Experience," *Journal of Asian Studies* 74, no. 1 (2015): 107–128.

58. Ong, *Neoliberalism as Exception*.

59. Ibid.

60. Nyíri, "Chinese Investors, Labour Discipline and Developmental Cosmopolitanism"; Ho and Chua, "Law and 'Race' in the Citizenship Spaces of Myanmar"; Roberts, *Mapping Chinese Rangoon*.

61. Thomas S. Mullaney, *Coming to Terms with the Nation: Ethnic Classification in Modern China* (Berkeley: University of California Press, 2011); Ke Fan, "Representation of Ethnic Minorities in Socialist China," *Ethnic and Racial Studies* 39, no. 12 (2016): 2091–2107.

62. Western-trained scholars argue that the Chinese state legitimizes its control of ethnic minority regions by portraying ethnic minority groups as primitive, exotic, or promiscuous. China-trained scholars published counterarguments critiquing such Western interpretations as attempts to entrench negative perceptions of China. The distinction between "Western-trained" and "China-trained" scholars used here loosely demarcates the academic influences and ideological leanings of the two camps. In reality, educational stints abroad and scholarly exchanges on both sides mean there is considerable ambiguity over how one's academic background is defined. For example, Frank Dikötter, *The Discourse of Race in Modern China* (London: Hurst, 1992); Dru C. Gladney, "Representing Nationality in China: Refiguring Majority/Minority Identities," *Journal of Asian Studies* 53, no. 1 (February 1994): 92–123; Tim Oakes, "Bathing in the Far Village: Globalization, Transnational Capital, and the Cultural Politics of Modernity in China," *Positions: East Asia Cultures Critique* 7, no. 2 (Fall 1999): 307–342; Pan Jiao, "Deconstructing China's Ethnic Minorities: Deorientalization or Reorientalization?," *Chinese Sociology & Anthropology* 42, no. 4 (Summer 2010): 46–61.

63. Chris Vasantkumar, "What Is This 'Chinese' in Overseas Chinese? Sojourn Work and the Place of China's Minority Nationalities in Extraterritorial Chinese-ness," *Journal of Asian Studies* 71, no. 2 (2012): 423–446.

64. On the international dimensions that impact the Chinese state's relations with ethnic minority groups such as the Dai, Korean-Chinese, Mongols, Tibetans, and Uyghurs, see Enze Han, who argues that the support of external kin-states augments domestic demands for separatism from China. Enze Han, *Contestation and Adaptation: The Politics of National Identity in China* (New York: Oxford University Press, 2013).

65. Muslim students of ethnic minority backgrounds in China choose Arab or Southeast Asian countries where Islam is widely practiced. Other Muslims also go to these countries for trade. For Malaysia, see Diana Wong and Pei Wen Ooi, "The Globalization of Tertiary Education and Intra-Asian Student Mobility: Mainland Chinese Student Mobility to Malaysia," *Asian and Pacific Migration Journal* 22, no. 1 (2013): 55–76; Chow Bing Ngeow and Hailong Ma, "More Islamic, No Less Chinese: Explorations into Overseas Chinese Muslim Identities in Malaysia," *Ethnic and Racial Studies* 39, no. 12 (2016): 2108–2128. For Sino–Arab connections, see Wai Yip Ho, "Mobilizing the Muslim Minority for China's Development: Hui Muslims, Ethnic Relations and Sino–Arab Connections," *Journal of Comparative Asian Development* 12, no. 1 (2013): 84–112.

66. This group of ethnic minority diasporic descendants are from neighboring states in Central Asia, South Asia, East Asia, and Southeast Asia.

67. Elena Barabantseva, "Who Are 'Overseas Chinese Ethnic Minorities'? China's Search for Transnational Ethnic Unity," *Modern China* 38, no. 1 (January 2012): 78–109.

68. The "New Silk Road" (also known as One Belt, One Road) refers to China's ambitious land and maritime plans to develop new trading routes through infrastructure investment that will link the country with Central Asia, Europe, Southeast Asia, and Africa. The development plans involve autonomous regions in China that are populated by ethnic minority groups such as the Hui in Ningxia and Uyghurs in Xinjiang (both are Muslims), leading to suspicions that the New Silk Road is meant to weaken ethnic minority power.

69. Ho, "Mobilizing the Muslim Minority for China's Development," p. 107.

70. Vasantkumar, "What Is This 'Chinese' in Overseas Chinese?"

71. Elena Barabantseva, *Overseas Chinese, Ethnic Minorities and Nationalism: Decentering China* (New York: Routledge, 2011).

72. Ibid.; Ngeow and Ma, "More Islamic, No Less Chinese."

73. Barabantseva, *Overseas Chinese, Ethnic Minorities and Nationalism*; Vasantkumar, "What Is This 'Chinese' in Overseas Chinese?"

74. Barabantseva, *Overseas Chinese, Ethnic Minorities and Nationalism*, p. 84.

75. Vasantkumar, "What Is This 'Chinese' in Overseas Chinese?," p. 423.

76. Barabantseva, *Overseas Chinese, Ethnic Minorities and Nationalism*. The Dungans are based in Central Asian countries that share a border with China. Dungan identity consists of Hui Chinese, Central Asian, and Russian influences.

77. Emile K. K. Yeoh, "From Dungans to Xinyimin: China, Chinese Migration and the Changing Sociopolitical Fabric of Central Asian Republics," *Contemporary Chinese Political Economy and Strategic Relations: An International Journal* 1, no. 2 (August 2015): 87–245.

Chapter 6: Contemporaneous Migration

1. Jørgen Carling and Kerilyn Schewel, "Revisiting Aspiration and Ability in International Migration," *Journal of Ethnic and Migration Studies* 44, no. 6 (2017): 945–963.

2. Arjun Appadurai, "The Capacity to Aspire: Culture and the Terms of Recognition," in *Culture and Public Action*, ed. Vijayendra Rao and Michael Walton (Stanford, CA: Stanford University Press, 2004), pp. 59–84.

3. Amartya Kumar Sen, *Development as Freedom* (New York: Anchor Books, 2000); Martha Craven Nussbaum, *Creating Capabilities: The Human Development Approach* (Cambridge, MA: Belknap Press of Harvard University Press, 2011); Vanessa L. Fong, *Paradise Redefined: Transnational Chinese Students and the Quest for Flexible Citizenship in the Developed World* (Stanford, CA: Stanford University Press, 2011).

4. Rainer Bauböck, "Studying Citizenship Constellations," *Journal of Ethnic and Migration Studies* 36, no. 5 (May 2010): 847–859.

5. This observation extends to other country examples too. For re-migration of Greek diasporic descendants from Germany and America, see Russell King and Anastasia Christou, "Second-Generation 'Return' to Greece: New Dynamics of Trans-nationalism and Integration," *International Migration* 52, no. 6 (December 2014): 85–99. For re-migration of "heritage migrants" of various ethnicities to South Africa, see Melissa Tandiwe Myambo, "Frontier Heritage Migration in the Global Ethnic Economy," *Public Culture* 29, no. 2/82 (May 2017): 261–285.

6. Janine Dahinden, "A Plea for the 'De-Migranticization' of Research on Migration and Integration," *Ethnic and Racial Studies* 39, no. 13 (2016): 2207–2225.

7. For Japan and Korea, see Eleana Jean Kim, *Adopted Territory: Transnational Korean Adoptees and the Politics of Belonging* (Durham, NC: Duke University Press, 2010); Caren Freeman, *Making and Faking Kinship: Marriage and Labor Migration Between China and South Korea* (Ithaca, NY: Cornell University Press, 2011); Jane H. Yamashiro, "Working Towards Conceptual Consistency in Discussing 'Diaspora' and 'Diaspora Strategies': Ethnicity and Affinity in the Case of Japan," *Geoforum* 59 (2015): 178–186. For Greece, see Anastasia Christou and Russell King, *Counter-Diaspora: The Greek Second Generation Returns "Home"* (Cambridge, MA: Harvard University Press, 2015). For Ireland, see Mary Gilmartin, "Changing Ireland, 2000–2012: Immigration, Emigration and Inequality," *Irish Geography* 46, no. 1–2 (2013): 91–111. For Germany, Sweden, Russia, and the former Soviet nations, see Takeyuki Tsuda, ed., *Diasporic Homecomings: Ethnic Return Migration in Comparative Perspective* (Stanford, CA: Stanford University Press, 2009). For Israel, see Nir Cohen, "Come Home, Be Professional: Ethno-Nationalism and Economic Rationalism in Israel's Return Migration Strategy," *Immigrants & Minorities* 27, no. 1 (March 2009): 1–28.

8. Filomeno V. Aguilar, *Migration Revolution: Philippine Nationhood and Class Relations in a Globalized Age* (Singapore and Kyoto: NUS Press and Kyoto University Press, 2014); Sin Yee Koh, "State-Led Talent Return Migration Programme and the Doubly Neglected 'Malaysian Diaspora': Whose Diaspora, What Citizenship, Whose Development?," *Singapore Journal of Tropical Geography* 36, no. 2 (July 2015): 183–200.

9. As Ayse Çağlar observes, placing migrants and alleged "natives" in different temporal frames results in "a denial of coevalness [that] disregards the experiences, norms and values [which] migrants and the natives share." Ayse Çağlar, "Still 'Migrants' After All Those Years: Foundational Mobilities, Temporal Frames and Emplacement of Migrants," *Journal of Ethnic and Migration Studies* 42, no. 6 (May 2016): 952–969.

10. For labor migration see Frank N. Pieke, ed., *Transnational Chinese: Fujianese Migrants in Europe* (Stanford, CA: Stanford University Press, 2004). For educational and skilled migration, see Fong, *Paradise Redefined*, and Xiang Biao, "A Ritual Economy of 'Talent': China and Overseas Chinese Professionals," *Journal of Ethnic and Migration Studies* 37, no. 5 (May 2011): 821–838. For new Chinese migration to Southeast Asia and Africa, see Pál Nyíri, "Chinese Investors, Labour Discipline and Developmental

Cosmopolitanism: Chinese Investors in Cambodia," *Development and Change* 44, no. 6 (2013): 1387–1405; and Karsten Giese, "Perceptions, Practices and Adaptations: Understanding Chinese–African Interactions in Africa," *Journal of Current Chinese Affairs* 43, no. 1 (2014): 3–8. For ethnic minority emigration from China, see Elena Barabantseva, "Who Are 'Overseas Chinese Ethnic Minorities?' China's Search for Transnational Ethnic Unity," *Modern China* 38, no. 1 (January 2012): 78–109; and Chris Vasantkumar, "What Is This 'Chinese' in Overseas Chinese? Sojourn Work and the Place of China's Minority Nationalities in Extraterritorial Chinese-ness," *Journal of Asian Studies* 71, no. 2 (2012): 423–446.

11. Gungwu Wang, *Chinese Overseas: From Earthbound China to the Quest for Autonomy* (Cambridge, MA: Harvard University Press, 2000).

12. Gerard Delanty and Baogang He, "Cosmopolitan Perspectives on European and Asian Transnationalism," *International Sociology* 23, no. 3 (May 2008): 323–344; Shan Chun, "On Chinese Cosmopolitanism (Tian Xia)," *Culture Mandala: The Bulletin of the Centre for East-West Cultural and Economic Studies* 8, no. 2 (December 2009): 20–29; Jilin Xu, "Tianxia Zhuyi/Yixia Zhi Bian Ji Qizai Jindai De Bianyi" [Cosmopolitanism, the debate of the civilized and the uncivilized, and their variations in modern times], *Journal of East China Normal University* 44, no. 6 (2012): 66–76; Sang-Jin Han, Young-Hee Shim, and Young-Do Park, "Cosmopolitan Sociology and Confucian Worldview: Beck's Theory in East Asia," *Theory, Culture & Society* 33, no. 7–8 (2016): 281–290.

13. Barabantseva suggests that the worldview of *tianxia* is one of several narratives through which China sees the world and its place in the world. She proposes *shijie* (the world) as a different vision promoted by the Chinese state that connotes "a world of relations always in the making where people experience the world in a variety of ways." Barabantseva, "Change vs. Order: *Shijie* Meets *Tianxia* in China's Interactions with the World," *Alternatives: Global, Local, Political* 34, no. 2 (2009): 129–155, quotation from p. 135. Compared to the hierarchal ordering connoted by *tianxia*, the notion of *shijie* is closer to cosmopolitan thought (*shijie zhuyi*). In her view, *tianxia* and *shijie* are not antithetical but can coexist in reflecting China's different ways of engaging with the world. Nonetheless, a realist reading of *shijie* would maintain that it functions as a mode of soft power for China by reinforcing its worldview of *tianxia*, which connotes a central source of authority with Chinese ethnocentrism at its core.

14. Nina Glick Schiller, "Situating Identities: Towards an Identities Studies Without Binaries of Difference," *Identities* 19, no. 4 (July 2012): 520–532.

15. Pietro Calogero, "Kabul Cosmopolitan: Geopolitical Empire from the Planner's Viewpoint," *Planning Theory* 10, no. 1 (February 2011): 66–78, quotation from p. 67, citing Chantal Mouffe's version of agonism as applied to cosmopolitanism: Chantal Mouffe, *The Return of the Political* (London: Verso, 1993).

16. Saranindranath Tagore, "Tagore's Conception of Cosmopolitanism: A Reconstruction," *University of Toronto Quarterly* 77, no. 4 (Fall 2008): 1070–1084, quotation from p. 1081.

17. Michael Burawoy, *The Extended Case Method: Four Countries, Four Decades, Four Great Transformations, and One Theoretical Tradition* (Berkeley: University of California Press, 1997); Anna Lowenhaupt Tsing, *Friction: An Ethnography of Global Connection* (Princeton, NJ: Princeton University Press, 2005).

18. AbdouMaliq Simone, *For the City Yet to Come: Changing African Life in Four Cities* (Durham, NC: Duke University Press, 2004), p. 17.

Glossary

Bairen Jihua	The "100 Talents" program.
Bumiputra	Malaysian policy that privileges the indigenous Malays.
Chayi	Disjuncture.
Da jiazu	Extended family.
Datongshu	Kang Youwei's philosophical treatise of "One World," under which darker races were considered unequal.
Fazhan guojia	Developed country.
Fei Cheng Wu Rao	Title of a dating game show in China (also known as *The One and Only*).
Fuza	Complicated.
Gaolao huanxiang	To spend one's golden years in China.
Gongmin	Citizens.
Guiguo nanqiao	Refugee-returnees.
Guiqiao	Returnee or return migrant in China (also see *huiliu zhongguo huaren*).
Guiqiao Qiaojuan Quanyi Baohu Fa	Law of the People's Republic of China on the Protection of the Rights and Interests of Returned Overseas Chinese and the Family Members of Overseas Chinese.
Guomin	Nationals.
Haigui	Translated as "sea turtles," this phrase is used in popular parlance to describe the overseas Chinese

	students or professionals who have returned to China. This category of returnees retain their Chinese nationality status (compare with *haiou*).
Haiou	Translated as "seagulls," this phrase is used in popular parlance to describe the overseas Chinese who have given up their Chinese nationality status to naturalize abroad but subsequently decided to return to China (also see *waiji huaren* or *waiji renyuan*).
Haiwai xuezhe	A specific cohort of overseas Chinese courted by the Chinese state for the intellectual or scientific knowledge they embody.
Heigui	Translated as "black ghost," this phrase is used in popular parlance to refer derogatorily to Africans as dark-skinned persons.
Hongweibing	Communist Red Guards.
Huaqiao	Overseas Chinese who consider China the natal land (also used to describe first-generation emigrants).
Huaqiao nongchang	State-owned farms established to resettle the voluntary and involuntary migrants who re-migrated to China during the period from 1949 to 1979.
Huaqiao Shiwu Weiyuanhui	Overseas Chinese Affairs Commission, predating the *Qiaoban*. Also known as the Overseas Chinese Affairs Office (OCAO).
Huaren	Persons of Chinese ethnicity.
Huayi	Chinese diasporic descendants who consider a country other than China their natal land and with nationality status outside of China.
Huiliu zhongguo huaren	Refers to persons of Chinese ethnicity who have returned or re-migrated to China.
Hukou	Household registration system.
Jingying	Cream of the crop.
Jishu yimin	Skilled migrant.
Jus sanguinis	Inheritance of nationality by bloodline.
Kristang	Creole language bearing Portuguese and Malay influences.

Kuajing minzu	Cross-border ethnic minority groups.
Laodong guannian	A "laboring outlook."
Lao xinyimin	An emic label that refers to Chinese migrants who left China soon after 1979 and settled in another country earlier than subsequent emigrants from China. They emigrated when China was a low-income developing country, and consider their personal wealth and family backgrounds to be less privileged than later cohorts of Chinese emigrants (compare with *xin xinyimin*).
Lihai	Formidable.
Longgyi	A roll of fabric wrapped and knotted around the waist securely to cover the lower body, as used in Myanmar.
Minzu	Refers to ethnicity but connotes "nationality" as used in China. The fifty-six ethnic groups in China are referred to as *minzu*.
Nanqiao	Refugee.
Nanyang	South China Sea.
Putonghua	Mandarin, the official language of China.
Qianren Jihua	The "1000 Talents" program.
Qiaoban (or *Qiaowu Bangongshi*)	Overseas Chinese Affairs Office (OCAO).
Qiaojuan	Dependents of overseas Chinese.
Qiaolian	All-China Federation of Returned Overseas Chinese.
Qiaosheng	Students who returned to China in the 1950s.
Qiaowu	Overseas Chinese affairs or policies and programs concerning the Chinese abroad.
Renmin	People.
Sanju huaren	Chinese diaspora (in China it is substituted with *huaqiao*, although the latter term connotes natal ties).
Shaoshu Minzu Huaqiao Huaren	Ethnic Minority Overseas Chinese.
Shijie	The world.
Shijie zhuyi	Cosmopolitan thought.
Shimin	Citizens.

Shou	Longevity.
Suzhi	A catch-all phrase used in China to refer to a person's "quality" or value, which can encompass cultural traits, consumption practices, social distinctions, human capital, and other attributes.
Tianxia	A Chinese geographical worldview known as "all-under-heaven."
Touzi yimin	Investor migrant.
Tuhao	The "crass rich."
Waiji huaren	Persons of Chinese ethnicity with foreign nationality status. It includes both the overseas Chinese who have naturalized abroad (see *haiou*) and Chinese diasporic descendants (see *huayi*).
Waiji renyuan	Persons of foreign nationality (regardless of their ethnic backgrounds).
Weiguo fuwu	Service to the country.
Xinfu	The "new rich."
Xinyimin	"New Chinese immigrants" who left China after 1979.
Xin xinyimin	An emic label that refers to Chinese migrants who left China after 1979 and when China had transitioned to a middle-income developing country. Their personal wealth and family backgrounds tend to be more privileged than an earlier cohort of Chinese migrants that left China when it was still a low-income developing country (compare with *lao xinyimin*).
Xuetong zhuyi	*Jus sanguinis* or nationality inheritance by bloodline.
Yangguizi	"Foreign devils"—white Westerners.
You wenhua	More "cultured."
Zhongdeng yimin	"Middling migrants" or migrants who belong neither to the high-skilled or low-skilled categories.
Zhongguo shou	"China Hand," an expert on bridging cultural differences.
Zhonghua minzu	The Chinese nation.
Zhonghua Renmin Gonghe Guo Churu Jing Guanli Fa	1985 Law of the People's Republic of China on the Administration of the Exit and Entry of Citizens.

Bibliography

Abraham, Itty. *How India Became Territorial: Foreign Policy, Diaspora, Geopolitics.* Stanford, CA: Stanford University Press, 2014.

Ackers, Louise. "Citizenship, Migration and the Valuation of Care in the European Union." *Journal of Ethnic and Migration Studies* 30, no. 2 (2004): 373–396.

Aguilar, Filomeno V. *Migration Revolution: Philippine Nationhood and Class Relations in a Globalized Age.* Singapore and Kyoto: NUS Press and Kyoto University Press, 2014.

Aidoo, Richard, and Steve Hess. "Non-Interference 2.0: China's Evolving Foreign Policy Towards a Changing Africa." *Journal of Current Chinese Affairs* 44, no. 1 (2015): 107–139.

Amin, Ash. *Land of Strangers.* Cambridge: Polity Press, 2012.

———. "Regions Unbound: Towards a New Politics of Place." *Geografiska Annaler: Series B, Human Geography* 86, no. 1 (March 2004): 33–44.

Anagnost, Ann. "The Corporeal Politics of Quality (*Suzhi*)." *Public Culture* 16, no. 2 (Spring 2004): 189–208.

Ang, Ien. "Together-in-Difference: Beyond Diaspora, into Hybridity." *Asian Studies Review* 27, no. 2 (June 2003): 141–154.

Appadurai, Arjun. "The Capacity to Aspire: Culture and the Terms of Recognition." In *Culture and Public Action*, edited by Vijayendra Rao and Michael Walton, pp. 59–84. Stanford, CA: Stanford University Press, 2004.

Arsene, Codrin. "Chinese Employers and Their Ugandan Workers: Tensions, Frictions and Cooperation in an African City." *Journal of Current Chinese Affairs* 43, no. 1 (2014): 139–176.

Balibar, Etienne. "Difference, Otherness, Exclusion." *Parallax* 11, no. 1 (2005): 19–34.

———. *Equaliberty: Political Essays.* Durham, NC: Duke University Press, 2014.

———. "The 'Impossible' Community of the Citizens: Past and Present Problems." *Environment and Planning D: Society and Space* 30, no. 3 (2012): 437–449.

———. "Is There a Neo-Racism?" In *Race, Nation, Class: Ambiguous Identities*, edited by Etienne Balibar and Immanuel Wallerstein, pp. 17–28. London: Verso, 1991.

———. "Strangers as Enemies: Further Reflections on the Aporias of Transnational Citizenship." Globalisation Working Papers 06/04, Institute on Globalization and the Human Condition, Hamilton, ON, May 2006.

Barabantseva, Elena. "Change vs. Order: *Shijie* Meets *Tianxia* in China's Interactions with the World." *Alternatives: Global, Local, Political* 34, no. 2 (2009): 129–155.

———. *Overseas Chinese, Ethnic Minorities and Nationalism: De-centering China.* New York: Routledge, 2011.

———. "Trans-nationalising Chineseness: Overseas Chinese Policies of the PRC's Central Government." *Asien* 96 (July 2005): 7–28.

———. "Who Are 'Overseas Chinese Ethnic Minorities'? China's Search for Transnational Ethnic Unity." *Modern China* 38, no. 1 (January 2012): 78–109.

Barker, Joshua, Erik Harms, and Johan Lindquist, eds. *Figures of Southeast Asian Modernity.* Honolulu: University of Hawai'i Press, 2014.

Barr, Michael D., and Jevon Low. "Assimilation as Multiracialism: The Case of Singapore's Malays." *Asian Ethnicity* 6, no. 3 (October 2005): 161–182.

Barry, Kim. "Home and Away: The Construction of Citizenship in an Emigration Context." *New York University Law Review* 81, no. 1 (April 2006): 11–59.

Basch, Linda G., Nina Glick Schiller, and Cristina Szanton Blanc. *Nations Unbound: Transnational Projects, Postcolonial Predicaments, and Deterritorialized Nation-States.* New York: Gordon and Breach, 1994.

Bauböck, Rainer. "The Rights and Duties of External Citizenship." *Citizenship Studies* 13, no. 5 (October 2009): 475–499.

———. "Studying Citizenship Constellations." *Journal of Ethnic and Migration Studies* 36, no. 5 (May 2010): 847–859.

———. *Transnational Citizenship: Membership and Rights in International Migration.* Aldershot, UK: Edward Elgar, 1994.

Bauböck, Rainer, and Virginie Guiraudon. "Introduction: Realignments of Citizenship: Reassessing Rights in the Age of Plural Memberships and Multi-Level Governance." *Citizenship Studies* 13, no. 5 (October 2009): 439–450.

Biao, Xiang. "Emigration from China: A Sending Country Perspective." *International Migration* 41, no. 3 (2003): 21–48.

———. "A Ritual Economy of 'Talent': China and Overseas Chinese Professionals." *Journal of Ethnic and Migration Studies* 37, no. 5 (May 2011): 821–838.

Bitran, Maurice, and Serene Tan. "Diaspora Nation: An Inquiry into the Economic Potential of Diaspora Networks in Canada." Mowat Centre for Policy Innovation,

Toronto, September 2013. Accessed on November 13, 2017, from https://mowatcentre.ca/diaspora-nation/.

Bork-Hüffer, Tabea, and Yuan Yuan-Ihle. "The Management of Foreigners in China: Changes to the Migration Law and Regulations During the Late Hu-Wen and Early Xi-Li Eras and Their Potential Effects." *International Journal of China Studies* 5, no. 3 (December 2014): 571–597.

Boyle, Mark, and Elaine Lynn-Ee Ho. "Sovereign Power, Biopower, and the Reach of the West in an Age of Diaspora-Centred Development." *Antipode* 49, no. 3 (June 2017): 577–596.

Boyle, Mark, and Rob Kitchin. "Diaspora-Centred Development: Current Practice, Critical Commentaries, and Research Priorities." In *Global Diasporas and Development: Socioeconomic, Cultural, and Policy Perspectives*, edited by Sadananda Sahoo and B. K. Pattanaik, pp. 17–37. New Delhi: Springer, 2014.

Brah, Avtar. *Cartographies of Diaspora: Contesting Identities.* New York: Routledge, 1998.

Brand, Laurie A. "Arab Uprisings and the Changing Frontiers of Transnational Citizenship: Voting from Abroad in Political Transitions." *Political Geography* 41 (July 2014): 54–63.

Brodie, Janine. "The Social in Social Citizenship." In *Recasting the Social in Citizenship*, edited by Engin F. Isin, pp. 20–43. Toronto: University of Toronto Press, 2008.

Bunnell, Tim, Jamie Gillen, and Elaine Lynn-Ee Ho. "The Prospect of Elsewhere: Engaging the Future Through Aspirations in Asia." *Annals of the Association of American Geographers* 108, no. 1 (2018): 35–51.

Burawoy, Michael. *The Extended Case Method: Four Countries, Four Decades, Four Great Transformations, and One Theoretical Tradition.* Berkeley: University of California Press, 1997.

Çağlar, Ayse. "Still 'Migrants' After All Those Years: Foundational Mobilities, Temporal Frames and Emplacement of Migrants." *Journal of Ethnic and Migration Studies* 42, no. 6 (May 2016): 952–969.

Callahan, William A. "Beyond Cosmopolitanism and Nationalism: Diasporic Chinese and Neo-Nationalism in China and Thailand." *International Organization* 57, no. 3 (Summer 2003): 481–517.

———. "Chinese Visions of World Order: Post-Hegemonic or a New Hegemony?" *International Studies Review* 10, no. 4 (December 2008): 749.

———. "Sino-Speak: Chinese Exceptionalism and the Politics of History." *Journal of Asian Studies* 71, no. 1 (February 2012): 33–55.

Calogero, Pietro. "Kabul Cosmopolitan: Geopolitical Empire from the Planner's Viewpoint." *Planning Theory* 10, no. 1 (February 2011): 66–78.

Carling, Jørgen, and Kerilyn Schewel. "Revisiting Aspiration and Ability in International Migration." *Journal of Ethnic and Migration Studies* 44, no. 6 (2017): 945–963.

Castillo, Roberto. "'Homing' Guangzhou: Emplacement, Belonging and Precarity Among Africans in China." *International Journal of Cultural Studies* 19, no. 3 (2016): 287–306.

Chan, Fiona. "Creating a More Welcoming Home for All Singaporeans." *The Straits Times*, March 11, 2015. Accessed on January 24, 2017, from http://news.asiaone.com /news/singapore/creating-more-welcoming-home-all-singaporeans.

Chan, Kam Wing. "China's Urbanisation 2020: A New Blueprint and Direction." *Eurasian Geography and Economics* 55, no. 1 (2014): 1–9.

Chan, Shelly. "The Case for Diaspora: A Temporal Approach to the Chinese Experience." *Journal of Asian Studies* 74, no. 1 (2015): 107–128.

———. "The Disobedient Diaspora: Overseas Chinese Students in Mao's China, 1958–66." *Journal of Chinese Overseas* 10, no. 2 (2014): 220–238.

Chang, Wen-Chien. *Beyond Borders: Stories of Yunnanese Chinese Migrants of Burma.* Ithaca, NY: Cornell University Press, 2014.

Cheah, Pheng. "Cosmopolitanism." *Theory, Culture and Society* 23, no. 2–3 (May 2006): 486–496.

Chen, Yun-Chung. "The Limits of Brain Circulation: Chinese Returnees and Technological Development in Beijing." *Pacific Affairs* 81, no. 2 (Summer 2008): 195–215.

Cheng, Xi. "The 'Distinctiveness' of the Overseas Chinese as Perceived in the People's Republic of China." In *Beyond Chinatown: New Chinese Migration and the Global Expansion of China*, edited by Mette Thunø, pp. 49–64. Copenhagen: NIAS Press, 2007.

Cheng, Ying Hong. "From Campus Racism to Cyber Racism: Discourse of Race and Chinese Nationalism." *The China Quarterly* 207 (Septemeber 2011): 561–579.

Cheuk, Ka-kin. "China." In *Brill's Encyclopedia of Hinduism*, edited by Knut A. Jacobsen, Helene Basu, Angelika Malinar, and Vasudha Narayanan, pp. 213–216. Leiden, The Netherlands: Brill, 2013.

Chow, Jermyn, and Amanda Tan. "New York to Draw 4,000 on S'pore Day." *The Straits Times*, April 7, 2012. Accessed on January 24, 2017, from http://articles.stclassifieds .sg/travel-and-holiday/new-york-to-draw-4000-on-spore-day/a/60632.

Christou, Anastasia, and Russell King. *Counter-Diaspora: The Greek Second Generation Returns "Home."* Cambridge, MA: Harvard University Press, 2015.

Chua, Beng Huat. *Communitarian Ideology and Democracy in Singapore*. London: Routledge, 1995.

Chun, Shan. "On Chinese Cosmopolitanism (Tian Xia)." *Culture Mandala: The Bulletin of the Centre for East-West Cultural and Economic Studies* 8, no. 2 (December 2009): 20–29.

Clayton, Cathryn H. *Sovereignty at the Edge: Macau and the Question of Chineseness.* Cambridge, MA: Harvard University Press, 2009.

Closs Stephens, Angharad, and Vicki Squire. "Politics Through a Web: Citizenship and Community Unbound." *Environment and Planning D: Society and Space* 30, no. 3 (2012): 551–567.

Cohen, Nir. "Come Home, Be Professional: Ethno-Nationalism and Economic Rationalism in Israel's Return Migration Strategy." *Immigrants & Minorities* 27, no. 1 (March 2009): 1–28.

Collyer, Michael. "A Geography of Extra-Territorial Citizenship: Explanations of External Voting." *Migration Studies* 2, no. 1 (March 2014): 55–72.

Collyer, Michael, and Russell King. "Producing Transnational Space: International Migration and the Extra-Territorial Reach of State Power." *Progress in Human Geography* 39, no. 2 (2015): 185–204.

Conradson, David, and Alan Latham. "Transnational Urbanism: Attending to Everyday Practices and Mobilities." *Journal of Ethnic and Migration Studies* 31, no. 2 (March 2005): 227–233.

Constable, Nicole. *Born Out of Place: Migrant Mothers and the Politics of International Labor.* Berkeley: University of California Press, 2014.

Conway, Dennis, and Robert B. Potter. "Return of the Next Generations: Transnational Migration and Development in the 21st Century." In *Return Migration of the Next Generations: 21st Century Transnational Mobility*, edited by Dennis Conway and Robert B. Potter, pp. 1–16. Farnham, UK: Ashgate, 2009.

Coutin, Susan Bibler. "Confined Within: National Territories as Zones of Confinement." *Political Geography* 29 (2010): 200–208.

——. *Nations of Emigrants: Shifting Boundaries of Citizenship in El Salvador and the United States.* Ithaca, NY: Cornell University Press, 2007.

Crang, Mike. "Rhythms of the City: Temporalised Space and Motion." In *TimeSpace: Geographies of Temporality*, edited by Jon May and Nigel Thrift, pp. 187–207. London: Routledge, 2001.

Cwerner, Saulo B. "The Times of Migration." *Journal of Ethnic and Migration Studies* 27, no. 1 (January 2001): 7–36.

Dahinden, Janine. "A Plea for the 'De-Migranticization' of Research on Migration and Integration." *Ethnic and Racial Studies* 39, no. 13 (2016): 2207–2225.

Dauvergne, Catherine. *The New Politics of Immigration and the End of Settler Societies.* New York: Cambridge University Press, 2016.

Davin, Della. *Internal Migration in Contemporary China.* New York: St. Martin's Press, 1999.

Dear, Michael, and Gustavo Leclerc. *Postborder City: Cultural Spaces of Bajalta California.* New York: Routledge, 2003.

Delano, Alexandra. "Immigrant Integration vs. Transnational Ties? The Role of the Sending State." *Social Research: An International Quarterly* 77, no. 1 (2010): 237–268.

———. *Mexico and Its Diaspora in the United States: Policies of Emigration Since 1848.* New York: Cambridge University Press, 2011.

Delanty, Gerard, and Baogang He. "Cosmopolitan Perspectives on European and Asian Transnationalism." *International Sociology* 23, no. 3 (May 2008): 323–344.

Department of Statistics Singapore. *Population Trends 2015.* 2015. Accessed on November 6, 2015, from http://www.singstat.gov.sg/publications/publications-and -papers/population-and-population-structure/population-trends.

Derrida, Jacques. *Politics of Friendship.* London: Verso, 1997.

DeVoretz, Don J. "Canada's Secret Province: 2.8 Million Canadians Abroad." Canadians Abroad Project Paper Series #09-5, Asia Pacific Foundation of Canada, Vancouver, BC, October 2009.

Dikötter, Frank. *The Discourse of Race in Modern China.* London: Hurst, 1992.

Ding, Sheng, and Rey Koslowski. "Chinese Soft Power and Immigration Reform: Can Beijing's Approach to Pursuing Global Talent and Maintaining Domestic Stability Succeed?" *Journal of Chinese Political Science* 22, no. 1 (2017): 97–116.

Dirlik, Arif. "Chinese History and the Question of Orientalism." *History and Theory* 35, no. 4 (December 1996): 96–118.

———. "Intimate Others: [Private] Nations and Diasporas in an Age of Globalization." *Inter-Asia Cultural Studies* 5, no. 3 (2004): 491–502.

Douglass, Mike. "Global Householding in Pacific Asia." *International Development Planning Review* 28, no. 4 (2006): 421–446.

Duara, Prasenjit. *The Crisis of Global Modernity: Asian Traditions and a Sustainable Future.* Cambridge: Cambridge University Press, 2015.

———. *Rescuing History from the Nation: Questioning Narratives of Modern China.* Chicago: University of Chicago Press, 1995.

Dzenovska, Dace. "The Great Departure: Rethinking National(ist) Common Sense." *Journal of Ethnic and Migration Studies* 39, no. 2 (2013): 201–218.

Elden, Stuart. *Terror and Territory: The Spatial Extent of Sovereignty.* Minneapolis: University of Minnesota Press, 2009.

Fabian, Johannes. *Time and the Other: How Anthropology Makes Its Object.* New York: Columbia University Press, 1983.

Faier, Lieba. *Intimate Encounters: Filipina Women and the Remaking of Rural Japan.* Berkeley: University of California Press, 2009.

Faist, Thomas. "Transnational Social Spaces." *Ethnic and Racial Studies* 38, no. 13 (2015): 2271–2274.

———. *The Volume and Dynamics of International Migration and Transnational Social Spaces.* Oxford: Oxford University Press, 2000.

Fan, Ke. "Representation of Ethnic Minorities in Socialist China." *Ethnic and Racial Studies* 39, no. 12 (2016): 2091–2107.

Farrer, James. "From 'Passports' to 'Joint Ventures': Intermarriage Between Chinese Nationals and Western Expatriates Residing in Shanghai." *Asian Studies Review* 32, no. 1 (2008): 7–29.

Fischer, Marilyn. "A Pragmatist Cosmopolitan Moment: Reconfiguring Nussbaum's Cosmopolitan Concentric Circles." *Journal of Speculative Philosophy* 21, no. 3 (2007): 151–165.

Fitzgerald, David. *A Nation of Emigrants: How Mexico Manages Its Migration.* Berkeley: University of California Press, 2009.

———. *Negotiating Extra-Territorial Citizenship: Mexican Migration and the Transnational Politics of Community.* San Diego, CA: Center for Comparative Immigration Studies, 2000.

Fitzgerald, Stephen. *China and the Overseas Chinese.* London: Cambridge University Press, 1972.

———. "China and the Overseas Chinese: Perceptions and Policies." *The China Quarterly* 44 (October–December 1970): 1–37.

———. "Overseas Chinese Affairs and the Cultural Revolution." *The China Quarterly* 40 (October–December 1969): 103–126.

Fogel, Joshua A., and Peter G. Zarrow, eds. *Imagining the People: Chinese Intellectuals and the Concept of Citizenship, 1890–1920.* Armonk, NY: M. E. Sharpe, 1997.

Fong, Vanessa L. *Paradise Redefined: Transnational Chinese Students and the Quest for Flexible Citizenship in the Developed World.* Stanford, CA: Stanford University Press, 2011.

Freeman, Caren. *Making and Faking Kinship: Marriage and Labor Migration Between China and South Korea.* Ithaca, NY: Cornell University Press, 2011.

Friedman, Sara. *Exceptional States: Chinese Immigrants and Taiwanese Sovereignty.* Oakland: University of California Press, 2015.

Frow, John. "A Politics of Stolen Time." In *TimeSpace: Geographies of Temporality*, edited by Jon May and Nigel Thrift, pp. 73–88. London: Routledge, 2001.

Gamlen, Alan. "The Emigration State and the Modern Geopolitical Imagination." *Political Geography* 27, no. 8 (2008): 840–856.

Geschiere, Peter. *The Perils of Belonging: Autochthony, Citizenship, and Exclusion in Africa and Europe.* Chicago: University of Chicago Press, 2009.

Giese, Karsten. "Perceptions, Practices and Adaptations: Understanding Chinese–African Interactions in Africa." *Journal of Current Chinese Affairs* 43, no. 1 (2014): 3–8.

Gillespie, Sandra. *South–South Transfer: A Study of Sino–African Exchanges.* New York: Routledge, 2001.

Gilmartin, Mary. "Changing Ireland, 2000–2012: Immigration, Emigration and Inequality." *Irish Geography* 46, no. 1–2 (2013): 91–111.

Giralt, Rosa Mas, and Adrian J. Bailey. "Transnational Familyhood and the Liquid Life Paths of South Americans in the UK." *Global Networks* 10, no. 3 (2010): 383–400.

Gladney, Dru C. "Representing Nationality in China: Refiguring Majority/Minority Identities." *Journal of Asian Studies* 53, no. 1 (February 1994): 92–123.

Glick Schiller, Nina. "Explanatory Frameworks in Transnational Migration Studies: The Missing Multi-Scalar Global Perspective." *Ethnic and Racial Studies* 38, no. 13 (2015): 2275–2282.

———. "Situating Identities: Towards an Identities Studies Without Binaries of Difference." *Identities* 19, no. 4 (July 2012): 520–532.

———. "Transnational Social Fields and Imperialism: Bringing a Theory of Power to Transnational Studies." *Anthropological Theory* 5, no. 4 (2005): 439–461.

Glick Schiller, Nina, Tsypylma Darieva, and Sandra Gruner-Domic. "Defining Cosmopolitan Sociability in a Transnational Age: An Introduction." *Ethnic and Racial Studies* 34, no. 3 (2011): 399–418.

Godley, Michael R. "The Sojourners: Returned Overseas Chinese in the People's Republic of China." *Pacific Affairs* 62, no. 3 (Autumn 1989): 330–352.

Goldman, Merle, and Elizabeth J. Perry, eds. *Changing Meanings of Citizenship in Modern China*. Cambridge, MA: Harvard University Press, 2002.

Grady, Patrick, and Herbert Grubel. "Immigration and the Welfare State Revisited: Fiscal Transfers to Immigrants in Canada." Vancouver, BC: Fraser Institute, May 31, 2015. Accessed on June 28, 2016, from http://ssrn.com/abstract=2612456.

Gray, Breda. "'Generation Emigration': The Politics of (Trans)national Social Reproduction in Twenty-First-Century Ireland." *Irish Studies Review* 21, no. 1 (2013): 20–36.

Grosz, Elizabeth A. *The Nick of Time: Politics, Evolution, and the Untimely*. Durham, NC: Duke University Press, 2004.

Guo, Shibao. "Toward Recognitive Justice: Emerging Trends and Challenges in Transnational Migration and Lifelong Learning." *International Journal of Lifelong Education* 29, no. 2 (March–April 2010): 149–167.

Hammer, Espen. *Philosophy and Temporality from Kant to Critical Theory*. Cambridge: Cambridge University Press, 2011.

Han, Enze. *Contestation and Adaptation: The Politics of National Identity in China*. New York: Oxford University Press, 2013.

Han, Sang-Jin, Young-Hee Shim, and Young-Do Park. "Cosmopolitan Sociology and Confucian Worldview: Beck's Theory in East Asia." *Theory, Culture & Society* 33, no. 7–8 (2016): 281–290.

Han, Xiaorong. "From Resettlement to Rights Protection: The Collective Actions of the Refugees from Vietnam in China Since the Late 1970s." *Journal of Chinese Overseas* 10, no. 2 (2014): 197–219.

——. "Spoiled Guests or Dedicated Patriots? The Chinese in North Vietnam, 1954–1978." *International Journal of Asian Studies* 6, no. 1 (2009): 1–36.

Harris, Peter. "The Origins of Modern Citizenship in China." *Asia Pacific Viewpoint* 43, no. 2 (August 2002): 181–203.

Haugen, Heidi Østbø. "Nigerians in China: A Second State of Immobility." *International Migration* 50, no. 2 (2012): 65–80.

Henry, Eric S. "Emissaries of the Modern: The Foreign Teacher in Urban China." *City & Society* 25, no. 2 (2013): 216–234.

Hickey, Maureen, Elaine Lynn-Ee Ho, and Brenda S. A. Yeoh. "Introduction to the Special Section on Establishing State-Led 'Diaspora Strategies' in Asia: Migration-As-Development Reinvented?" *Singapore Journal of Tropical Geography* 36, no. 2 (July 2015): 139–146.

Hill, Michael, and Kwen Fee Lian. *The Politics of Nation Building and Citizenship in Singapore.* London: Routledge, 1995.

Ho, Elaine Lynn-Ee. "Caught Between Two Worlds: Mainland Chinese Return Migration, Hukou Considerations and the Citizenship Dilemma." *Citizenship Studies* 15, no. 6–7 (October 2011): 643–658.

——. "'Claiming' the Diaspora: Sending State Strategies, Elite Mobility and the Spatialities of Citizenship." *Progress in Human Geography* 35, no. 6 (December 2011): 757–772.

——. "The Geo-Social and Global Geographies of Power: Urban Aspirations of 'Worlding' African Students in China." *Geopolitics* 22, no. 1 (2017): 15–33.

——. "Identity Politics and Cultural Asymmetries: Singaporean Transmigrants 'Fashioning' Cosmopolitanism." *Journal of Ethnic and Migration Studies* 37, no. 5 (May 2011): 729–746.

——. "Incongruent Migration Categorisations and Competing Citizenship Claims: 'Return' and Hypermigration in Transnational Migration Circuits." *Journal of Ethnic and Migration Studies* 42, no. 14 (November 2016): 2379–2394.

——. "Transnational Identities, Multiculturalism or Assimilation? China's 'Refugee-Returnees' and Generational Transitions." *Modern Asian Studies* 49, no. 2 (March 2015): 525–545.

Ho, Elaine Lynn-Ee, and Lynette J. Chua. "Law and 'Race' in the Citizenship Spaces of Myanmar: Spatial Strategies and the Political Subjectivity of the Burmese Chinese." *Ethnic and Racial Studies* 39, no. 5 (2016): 896–916.

Ho, Elaine Lynn-Ee, and Fangyu Foo. "Debating Integration in Singapore, Deepening the Variegations of the Chinese Diaspora." In *Contemporary Chinese Diasporas*, edited by Min Zhou, pp. 105–126. Singapore: Palgrave Macmillan, 2017.

Ho, Eng Seng. The *Graves of Tarim: Genealogy and Mobility Across the Indian Ocean.* Berkeley: University of California Press, 2006.

Ho, Wai Yip. "Mobilizing the Muslim Minority for China's Development: Hui Muslims, Ethnic Relations and Sino–Arab Connections." *Journal of Comparative Asian Development* 12, no. 1 (2013): 84–112.

Hooker, Michael B., ed. *Law and the Chinese in Southeast Asia*. Singapore: Institute of Southeast Asian Studies, 2002.

Huang, Matt, and Grace Hsu. *Young China Hand*. Bloomington, IN: Archway Publishing, 2016.

Hunter, Alistair. "Theory and Practice of Return Migration at Retirement: The Case of Migrant Worker Hostel Residents in France." *Population, Space and Place* 17, no. 2 (2011): 179–192.

Isin, Engin F. *Being Political: Genealogies of Citizenship*. Minneapolis: University of Minnesota Press, 2002.

———. "Citizens Without Nations." *Environment and Planning D: Society and Space* 30, no. 3 (2012): 450–467.

Jacobs, Jane M. *Edge of Empire: Postcolonialism and the City*. London: Routledge, 1996.

Jacobsen, Michael. "Navigating Between Disaggregating Nation States and Entrenching Processes of Globalisation: Reconceptualising the Chinese Diaspora in Southeast Asia." *Journal of Contemporary China* 18, no. 58 (January 2009): 69–91.

Jakimów, Małgorzata. "Chinese Citizenship 'After Orientalism': Academic Narratives on Internal Migrants in China." *Citizenship Studies* 169, no. 5–6 (August 2012): 657–671.

Jiao, Pan. "Deconstructing China's Ethnic Minorities: Deorientalization or Reorientalization?" *Chinese Sociology & Anthropology* 42, no. 4 (Summer 2010): 46–61.

Kang, David C. *China Rising: Peace, Power, and Order in East Asia*. New York: Columbia University Press, 2007.

Karl, Rebecca E. *Staging the World: Chinese Nationalism at the Turn of the Twentieth Century*. Durham, NC: Duke University Press, 2002.

Kawashima, Kumiko. "Service Outsourcing and Labour Mobility in a Digital Age: Transnational Linkages Between Japan and Dalian, China." *Global Networks* 17, no. 4 (2017): 483–499.

Keane, Michael. "Redefining Chinese Citizenship." *Economy and Society* 30, no. 1 (2001): 1–17.

Khalik, Salma. "Quality of Healthcare 'Not Tied to Workforce Numbers.'" *The Straits Times*, March 2, 2016. Accessed on January 24, 2017, from http://www.straitstimes.com/singapore/quality-of-healthcare-not-tied-to-workforce-numbers.

Kim, Eleana Jean. *Adopted Territory: Transnational Korean Adoptees and the Politics of Belonging*. Durham, NC: Duke University Press, 2010.

King, Russell, and Anastasia Christou. "Second-Generation 'Return' to Greece: New Dynamics of Transnationalism and Integration." *International Migration* 52, no. 6 (December 2014): 85–99.

King, Russell, Anthony M. Warnes, and Allan M. Williams. "International Retirement Migration in Europe." *International Journal of Population Geography* 4, no. 2 (1998): 91–111.

Kivisto, Peter. "Theorizing Transnational Immigration: A Critical Review of Current Efforts." *Ethnic and Racial Studies* 24, no. 4 (2001): 549–577.

Kobayashi, Audrey, and Valerie Preston. "Transnationalism Through the Life Course: Hong Kong Immigrants to Canada." *Asia-Pacific Viewpoint* 48, no. 2 (August 2007): 151–167.

Kofman, Eleonore. "Rethinking Care Through Social Reproduction: Articulating Circuits of Migration." *Social Politics: International Studies in Gender, State & Society* 19, no. 1 (Spring 2012): 142–162.

Koh, Sin Yee. "State-Led Talent Return Migration Programme and the Doubly Neglected 'Malaysian Diaspora': Whose Diaspora, What Citizenship, Whose Development?" *Singapore Journal of Tropical Geography* 36, no. 2 (July 2015): 183–200.

Kretsedemas, Philip. *Migrants and Race in the US: Territorial Racism and the Alien/Outside*. New York: Routledge, 2014.

Kuhn, Philip A. *Chinese Among Other: Emigration in Modern Times*. Singapore: NUS Press, 2008.

Kwok, Melissa. "Return of the Native." *The Straits Times*, October 23, 2011. Accessed on January 24, 2017, from http://sglinks.com/pages/1796908-return-native-singaporean-home-feels-foreign.

Lan, Shanshan. "State Regulation of Undocumented African Migrants in China: A Multi-Scalar Analysis." *Journal of Asian and African Studies* 50, no. 3 (2015): 289–304.

Lee, Pearl. "Improved Support for Postgrads." *The Straits Times*, August 6, 2015. Accessed on January 24, 2017, from http://www.straitstimes.com/singapore/education/improved-support-for-postgrads.

Lehman, Angela. *Transnational Lives in China: Expatriates in a Globalizing City*. Basingstoke, UK: Palgrave Macmillan, 2014.

Ley, David. *Millionaire Migrants: Trans-Pacific Life Lines*. Oxford: Wiley-Blackwell, 2010.

Ley, David, and Audrey Kobayashi. "Back to Hong Kong: Return Migration or Transnational Sojourn?" *Global Networks* 5, no. 2 (2005): 111–127.

Li, Zhigang, Laurence J. C. Ma, and Desheng Xue. "An African Enclave in China: The Making of a New Transnational Urban Space." *Eurasian Geography and Economics* 50, no. 6 (2009): 699–719.

Lin, Ping. "Chinese Diaspora 'At Home': Mainlander Taiwanese in Dongguan and Shanghai." *The China Review* 11, no. 2 (Fall 2011): 43–64.

Liu, Guofu. "Changing Chinese Migration Law: From Restriction to Relaxation." *Journal of International Migration and Integration* 10, no. 3 (2009): 311–333.

————. *The Right to Leave and Return and Chinese Migration Law.* Boston: Martinus Nijhoff, 2007.

Liu, Hong. "An Emerging China and Diasporic Chinese: Historicity, State, and International Relations." *Journal of Contemporary China* 20, no. 72 (November 2011): 813–832.

Liu, Hong, and Els van Dongen. "China's Diaspora Policies as a New Mode of Transnational Governance." *Journal of Contemporary China* 25, no. 102 (2016): 805–821.

Loh, Keng Fatt. "Engage Public on Singapore's Maritime Future." *The Straits Times,* November 22, 2015. Accessed on January 24, 2017, from http://www.straitstimes.com/singapore/engage-public-on-singapores-maritime-future.

Luo, Wangshu. "African Students Get Real-Life Experience." *China Daily,* March 29, 2013. Accessed on January 24, 2017, from http://www.chinadaily.com.cn/china/2013-03/25/content_16344269.htm.

Ma, Enyu, and Adams Bodomo. "We Are What We Eat: Food in the Process of Community Formation and Identity Shaping Among African Traders in Guangzhou and Yiwu." *African Diaspora* 5, no. 1 (2012): 3–26.

Ma, Laurence J. C., and Carolyn Cartier, eds. *The Chinese Diaspora: Space, Place, Mobility, and Identity, Why of Where.* Lanham, MD: Rowman and Littlefield, 2003.

Ma Mung, Emmanuel. "Dispersal as a Resource." *Diaspora: A Journal of Transnational Studies* 13, no. 2 (Fall 2004): 211–225.

Massey, Doreen B. *For Space.* London: Sage, 2005.

Mathews, Gordon, Dan Lin, and Yang Yang. "How to Evade States and Slip Past Borders: Lessons from Traders, Overstayers, and Asylum Seekers in Hong Kong and China." *City & Society* 26, no. 2 (2014): 217–238.

Mathews, Mathew, Leonard Lim, Shanthini Selvarajan, and Nicole Cheung. "CNA-IPS Survey on Ethnic Attitudes in Singapore." IPS Working Papers No. 28, Institute of Policy Studies, Singapore, November 2017. Accessed on November 13, 2017, from http://lkyspp2.nus.edu.sg/ips/wp-content/uploads/sites/2/2017/11/IPS-Working-Paper-28_081117.pdf.

McKeown, Adam M. *Melancholy Order: Asian Migration and the Globalization of Borders.* New York: Columbia University Press, 2008.

Mezzadra, Sandro, and Brett Nielson. *Border as Method, or, the Multiplication of Labor.* Durham, NC: Duke University Press, 2013.

Ministry of Education of the People's Republic of China. *Nian Quanguo Laihua Liuxuesheng Shuju Fabu* [Statistical report on the number of international students in China 2015]. April 14, 2016. Accessed on January 3, 2017, from http://www.moe.edu.cn/jyb_xwfb/gzdt_gzdt/s5987/201604/t20160414_238263.html/.

Mohan, Giles, and Ben Lampert. "Negotiating China: Reinserting African Agency into China–Africa Relations." *African Affairs* 112, no. 446 (2013): 92–110.

Montsion, Jean Michel. "Chinese Ethnicities in Neoliberal Singapore? State Designs and Dialect(ical) Struggles of Community Associations." *Ethnic and Racial Studies* 37, no. 9 (2014): 1486–1504.

Mouffe, Chantal. *The Return of the Political*. London: Verso, 1993.

Mullaney, Thomas S. *Coming to Terms with the Nation: Ethnic Classification in Modern China*. Berkeley: University of California Press, 2011.

Myambo, Melissa Tandiwe. "Frontier Heritage Migration in the Global Ethnic Economy." *Public Culture* 29, no. 2/82 (May 2017): 261–285.

National Bureau of Statistics of China. *Major Figures on Residents from Hong Kong, Macao and Taiwan and Foreigners Covered by 2010 Population Census*. April 29, 2011. Accessed on December 28, 2016, from http://www.stats.gov.cn/english /NewsEvents/201104/t20110429_26451.html.

National People's Congress of the People's Republic of China. *Law of the People's Republic of China on the Protection of the Rights and Interests of Returned Overseas Chinese and the Family Members of Overseas Chinese*. N.d. Accessed on December 28, 2016, from http://www.npc.gov.cn/englishnpc/Law/2007-12/12/content _1383902.htm.

National Population and Talent Division (NPTD), Singapore Department of Statistics, Ministry of Home Affairs, and Immigration and Checkpoints Authority. *2014 Population Brief*. September 2014. Accessed on January 13, 2017, from http:// population.sg/population-in-brief/files/population-in-brief-2014.pdf.

Newendorp, Nicole DeJong. *Uneasy Reunions: Immigration, Citizenship, and Family Life in Post-1997 Hong Kong*. Stanford, CA: Stanford University Press, 2008.

Ngeow, Chow Bing, and Hailong Ma. "More Islamic, No Less Chinese: Explorations into Overseas Chinese Muslim Identities in Malaysia." *Ethnic and Racial Studies* 39, no. 12 (2016): 2108–2128.

Noble, Greg. "'Bumping into Alterity': Transacting Cultural Complexities." *Continuum* 25, no. 6 (December 2011): 827–840.

———. "Cosmopolitan Habits: The Capacities and Habitats of Intercultural Conviviality." *Body & Society* 19, no. 2–3 (2013): 162–185.

Nussbaum, Martha Craven. *Creating Capabilities: The Human Development Approach*. Cambridge, MA: Belknap Press of Harvard University Press, 2011.

Nyíri, Pál. "Chinese Investors, Labour Discipline and Developmental Cosmopolitanism: Chinese Investors in Cambodia." *Development and Change* 44, no. 6 (2013): 1387–1405.

———. *Mobility and Cultural Authority in Contemporary China*. Seattle: University of Washington Press, 2010.

———. "The Yellow Man's Burden: Chinese Migrants on a Civilizing Mission." *China Journal* 56 (July 2006): 83–106.

Oakes, Tim. "Bathing in the Far Village: Globalization, Transnational Capital, and the Cultural Politics of Modernity in China." *Positions: East Asia Cultures Critique* 7, no. 2 (Fall 1999): 307–342.

Ong, Aihwa. "Cyberpublics and Diaspora Politics Among Transnational Chinese." *Interventions* 5, no. 1 (2003): 82–100.

———. *Flexible Citizenship: The Cultural Logics of Transnationality*. Durham, NC: Duke University Press, 1999.

———. "Mutations in Citizenship." *Theory, Culture & Society* 23, no. 2–3 (2006): 499–505.

———. *Neoliberalism as Exception: Mutations in Citizenship and Sovereignty*. Durham, NC: Duke University Press, 2006.

Overseas Chinese Affairs Office of the State Council. *Guanyu Waiji Huaren Qianzheng, Juliu Ji Yongjiu Juming Liu De Zhengce Jing* [Policy concerning the visa and permanent residency status of the Chinese who have foreign nationality status]. August 17, 2015. Accessed on June 23, 2016, from http://www.gqb.gov.cn/news/2015/0817/36451.shtml.

Painter, Joe. "Rethinking Territory." *Antipode* 42, no. 5 (2010): 1090–1118.

Parliament of Canada. *Second Session, Forty-First Parliament, 62–63 Elizabeth II, 2013–2014 House of Commons Canada Bill C-24*. June 4, 2014. Accessed on June 23, 2016, from http://www.parl.gc.ca/HousePublications/Publication.aspx?Language=E&Mode=1&DocId=6646338.

Parrish, Austen L. "Reclaiming International Law from Extraterritoriality." Indiana University Maurer School of Law Paper 894, 2009. Accessed on February 5, 2015, from http://www.repository.law.indiana.edu/facpub/894.

Pellerin, Hélène, and Beverley Mullings. "The 'Diaspora Option,' Migration and the Changing Political Economy of Development." *Review of International Political Economy* 20, no. 1 (2013): 89–120.

Percival, John. *Return Migration in Later Life: International Perspectives*. Bristol, UK: Policy Press, 2013.

Peterson, Glen. *Overseas Chinese in the People's Republic of China*. New York: Routledge, 2012.

———. "Socialist China and the Huaqiao: The Transition to Socialism in the Overseas Chinese Areas of Rural Guangdong, 1949–1956." *Modern China* 14, no. 3 (July 1988): 309–335.

Pieke, Frank N. "Emerging Markets and Migration Policy: China." The Emerging Markets and Migration Policy Publication Series, Center for Migrations and Citizenship, Paris, July 2014. Accessed on January 3, 2017, from http://www.ifri.org/sites/default/files/atoms/files/ifri_migrationpolicychina_2.pdf.

———. "Immigrant China." *Modern China* 38, no. 1 (2012): 40–77.

———. ed. *Transnational Chinese: Fujianese Migrants in Europe.* Stanford, CA: Stanford University Press, 2004.

Pina-Guerassimoff, Carine, and Eric Guerassimoff. "The 'Overseas Chinese': The State and Emigration from the 1890s through the 1990s." In *Citizenship and Those Who Leave: The Politics of Emigration and Expatriation*, edited by Nancy L. Green and François Weil, pp. 245–264. Urbana: University of Illinois Press, 2007.

Pratt, Geraldine. *Families Apart: Migrant Mothers and the Conflicts of Labor and Love.* Minneapolis: University of Minnesota Press, 2012.

Preston, Valerie, Audrey Kobayashi, and Guida Man. "Transnationalism, Gender, and Civic Participation: Canadian Case Studies of Hong Kong Immigrants." *Environment and Planning A* 38, no. 9 (2006): 1633–1651.

Roberts, Jayde Lin. *Mapping Chinese Rangoon: Place and Nation Among the Sino-Burmese.* Seattle: University of Washington Press, 2016.

Rosaldo, Renato. "Cultural Citizenship and Educational Democracy." *Cultural Anthropology* 9, no. 3 (August 1994): 402–411.

Roy, Ananya. "The 21st-Century Metropolis: New Geographies of Theory." *Regional Studies* 43, no. 6 (July 2009): 819–830.

Sack, Robert D. "Human Territoriality: A Theory." *Annals of the Association of American Geographers* 73, no. 1 (March 1983): 55–74.

Salaff, Janet, Angela Shik, and Arent Greve. "Like Sons and Daughters of Hong Kong: The Return of the Young Generation." *The China Review* 8, no. 1 (Spring 2008): 31–57.

Salazar, Noel B. "Key Figures of Mobility: An Introduction." *Social Anthropology* 25, no. 1 (2017): 5–12.

Saldanha, Arun. "Reontologising Race: The Machinic Geography of Phenotype." *Environment and Planning D: Society and Space* 24, no. 1 (2006): 9–24.

Sandercock, Leonie, and Peter Lyssiotis. *Cosmopolis II: Mongrel Cities of the 21st Century.* New York: Continuum, 2003.

Sassen, Saskia. *Territory, Authority, Rights: From Medieval to Global Assemblages.* Princeton, NJ: Princeton University Press, 2006.

———. "When Territory Deborders Territoriality." *Territory, Politics, Governance* 1, no. 1 (2013): 21–45.

Sautman, Barry. "Anti-Black Racism in Post-Mao China." *The China Quarterly* 138 (June 1994): 413–437.

Sautman, Barry, and Hairong Yan. "African Perspectives on China–Africa Links." *The China Quarterly* 199 (September 2009): 728–759.

Saxenian, AnnaLee. *The New Argonauts: Regional Advantage in a Global Economy.* Cambridge, MA: Harvard University Press, 2006.

Schmitz, Cheryl M. T. "Significant Others: Security and Suspicion in Chinese–Angolan Encounters." *Journal of Chinese Current Affairs* 43, no. 1 (2014): 41–69.

Sen, Amartya Kumar. *Development as Freedom*. New York: Anchor Books, 2000.

Sevenhuijsen, Selma. "The Place of Care: The Relevance of the Feminist Ethic of Care for Social Policy." *Feminist Theory* 4, no. 2 (2003): 179–197.

Shachar, Ayelet. *The Birthright Lottery: Citizenship and Global Inequality*. Cambridge, MA: Harvard University Press, 2009.

Shao, Dan. "Chinese by Definition: Nationality Law, Jus Sanguinis, and State Succession, 1909–1980." *Twentieth-Century China* 35, no. 1 (November 2009): 4–28.

Shapiro, Michael J. "National Times and Other Times: Re-thinking Citizenship." *Cultural Studies* 14, no. 1 (2000): 79–98.

Simone, AbdouMaliq. *For the City Yet to Come: Changing African Life in Four Cities*. Durham, NC: Duke University Press, 2004.

Smart, Alan, and Jinn-Yuh Hsu. "The Chinese Diaspora, Foreign Investment and Economic Development in China." *Review of International Affairs* 3, no. 4 (Summer 2004): 544–566.

Smith, Michael Peter. "Transnationalism, the State, and the Extraterritorial Citizen." *Politics and Society* 31, no. 4 (December 2003): 467–502.

Smith, Robert C. "Migrant Membership as an Instituted Process: Transnationalization, the State and the Extra-territorial Conduct of Mexican Politics." *International Migration Review* 37, no. 2 (Summer 2003): 297–343.

Soon, Debbie, and Chan-Hoong Leong. "A Study on Emigration Attitudes of Young Singaporeans." IPS Working Papers No. 19, Institute of Policy Studies, March 2011. Accessed on November 13, 2017, from http://lkyspp.nus.edu.sg/ips/publications /working-papers?y=2011.

Staeheli, Lynn A., Patricia Ehrkamp, Helga Leitner, and Caroline R. Nagel. "Dreaming the Ordinary: Daily Life and the Complex Geographies of Citizenship." *Progress in Human Geography* 36, no. 5 (2012): 628–644.

Stanley, Phiona. "Superheroes in Shanghai: Constructing Transnational Western Men's Identities." *Gender, Place & Culture* 19, no. 2 (2012): 213–231.

Stasiulis, Daiva. "The Migration-Citizenship Nexus." In *Recasting the Social in Citizenship*, edited by Engin F. Isin, pp. 134–161. Toronto: University of Toronto Press, 2008.

Statistics Canada. *Place of Birth for the Immigrant Population by Period of Immigration, 2006 Counts and Percentage Distribution, for Canada, Provinces and Territories—20% Sample Data*. Last modified on March 27, 2009. Accessed on January 26, 2016, from https://www12.statcan.gc.ca/census-recensement/2006 /dp-pd/hlt/97-557/T404-eng.cfm?Lang=E&T=404&GH=4&GF=1&SC=1&S =1&O=D.

Sullivan, Michael J. "The 1988–89 Nanjing Anti-African Protests: Racial Nationalism or National Racism?" *The China Quarterly* 138 (June 1994): 438–457.

Sun, Ken Chih-Yan. "Transnational Healthcare Seeking: How Ageing Taiwanese Return Migrants View Homeland Public Benefits." *Global Networks* 14, no. 4 (2014): 533–550.

Suryadinata, Leo. "China's Citizenship Law and the Chinese in Southeast Asia." In *Law and the Chinese in Southeast Asia*, edited by Michael B. Hooker, pp. 169–202. Singapore: Institute of Southeast Asia Studies, 2002.

———. *The Ethnic Chinese as Southeast Asians*. Singapore: World Scientific Publishing, 1997.

———. "Ethnic Chinese in Southeast Asia: Overseas Chinese, Chinese Overseas or Southeast Asians?" In *The Ethnic Chinese as Southeast Asians*, edited by Leo Suryadinata, pp. 1–24. Singapore: World Scientific Publishing, 1997.

Tagore, Saranindranath. "Tagore's Conception of Cosmopolitanism: A Reconstruction." *University of Toronto Quarterly* 77, no. 4 (Fall 2008): 1070–1084.

Tan, Chee-Beng. "Indonesian Chinese in Hong Kong: Re-migration, Re-establishment of Livelihood and Belonging." *Asian Ethnicity* 12, no. 1 (February 2011): 101–119.

———. "Reterritorialization of a Balinese Chinese Community in Quanzhou, Fujian." *Modern Asian Studies* 44, no. 3 (May 2010): 547–566.

Tham, Irene. "$120m to Help Arm S'poreans with IT Skills as Demand Rises." *The Straits Times*, April 12, 2016. Accessed on January 24, 2017, from http://www .straitstimes.com/singapore/120m-to-help-arm-sporeans-with-it-skills-as -demand-rises.

Thang, Leng Leng, Sachiko Sone, and Mika Toyota. "Freedom Found? The Later-Life Transnational Migration of Japanese Women to Western Australia and Thailand." *Asia and Pacific Migration Journal* 21, no. 2 (2012): 239–261.

Thunø, Mette. "Reaching Out and Incorporating Chinese Overseas: The Trans-Territorial Scope of the PRC by the End of the 20th Century." *The China Quarterly* 168 (December 2001): 910–929.

Tronto, Joan C. *Caring Democracy: Markets, Equality, and Justice*. New York: New York University Press, 2013.

Tsing, Anna Lowenhaupt. *Friction: An Ethnography of Global Connection*. Princeton, NJ: Princeton University Press, 2005.

Tsuda, Takeyuki, ed. *Diasporic Homecomings: Ethnic Return Migration in Comparative Perspective*. Stanford, CA: Stanford University Press, 2009.

———. *Strangers in the Ethnic Homeland: Japanese Brazilian Return Migration in Transnational Perspective*. New York: Columbia University Press, 2003.

United Nations (UN) Department of Economic and Social Affairs, Population Division. *International Migration Report 2015: Highlights*. 2016. Accessed on January 3, 2017, from http://www.un.org/en/development/desa/population/migration/publi cations/migrationreport/docs/MigrationReport2015_Highlights.pdf.

van Dongen, Els. "Behind the Ties That Bind: Diaspora-Making and Nation-Building in China and India in Historical Perspective, 1850s–2010s." *Asian Studies Review* 41, no. 1 (2017): 1–19.

Vasantkumar, Chris. "Unmade in China: Reassembling the Ethnic on the Gansu–Tibetan Border." *Ethnos* 79, no. 2 (May 2014): 261–286.

———. "What Is This 'Chinese' in Overseas Chinese? Sojourn Work and the Place of China's Minority Nationalities in Extraterritorial Chinese-ness." *Journal of Asian Studies* 71, no. 2 (2012): 423–446.

Vijayan, K. C. "The Extent of Yang Yin's Manipulation." *The Straits Times*, August 30, 2015. Accessed on January 24, 2017, from http://www.straitstimes.com/singapore /courts-crime/the-extent-of-yang-yins-manipulation.

Waldinger, Roger David. *The Cross-Border Connection: Immigrants, Emigrants and Their Homelands.* Cambridge, MA: Harvard University Press, 2015.

Wang, Gungwu. *China and the Chinese Overseas.* Singapore: Times Academic Press, 1991.

———. "China and Singapore: Looking Back to Understand the Future." *The Straits Times*, October 22, 2016. Accessed on January 24, 2017, from http://www .straitstimes.com/opinion/china-and-spore-looking-back-to-understand-the -future.

———. "The Chinese as Immigrants and Settlers." In *Management of Success: The Moulding of Modern Singapore*, edited by Kernial Singh Sandhu and Paul Wheatley, pp. 552–562. Singapore: Institute of Southeast Asian Studies, 1989.

———. *Chinese Overseas: From Earthbound China to the Quest for Autonomy.* Cambridge, MA: Harvard University Press, 2000.

Wang, Pan. *Love and Marriage in Globalizing China.* New York: Routledge, 2014.

Waters, Johanna L. *Education, Migration, and Cultural Capital in the Chinese Diaspora: Transnational Students Between Hong Kong and Canada.* Amherst, NY: Cambria Press, 2008.

Wong, Diana, and Pei Wen Ooi. "The Globalization of Tertiary Education and Intra-Asian Student Mobility: Mainland Chinese Student Mobility to Malaysia." *Asian and Pacific Migration Journal* 22, no. 1 (2013): 55–76.

Wong, Wei Han. "New Panel to Advise MAS on Strategies." *The Straits Times*, July 29, 2015. Accessed on January 24, 2017, from http://www.straitstimes.com/business /new-panel-to-advise-mas-on-strategies.

Xu, Jilin. "Tianxia Zhuyi/Yixia Zhi Bian Ji Qizai Jindai De Bianyi" [Cosmopolitanism, the debate of the civilized and the uncivilized, and their variations in modern times]. *Journal of East China Normal University* 44, no. 6 (2012): 66–76.

Yamashiro, Jane H. "Working Towards Conceptual Consistency in Discussing 'Diaspora' and 'Diaspora Strategies': Ethnicity and Affinity in the Case of Japan." *Geoforum* 59 (2015): 178–186.

Yan, Hairong. "Neoliberal Governmentality and Neohumanism: Organizing Suzhi/ Value Flow Through Labor Recruitment Networks." *Cultural Anthropology* 18, no. 4 (2003): 493–523.

Yap, Mui Teng. "Brain Drain or Links to the World: Views on Emigrants from Singapore." *Asian and Pacific Migration Journal* 3, no. 2–3 (1994): 411–429.

Yen, Ching-hwang. *Coolies and Mandarins: China's Protection of Overseas Chinese During the Late Ch'ing Period (1985–1911).* Singapore: Singapore University Press, 1985.

———. *Studies in Modern Overseas Chinese History.* Singapore: Times Academic Press, 1995.

Yeoh, Brenda S. A., and Katie Willis. "Singapore Unlimited: Configuring Social Identity in the Regionalisation Process." Transnational Communities Programme, University of Oxford, 1998. Accessed on December 28, 2016, from http://www.trans comm.ox.ac.uk/working%20papers/nottitc.pdf.

Yeoh, Emile K. K. "From Dungans to Xinyimin: China, Chinese Migration and the Changing Sociopolitical Fabric of Central Asian Republics." *Contemporary Chinese Political Economy and Strategic Relations: An International Journal* 1, no. 2 (August 2015): 87–245.

Young, Ian. "Canada Floats New Citizenship Rules that Could Affect Thousands of Chinese." *South China Morning Post*, February 7, 2014. Accessed on January 24, 2017, from http://www.scmp.com/news/china/article/1423485/canada-floats-new-citizen ship-rules-could-affect-thousands-chinese.

———. "Canada Scraps Millionaire Visa Scheme, 'Dumps 46,000 Chinese Applications.'" *South China Morning Post*, February 12, 2014. Accessed on January 24, 2017, from http://www.scmp.com/news/world/article/1426368/canada-scraps-millionaire -visa-scheme-dumps-46000-chinese-applications.

Zhang, Kenny. "Canadians Abroad: Foreigners with Canadian Passports or the New Canadian Diaspora?" Working Paper Series #09-2, Asia Pacific Foundation of Canada, Vancouver, BC, 2009.

———. "Chinese in Canada and Canadians in China: The Human Platform for Relationships Between China and Canada." In *The China Challenge: Sino–Canadian Relations in the 21st Century*, edited by Huhua Cao and Vivienne Poy, pp. 158–182. Ottawa: University of Ottawa Press, 2011.

Zhang, Li. "Economic Migration and Urban Citizenship in China: The Role of Points Systems." *Population and Development Review* 38, no. 3 (September 2012): 503–533.

———. *Strangers in the City: Reconfigurations of Space, Power, and Social Networks Within China's Floating Population.* Stanford, CA: Stanford University Press, 1998.

Zhang, Yan. "Green Card Threshold Lowered." *China Daily*, June 9, 2015. Accessed on January 24, 2017, from http://www.chinadaily.com.cn/china/2015-06/09/content _20944896.htm.

Zhao, Tingyang. "Rethinking Empire from a Chinese Concept 'All-Under-Heaven' (Tian-Xia)." *Social Identities* 12, no. 1 (January 2006): 29–41.

———. *Tianxia Tixi: Shijie Zhidu Zhexue Daolun* [The *tianxia* system: An introduction to the philosophy of a world institution]. Beijing: Zhongguo Renmin Daxue Chuban She, 2011.

Zhou, Min, Shabnam Shenasi, and Tao Xu. "Chinese Attitudes Toward African Migrants in Guangzhou, China." *International Journal of Sociology* 46, no. 2 (2016): 141–161.

Zweig, David, and Huiyao Wang. "Can China Bring Back the Best? The Communist Party Organises China's Search for Talent." *The China Quarterly* 215 (September 2013): 590–615.

Index

Lin, Ping, 79
Low, Jevon, 120n56

Ma, Laurence, 11, 29
Macau, 7, 98n10, 127n49. *See also* alterity;
    co-ethnicity; fraternity
Mainland Chinese migrants, 111n2. *See also*
    Canada; *huaqiao*; *laoyimin*; Singapore;
    xinyimin
Malaya, 14, 18, 22, 24, 105n7, 108n34,
    117n13. See also *guiqiao*; refugee-
    returnees; Singapore
Malaysia, 53, 61, 90–91, 105n7
Mandarin (*Putonghua*), 122n1
Mao Zedong, 9, 109n49
McKeown, Adam, 6, 99n23
Mekong region, 79–81. *See also* Cambodia;
    Myanmar; Southeast Asian Chinese;
    Vietnam
middling migrants (*zhongdeng yimin*),
    39, 40
migrant-receiving countries, expectations
    for migrants, 37, 42–43, 44, 45–46
Mowat Centre (Canada), 41
multiple diasporas, 52–53. *See also*
    Singapore
Myanmar (Burma), 24, 78, 79, 80–81, 105n6,
    127n48. *See also* alterity; co-ethnicity;
    fraternity; Mekong region; refugee-
    returnees; *suzhi*

Newendorp, Nicole, 12
New Silk Road, 31, 82, 129n68. *See also*
    ethnic minorities: as emigrants
Noble, Greg, 60
Nussbaum, Martha, 8
Nyíri, Pál, 70

One Belt, One Road. *See* China; New Silk
    Road
one-child policy, 58, 119n46. *See also* China
"100 Talents" program (*qianren jihua*), 30,
    110n74. *See also* diaspora engagement;
    scientific diaspora
Ong, Aihwa, 36, 70, 73, 77, 79
Open Door Policy, 28, 29. *See also* China
orientalism, 70
overseas Chinese (*huaqiao*): engagement by
    China, 6; refugee-returnees (*guiguo
    nanqiao*) as, 22, 27, 31; use of term, 4, 5,
    17, 106n13

Overseas Chinese Affairs Commission
    (OCAC), 20, 21, 27, 104n4
Overseas Chinese Affairs Office (*Qiaoban*),
    17, 28, 71, 83, 104n4
Overseas Chinese Ethnic Minorities
    Association, 83
Overseas Chinese Muslim Association, 83
Overseas Singaporean Unit (OSU), 62–63.
    See also diaspora engagement; extra-
    territorial (external) citizenship;
    extraterritorial reach

Pakistan, 88–89
panicked multiculturalism, 59–61
periodization, 3, 59, 67, 90, 98n9. *See also*
    time
Peterson, Glen, 26
phenotypical racism, 55
Philippines, 105n6
Pratt, Geraldine, 35

Qing dynasty, 19, 22, 69, 100n29, 106n17,
    106n19

racism: alterity, 23; explanation of, 23;
    phenotypical approach to Africans, 9,
    75–77, 84, 126n42, 126n44; phenotypical
    racism, 55; territorial racism, 52. *See
    also* ethnic minorities
refugee-returnees (*guiguo nanqiao*):
    introduction and conclusion, 14–15,
    17–18, 31; agriculture reforms, 22–27;
    alterity of, 22–23, 26; author's
    encounter with, 23–24; Cultural
    Revolution, 27–28; Great Leap
    Forward, 26–27; heterogeneous
    clusters of time and, 28; historical
    context, 19–20, 105n6, 107n22,
    107n24, 108n31; periodization, 3, 59,
    67, 90, 98n9; recreation of Southeast
    Asia by, 25–26, 109n53; state farms, 26;
    status in China, 22, 24–25, 28–29,
    108n38, 109n47, 109n49; timeline and
    reasons for migration, 21–22, 24, 87,
    108nn33–34, 117n13
re-migration, 2, 3, 11. *See also* counter-
    diasporic migration; diaspora
    engagement; refugee-returnees;
    secondary diaspora; transnational
    sojourning
returnees (*guiqiao*), 19, 20, 22, 27, 31

Lightning Source UK Ltd.
Milton Keynes UK
UKHW040814020220
358006UK00003B/229